Voice of the People

Elections and Voting in the United States

Alan Abramowitz

Emory University

Boston   Burr Ridge, IL   Dubuque, IA   Madison, WI   New York
San Francisco   St. Louis   Bangkok   Bogotá   Caracas   Kuala Lumpur
Lisbon   London   Madrid   Mexico City   Milan   Montreal   New Delhi
Santiago   Seoul   Singapore   Sydney   Taipei   Toronto

Higher Education

VOICE OF THE PEOPLE: ELECTION AND VOTING IN THE UNITED STATES

Published by McGraw-Hill, a business unit of The McGraw-Hill Companies, Inc., 1221 Avenue of the Americas, New York, NY, 10020. Copyright © 2004, by The McGraw-Hill Companies, Inc. All rights reserved. No part of this publication may be reproduced or distributed in any form or by any means, or stored in a database or retrieval system, without the prior written consent of The McGraw-Hill Companies, Inc., including, but not limited to, in any network or other electronic storage or transmission, or broadcast for distance learning.

Some ancillaries, including electronic and print components, may not be available to customers outside the United States.

This book is printed on acid-free paper.

1 2 3 4 5 6 7 8 9 0 DOC/DOC 0 9 8 7 6 5 4 3

ISBN 0-07-249065-9

Publisher: *Lyn Uhl*
Senior sponsoring editor: *Monica Eckman*
Developmental editor: *Kate Scheinman*
Marketing manager: *Katherine Bates*
Senior project manager: *Jean Hamilton*
Production supervisor: *Janean A. Utley*
Associate designer: *George J. Kokkonas*
Supplement associate: *Kathleen Boylan*
Cover design: *George J. Kokkonas*
Interior design: *George J. Kokkonas*
Typeface: *10/12 Palatino*
Compositor: *G & S Typesetters*
Printer: *R. R. Donnelley*

Library of Congress Cataloging-in-Publication Data

Abramowitz, Alan.
　Voice of the people : elections and voting in the United States / Alan Abramowitz.
　　　p.　cm. — (Critical topics in American government series)
　　Includes bibliographical references and index.
　　ISBN 0-07-249065-9 (softcover : alk. paper)
　　1. Elections—United States.　2. Voting—United States.　3. Democracy—United States.　I. Title.　II. Series.
JK1965.A274 2004
324.973—dc21

2003052657

www.mhhe.com

Fig. 4.1 From Michael P. McDonald and Samuel L. Popkin, "The Myth of the Vanishing Voter," *American Political Science Review*, Vol. 95, December 2001. Reprinted with the permission of Cambridge University Press.

Critical Topics in American Government Series

Understanding the U.S. Supreme Court: Cases and Controversies
By Kevin McGuire

Organized Interests and American Government
By David Lowery and Holly Brasher

Voice of the People: Elections and Voting in the United States
By Alan Abramowitz

ALAN I. ABRAMOWITZ is the Alben W. Barkley Professor of Political Science at Emory University. He received his PhD in Political Science from Stanford University in 1976 and specializes in American elections, voting behavior, and public opinion. He has published more than 40 articles in scholarly journals including *The American Political Science Review, The American Journal of Political Science,* and *The Journal of Politics.* He is co-author of several books on electoral politics in the United States, including *The Life of the Parties* (with John McGlennon and Ronald Rapoport), *Nomination Politics* (with Walter Stone), and *Senate Elections* (with Jeffrey Segal).

For Jack and Isabel Abramowitz
who showed me the way

Man's capacity for justice makes democracy possible, but man's inclination to injustice makes democracy necessary.

—Reinhold Niebuhr
The Children of Light and the Children of Darkness, foreword (1944).

Contents

Contents

Preface

I decided to write this book about elections and voting in the Unites States for two major reasons. First, this is an especially interesting time to study the electoral process in the United States because of important changes affecting elections and voting behavior in the first decade of the twenty-first century; second, I did not find any existing book that provided a comprehensive perspective on the contemporary electoral process in the United States.

The extraordinary presidential election of 2000 underscored some of the changes that have affected the electoral process in recent years. Not since the beginning of the twentieth century has the American electorate been so closely divided in its partisan loyalties and not since the 1930s has the ideological gulf separating the Democratic and Republican parties been as wide. The 2000 election ended in a dead heat in the popular vote for president, a 50-50 tie in the Senate, and the narrowest majority in the House of Representatives in almost 50 years. However, despite the intensity of the battle for control of Congress and the White House and despite the growing ideological division between the two major parties, almost half of the eligible voters chose to stay on the sidelines. Two years later, with control of both the Senate and House of Representatives on the line, 60 percent of eligible voters stayed away from the polls. This book is intended to help students understand the reasons for the ongoing ideological realignment of the Democratic and Republican parties and the continuing disengagement of so many American citizens from the electoral process.

The book is divided into three major sections. The first two chapters provide the background and context necessary to understand the changes affecting American elections and voting behavior in the twenty-first century. Chapter 1 provides a historical perspective on the electoral process by examining the influence of fundamental American values on the development of voting and elections in the United States from the early nineteenth century until the present day. Then Chapter 2 examines the social and institutional contexts within which campaigns and elections take place. A unique feature of this book is that it includes an in-depth examination of the consequences of long-term trends in American society for the electoral process. While our political institutions have been quite stable, American society has been experiencing significant changes as a result of demographic trends, economic transformations, internal migration, and immigration, and these changes have important implications for the future of American elections and voting behavior.

The second major section of the book focuses on the characteristics, beliefs, and behavior of the American electorate. Chapter 3 examines the changing bases of support of the Democratic and Republican parties while Chapter 4 analyzes popular participation in the electoral process. Another unusual feature of this book is that it examines electoral participation beyond the basic act of voting. Opinion leaders and activists play an important role in the electoral process and their social background characteristics and political attitudes are different from those of less active citizens.

The third section of the book examines campaigns and elections at the national level. Chapter 5 focuses on the contemporary presidential nominating process. This chapter seeks to explain why George W. Bush and Al Gore won the Republican and Democratic presidential nominations in 2000 and how the rules of the nomination process will affect which Democrat gets to challenge George W. Bush in the 2004 presidential election. Chapter 6 turns to the presidential general election, examining the influence of the Electoral College, media, money, and the mood of the electorate on the campaign and the outcome. Chapter 7 examines congressional campaigns and elections. Congressional elections are both national and local events and this chapter therefore examines the influence of national and local forces on congressional elections. Chapter 7 also explores the reasons for the growing advantage of incumbency in House and Senate elections.

The concluding chapter of the book examines the outlook for electoral reform in the United States. In the absence of a major scandal or crisis, the prospects for reform in the near future appear to be much greater at the state and local level than at the national level. This chapter therefore focuses on recent efforts to increase participation, control the influence of money, and promote competition in state and local elections.

An important goal of this book is to introduce students to some of the theoretical approaches and analytic techniques that are commonly used in scholarly research on elections and voting behavior. Rational choice, sociological, and psychological approaches are incorporated in various chapters where they are relevant. Throughout the book, both survey and aggregate-level data are utilized to illustrate major themes and concepts. Data from the 1952 through 2000 American National Election Studies as well as the 2000 Voter News Service exit polls are used extensively along with data provided by the Census Bureau, Immigration and Naturalization Service, Federal

Election Commission, and other government agencies. A variety of statistical techniques are utilized in the book, including contingency table analysis, correlation analysis, and regression analysis. Where appropriate, line graphs and bar graphs are also employed to illustrate important comparisons and trends. The purposes for which these techniques are being used are explained and the results are interpreted in the body of the text.

Several special pedagogical tools are included in each chapter to assist students in understanding and using the material. Key terms and concepts are identified in the text. Questions to guide classroom discussion are provided at the end of each chapter along with a list of books and articles for additional reading and a list of websites with useful information.

Many people have contributed to this book. The ideas of several generations of scholars of electoral behavior are reflected in these chapters. I am especially grateful to my dissertation advisor at Stanford University, Heinz Eulau, who taught me that the individual was at the heart of the political process, and to my colleagues and research collaborators at the College of William and Mary, the State University of New York at Stony Brook, Emory University, and elsewhere. I would especially like to thank Ronald Rapoport, John McGlennon, Walter Stone, Merle Black, Micheal Giles, and Kyle Saunders for many helpful ideas and sometimes for just listening. Data from the National Election Studies and the Voter News Service exit polls was provided by the Inter-University Consortium for Political and Social Research.

I would like to thank the members of the editorial staff at McGraw-Hill who devoted many hours to bringing this project to fruition. Political Science Editor Monica Eckman encouraged me to undertake this project and provided regular advice and feedback along the way. Kate Scheinman kept me on track and on schedule. Jean Hamilton supervised the book's production and Carol Rose handled the copy-editing process with maximum efficiency.

I would also like to thank the outside reviewers who examined drafts of various chapters and provided many valuable suggestions that are incorporated in the book: Ken Kollman, University of Michigan; Richard Niemi, University of Rochester; Mark Rozell, Catholic University of America; Gary Segura, University of Iowa; Peverill Squire, University of Iowa; Paul Watanabe, University of Massachusetts, Boston; Clyde Wilcox, Georgetown University; and Kenneth Williams, Michigan State University.

Finally, I would like to thank my wife, Ann Abramowitz, for her encouragement and emotional support at every stage of this project.

CHAPTER 1

Elections and American Democracy

ELECTIONS AND THE AMERICAN CREED

The role of elections in American politics has been profoundly shaped by certain widely shared ideas about government and society—ideas that make up what is often described as the American creed. But while these ideas enjoy broad support among the American people, they do not constitute a coherent ideology. In fact, the American creed includes two distinct and sometimes contradictory elements. One element is a belief in egalitarianism and populism. The other element is a belief in personal freedom and self-reliance.[1] It is the tension between these beliefs that largely explains Americans' fundamental ambivalence about elections and voting. On the one hand, Americans place a very high value on elections as a tool for ensuring popular control of government. On the other hand, Americans tolerate a very low rate of voter turnout and vast differences in resources and influence among participants in the electoral process.

---

[1] Everett C. Ladd, *The American Ideology* (Storrs, CT: The Roper Center, 1994); Stanley Feldman, "Structure and Consistency in Public Opinion: The Role of Core Beliefs and Values," *American Journal of Political Science* 32 (1988), pp. 416–40; Herbert McClosky and John Zaller, *The American Ethos* (Cambridge, MA: Harvard University Press, 1981). For a theoretical treatment of the tension between liberal individualism and egalitarianism, see William H. Riker, *Liberalism Against Populism: A Confrontation Between the Theory of Democracy and the Theory of Social Choice* (Prospect Heights, IL: Waveland Press, 1988).

Egalitarianism and Populism

Popular support for democratic institutions and practices in the
United States rests largely on two interrelated sets of ideas that can
be traced back to the country's revolutionary origins and its frontier
experience—**egalitarianism** and **populism**.[2] American egalitarianism is embodied by the ringing statement in the Declaration of Independence that "all men are created equal" and are "endowed by their
Creator with certain unalienable Rights," including "Life, Liberty,
and the pursuit of Happiness." It is the widely shared belief that all
citizens should be equal before the law and should have an equal opportunity to pursue material success and personal fulfillment. While
this belief often appears to conflict with the realities of American society, it provides an important moral underpinning to the right of all
citizens to participate in the political process.

Populism involves a belief in the wisdom and virtue of the common people and a corresponding mistrust of political and economic
elites. Like egalitarianism, the roots of populism can be traced back
to the revolutionary era and the American colonists' mistrust of a
king and Parliament in London who seemed out of touch with their
problems and needs and who sought to impose taxes and regulations on the colonists without their consent.[3] But American populism
was also nurtured during the nineteenth century by the experience
of the frontier—a place where citizens often felt that the political establishment in Washington was as far removed from their problems
and needs as the British government had been during the colonial
period.[4]

Long after both George III and the frontier had disappeared,
mistrust of elites and faith in the wisdom and virtue of the common

[2] For a discussion of American beliefs about equality, see Sidney Verba and Gary Orren,
Equality in America (Cambridge, MA: Harvard University Press, 1985). A discussion of
American attitudes toward equality in the early years of the republic is found in Alexis
de Tocqueville, *Democracy in America* (Chicago: University of Chicago Press, 2000).
[3] These ideas were set forth in Thomas Paine's influential pamphlet, *Common Sense*,
first published in 1776. See Thomas Paine, *Common Sense* (New York: Penguin Books,
1986). See also Gordon S. Wood, *The Creation of the American Republic, 1776–1787*
(Chapel Hill, NC: University of North Carolina Press, 1969); and Merrill Jensen, *The
Founding of a Nation* (New York: Oxford University Press, 1968).
[4] The classic statement of the influence of the frontier on American political ideas is
found in Frederick Jackson Turner, *The Frontier in American History* (New York: Holt,
1920). For a collection of American populist writings from the eighteenth century
through the mid-twentieth century, see George McKenna, ed., *American Populism*
(New York: Putnam, 1974).

people remained deeply ingrained in the American belief system. Thus, during the 1950s, when political scientists Gabriel Almond and Sidney Verba conducted their pioneering research on mass belief systems in four democracies, they found that the most dramatic difference between the **political culture** of the United States and that of Great Britain was that American citizens generally displayed much greater support for popular participation in political decision-making and much less deference toward political elites than their British counterparts.[5] This faith in the common people and mistrust of political elites underlies the American belief in the value of elections as a mechanism for ensuring that government decisions reflect the will of the people.

Freedom and Self-Reliance

Egalitarianism and populism help to explain the vital role played by elections in contemporary American politics. However, two other elements of the American creed, **personal freedom** and **self-reliance,** help to explain some of the limitations of the electoral process in the United States. Personal freedom refers to the widely shared belief that citizens should be allowed to engage in economic and political activity free from excessive government regulation and taxation. Self-reliance refers to the closely related belief that the individual citizen, rather than the government or society, is primarily responsible for his or her own well-being.[6]

Like egalitarianism and populism, the American values of personal freedom and self-reliance were shaped first by the revolt against British rule and later by the experience of the frontier. The American Revolution was, to a considerable extent, a rebellion against what the colonists regarded as excessive taxation and regulation by the Crown and Parliament.[7] On the frontier, self-reliance was seen as crucial to survival in the face of threats from hostile natives, unpredictable weather, and disease. Government, especially the federal government, was generally viewed as far removed from the everyday

---

[5] Gabriel A. Almond and Sidney Verba, *The Civic Culture* (Princeton, NJ: Princeton University Press, 1963), especially pp. 161–79.

[6] See Feldman, "Structure and Consistency in Public Opinion." See also Ladd, *The American Ideology.*

[7] Bernard Bailyn, *The Ideological Origins of the American Revolution* (Cambridge, MA: Harvard University Press, 1967). See also Jensen, *The Founding of a Nation;* and Wood, *The Creation of the American Republic, 1776–1787.*

problems of the settlers. It mattered little that the settlers on the frontier, like the American colonists during the eighteenth century, benefited enormously from government subsidies. By the mid-nineteenth century, rugged individualism was firmly established in the pantheon of American values.[8]

Belief in personal freedom and self-reliance has had important consequences for many aspects of American politics. Perhaps the most important consequences for the electoral process have been an emphasis on individual responsibility for voting and minimal regulation of political campaigns. In the United States, to a greater extent than any other industrial democracy, the responsibility for voting rests with the individual citizen. The United States is the only major democracy that relies entirely on personal voter registration instead of a government census to determine who is eligible to vote. As a result, despite recent efforts to ease registration rules and requirements, the percentage of citizens eligible to vote in national elections is substantially smaller in the United States than in any of these other democracies.[9] Moreover, the United States, unlike many other democracies, does not hold elections on a national holiday or a weekend, further increasing the cost of voting to many citizens and reducing turnout.

The consequences of hostility to government regulation in the United States extend beyond the economic realm to the electoral arena. Before the 1970s, there was almost no meaningful regulation of how political parties or individual candidates raised or spent campaign funds. Parties and candidates were not required to disclose how much money they had raised, who had contributed to their campaigns, or how they had spent their campaign funds. All of that changed in 1974. In response to revelations of major fund-raising abuses by the 1972 Nixon presidential campaign, Congress passed a series of amendments to the **Federal Election Campaign Act** that provided for limits on the size of contributions to federal candidates, public disclosure of all campaign expenditures and all campaign contributions of more than $100, overall spending limits for congres-

---

[8]Seymour Martin Lipset, *American Exceptionalism* (New York: Norton, 1996). See also Lipset, "Why No Socialism in the United States?" in Seweryn Bialer and Sophia Sluzar, eds., *Sources of Contemporary Radicalism* (New York: Westview Press, 1977).

[9]See Stanley Kelley, Jr. Richard E. Ayres; and William G. Bowden, "Registration and Voting: Putting First Things First," *American Political Science Review* 61 (1967), pp. 359–77. For a more recent analysis of the reasons for low and declining turnout in the United States, see Ruy Teixeira, *The Disappearing American Voter* (Washington, DC: Brookings Institution: 1992).

sional candidates, and public financing of presidential nomination and general election campaigns.[10]

The 1974 amendments to the Federal Election Campaign Act were the most far-reaching attempt to regulate campaign finance in American history. However, in the three decades since these regulations were enacted, their effectiveness has eroded considerably. First, the United States Supreme Court struck down several major provisions of the new law. In *Buckley v. Valeo* (1976), the Court held that limits on campaign spending by candidates, as well as limits on spending by individuals and groups supporting or opposing candidates, violated the First Amendment's guarantee of freedom of speech.[11] More recently, decisions by the courts and the **Federal Election Commission** have allowed individuals and groups to make unlimited contributions to party organizations. Although the party organizations were supposed to use this "soft money" exclusively for "party-building" activities, in practice they spent most of it directly on behalf of individual candidates.[12]

In 2002, Congress passed and President Bush signed into law the **Bipartisan Campaign Reform Act** (better known as the **McCain-Feingold Law**) to eliminate soft money from federal elections. However, the effectiveness of this legislation remains to be seen. The McCain-Feingold regulations are being challenged in the courts even as party leaders seek new ways of funneling unregulated cash into federal campaigns.[13]

Today, the United States is one of the few major democracies in which parties and candidates rely on private contributions for the large majority of their campaign funds. Just as importantly, the United States is the only major democracy in which parties, candidates, and their supporters are allowed to spend unlimited amounts of money on political advertising.[14] The result is that inequalities of

---

[10]For a discussion of the background and provisions of the Federal Election Campaign Act, see Frank J. Sorauf, *Money in American Elections* (Boston: Scott, Foresman and Company, 1988). More recent developments are described in Anthony Gierzynski, *Money Rules: Financing Elections in America* (Boulder, CO: Westview Press, 2000).

[11]Sorauf, *Money in American Elections*, pp. 39–43.

[12]Gierzynski, *Money Rules*.

[13]For a pessimistic assessment of the likely effects of the new law, see Ellen Miller and Nick Penniman, "The Road to Nowhere: Thirty Years of Campaign Finance Reform Yield Precious Little," *The American Prospect*, August 12, 2002, p. 14.

[14]See Richard Katz, "Party Organizations and Finance," in Lawrence LeDuc, Richard Niemi, and Pippa Norris, eds., *Comparing Democracies* (Thousand Oaks, CA: Sage Publications, 1996).

wealth in the economic arena are reflected by inequalities of resources and influence in the electoral arena.

THE DARK SIDE OF THE AMERICAN CREED: RACISM, SEXISM, AND ETHNOCENTRISM

For much of American history, the ideals of individual freedom and equality applied almost exclusively to white males of European descent. During the first century of the nation's existence, the most glaring limitation of the American creed was the acceptance of African American slavery in the southern states. Some of the delegates to the Constitutional Convention were outspoken opponents of slavery. In the end, however, the opponents of slavery gave in on almost every major issue in order to ensure that the southern states would ratify the Constitution.[15] Thus, the Constitution not only allowed slavery to continue in the South but also guaranteed that slaves who escaped to the North would be returned to their owners and allowed the brutal and notorious slave trade to continue until at least 1808. In addition, the framers agreed to count three-fifths of the number of slaves in each state for the purpose of determining representation in the U.S. House, thus increasing the power of the slave-holding states in both Congress and the Electoral College.

The Emancipation Proclamation and the defeat of the South in the Civil War ended the institution of slavery. Long after the emancipation of the slaves, however, racist attitudes remained deeply ingrained among the majority of whites in the North as well as the South.[16] These beliefs reflected and reinforced a social system in which African Americans were economically exploited and denied fundamental human rights including the right to vote.

Of course, African Americans were not the only victims of prejudice and discrimination. During the nineteenth century, thousands of American Indians were driven from their traditional homelands to make room for white settlers even when this required violating

---

[15] Donald Robinson, *Slavery in the Structure of American Politics* (New York: Basic Books, 1991). For an analysis of the issue of slavery at the Constitutional Convention from an African American perspective, see Hanes Walton, Jr., and Robert C. Smith, *American Politics and the African American Quest for Universal Freedom* (New York: Longman, 2000), pp. 11–15.

[16] Howard Schuman, C. Steeth, and L. Bobo, *Racial Attitudes in America: Trends and Interpretations* (Cambridge, MA: Harvard University Press, 1985).

treaties between the Indian tribes and the federal government.[17] Throughout much of the nineteenth and early twentieth century, there was frequent hostility and occasional violence directed at recent immigrants, especially those whose race or religion differed from the majority of native whites.[18] Finally, until well into the twentieth century, women were generally regarded as morally and intellectually inferior to men and denied access to equal educational and economic opportunities.[19]

During the nineteenth and early twentieth centuries, attitudes of racism, sexism, and ethnocentrism were prevalent throughout the Western world, not just in the United States. Indeed, the contradiction between these attitudes and Americans' fundamental beliefs in individual freedom and equality provided a powerful impetus for reform movements aimed at bringing social and political realities into line with American ideals.[20] Nevertheless, such attitudes have exerted a powerful influence on the electoral process in the United States.

Restrictions on the Right to Vote

Probably the most important consequence of racism, sexism, and ethnocentrism for the electoral process has been restrictions on the right to vote. Needless to say, African American slaves were denied this fundamental right, even though they were counted in apportioning seats in the House of Representatives. In 1870, following the Civil War, the **Fifteenth Amendment** to the Constitution prohibited denial of the right to vote on the basis of "race, color, or previous condition of servitude," and, for a relatively brief period, freed male slaves in the South were able to exercise the franchise and even hold elected office. After the end of Reconstruction in 1876, however, most of the restored, white-controlled state governments in the South moved quickly to disenfranchise African Americans through

---

[17] Dee Brown, *Bury My Heart at Wounded Knee: An Indian History of the American West* (New York: Henry Holt and Company, 2001).

[18] The immigrant experience during the late nineteenth and early twentieth centuries is chronicled in Oscar Handlin, *The Uprooted,* 2nd ed. (Boston: Little, Brown, 1990).

[19] See Eleanor Flexner, *Century of Struggle: The Woman's Rights Movement in the United States,* rev. ed. (Cambridge, MA: Harvard University Press, 1975).

[20] The classic statement of this argument with regard to race relations in the United States is found in Gunnar Myrdal, *An American Dilemma: The Negro Problem and Modern Democracy* (New York: Harper and Brothers, 1944).

a combination of poll taxes, literacy tests, and, where necessary, intimidation and violence.[21]

Not all of the former Confederate states were equally aggressive in purging African Americans from the voting rolls. During the first half of the twentieth century, some African Americans continued to exercise the franchise, especially in the states of the Rim South. In the Deep South, however, where they comprised a much larger proportion of the population, very few African Americans were able to vote between the 1890s and the passage of the federal Voting Rights Act in 1965.

As recently as the 1960s, civil rights workers who sought to help blacks register and vote in the Deep South were regularly arrested and beaten and occasionally killed. One of the most infamous incidents involved the 1964 murders of three civil rights workers participating in a voter registration drive in Mississippi. Michael Schwerner, Andrew Goodman, and James Chaney were beaten and murdered near the small town of Philadelphia, Mississippi, by a Ku Klux Klan mob aided by local law enforcement officials. Public outrage over this incident contributed to the passage of the **Voting Rights Act of 1965**.[22]

With only a few minor exceptions, women were also excluded from voting from the time of the American Revolution until 1920, when the **Nineteenth Amendment** to the U.S. Constitution finally ended the disenfranchisement of almost half the population. The adoption of the Nineteenth Amendment was the outgrowth of a long and difficult struggle by women's rights advocates like Elizabeth Cady Stanton and Susan B. Anthony who had to overcome deeply entrenched attitudes of male superiority and intense opposition by the liquor and tobacco industries which feared that women's suffrage would lead to restrictions on their products.[23]

In contrast to the situation that confronted African Americans during the late nineteenth and early twentieth centuries, there was

---

[21] Alexander Keyssar, *The Right to Vote: The Contested History of Democracy in the United States* (New York: Basic Books, 2000), pp. 105–16.

[22] For an account of the murder of Goodman, Schwerner, and Chaney and its impact on the nation, see William Bradford Huie, *Three Lives for Mississippi* (Oxford, MS: University Press of Mississippi, 2000); and Seth Cagin and Philip Dray, *We Are Not Afraid: The Story of Goodman, Schwerner, and Chaney and the Civil Rights Campaign for Mississippi* (New York: Macmillan, 1988). For a general discussion of white resistance to black registration and voting in the South, see James W. Prothro and Donald W. Matthews, *Negroes and the New Southern Politics* (New York: Harcourt, Brace, and World, 1966).

[23] Flexner, *Century of Struggle*. See also Keyssar, *The Right to Vote*, chapter 6.

very little organized resistance to efforts by women to exercise the franchise following the adoption of the Nineteenth Amendment. However, due largely to the persistence of traditional views about gender roles among older women, the rate of voting among women remained far below that among men for several decades. Not until the 1980s and 1990s did women begin to turn out at a rate equal to or higher than that of men.[24]

In addition to African Americans and women, other minority groups such as American Indians, Asian Americans, and Hispanics have, from time to time, encountered legal and extra legal barriers to voting. These barriers have ranged from relatively subtle legal provisions, such as lengthy residency requirements, to English-only literacy tests and ballots, to physical intimidation and violence.[25] Although many of these barriers have been reduced or eliminated in recent years as a result of civil rights laws and court decisions, their effects may still be evident in lower rates of political participation among the members of some of these groups.

THE CENTRALITY OF ELECTIONS IN AMERICAN POLITICS

Attitudes such as racism, sexism, and ethnocentrism, along with the American belief in individual responsibility and self-reliance, have sometimes limited popular participation in the electoral process. Despite these limitations, however, the American values of egalitarianism and populism have contributed to the development of a political system in which elections play a larger role than in any other major democracy.

The Number, Variety, and Frequency of Elections

One indicator of the importance of elections in American politics is the sheer number and variety of elected offices. The United States has by far the largest number of elected officials of any nation. Of course, the large majority of these officials are found at the local level

---

[24]For a discussion of the gender gap in turnout see Linda L. M. Bennett and Stephen E. Bennett, "Changing Views about Gender Equality in Politics: Gradual Change and Lingering Doubts," in Lois D. Whitaker, ed., *Women in Politics,* 3rd ed. (Upper Saddle River, NJ: Prentice-Hall, 1999).

[25]Keyssar, *The Right to Vote,* especially pp. 82–86, and 252–55.

of government. In 1992, according to the Census of Governments conducted by the U.S. Census Bureau, there were 493,830 local elected officials in the United States—approximately 1 for every 400 adult citizens.[26] These included thousands of mayors, city council members, county commissioners, local school board members, and officials of special districts such as water and fire commissioners. Also included were thousands of county and municipal judges and other court officials such as clerks and coroners. In every other major democracy, the overwhelming majority of such positions are filled by appointed officials or career civil servants.

At the state level, as well, the number and variety of elected offices is quite impressive. In most states, in addition to the governor and upper and lower houses of the state legislature, voters elect a lieutenant governor, an attorney general, and a secretary of state, who is usually responsible for overseeing the conduct of elections. In the large majority of states, each of these statewide officeholders is elected separately. In addition, in many states, voters choose commissioners of education, agriculture, and insurance, and members of other key regulatory agencies such as public utility commissions.

At the federal level, in addition to voting for their state's electors for president and vice president, voters get to choose one member of the House of Representatives and, since the adoption of the **Seventeenth Amendment** to the Constitution in 1913, two U.S. senators. While the number of federal elected officials is fairly limited, national elections take place much more frequently in the United States than in other industrial democracies. The president and vice president are elected every 4 years, but the entire House of Representatives and one-third of the Senate are chosen every 2 years. In addition, state and local elections often take place at different times from federal elections and primary elections to designate party nominees usually take place from 2 to 6 months before general elections. As a result, Americans not only elect many more public officials than do citizens of other democracies, they also get to vote much more frequently. In fact, elections take place so frequently in some parts of the United States that voting fatigue is often cited as a factor contributing to low voter turnout.

---

[26]U.S. Census Bureau, *Statistical Abstract of the United States: The National Data Book* (Washington, DC: U.S. Census Bureau, 2000), p. 287.

Primary Elections

Nothing more clearly demonstrates the central role of elections in American politics than the use of primary elections to choose party nominees. This practice is unique to the United States.[27] Political parties in a few other democracies have experimented in recent years with allowing dues-paying members to choose nominees from candidates who have been carefully screened by party leaders. However, no other major democracy allows ordinary voters to choose party nominees. In every other democracy, control of nominations is a closely guarded prerogative of party organizations and their leaders. Indeed, the selection of candidates for public office is generally regarded as the most vital function of a political party.

The **direct primary** was perhaps the most far-reaching reform promoted by the **progressive movement** in the United States during the late nineteenth and early twentieth centuries. For the almost exclusively white, middle-class leaders of the progressive movement, the goal of the direct primary was to wrest control of nominations, and thereby control of local and state governments, from party organizations like New York's infamous Tammany Hall.[28] The reformers viewed these organizations and their bosses as corrupt and overly dependent on low-income, immigrant voters whose support could be "bought" with patronage and appeals to ethnic solidarity.

Although a few state parties had experimented with primary elections during the mid-nineteenth century, it was not until the 1890s that states began enacting laws mandating the use of primary elections to nominate candidates for local and state office. By 1917, 44 of the 48 states had enacted some sort of primary law, with 32 states making the use of primaries mandatory.[29] In less than 30 years, the direct primary had replaced the party convention as the dominant method of nominating candidates for state and local office in the United States.

[27] V. O. Key, Jr., *Politics, Parties, and Pressure Groups*, 5th ed. (New York: Thomas Y. Crowell, 1964), chapter 14. For more recent analyses of the role of primary elections in American politics, see John S. Jackson III and William Crotty, *The Politics of Presidential Selection* (New York: Longman, 2001); and Peter F. Galderisi, Marni Ezra, and Michael Lyons, eds., *Congressional Primaries and the Politics of Representation* (Lanham, MD: Rowman and Littlefield, 2001).

[28] For a statement of the views of one of the leading progressive reformers concerning the direct primary, see Ellen Torelle, ed., *The Political Philosophy of Robert M. LaFollette* (Madison, WI: Robert M. LaFollete Co., 1920), pp. 29–31.

[29] William J. Crotty, *Political Reform and the American Experiment* (New York: Thomas Y. Crowell, 1977), pp. 203–7.

In 1905, Wisconsin, the home state of Robert LaFollette, one of the leading progressive reformers, established the nation's first presidential primary and, by 1916, 24 states had adopted some type of presidential primary. Many of these early presidential primaries were advisory in nature, allowing voters to express a preference for a presidential candidate but not binding the state's convention delegates to support that candidate, and the number of states holding presidential primaries actually decreased between the 1920s and the 1960s. During the 1970s, however, spurred by criticism of the Democratic Party's disastrous 1968 convention at which Hubert Humphrey received the presidential nomination without running in a single primary, many more states adopted binding presidential primaries.[30] By 1976, a majority of delegates to the Democratic and Republican presidential nominating conventions were chosen in primary elections.

Today, almost all nominees for state and federal office, and the overwhelming majority of delegates to the Democratic and Republican presidential nominating conventions, are chosen in primary elections. The rules governing who is eligible to vote in these primaries vary considerably from state to state. According to information compiled by the Federal Election Commission,[31] 13 states currently hold **closed primaries** to select party nominees. These states allow only registered Republicans and Democrats to vote in their respective party's primary. Ten states allow registered independents to vote in either party's primary, two states allow independents to vote in the Republican primary only, and one state allows independents to vote in the Democratic primary only.

Twenty-three states have **open primaries.** These states have no **party registration.** In these states, any registered voter can vote in either party's primary simply by asking for that party's primary ballot. Three of these states—Alaska, California, and Washington—use what is known as a **blanket primary** in which voters can participate in the Democratic and Republican primaries for different offices in the same election. Finally, Louisiana has a unique system in which all Democratic and Republican candidates run together in a single open primary. If any candidate receives a majority of the vote in the primary, that candidate is elected; if no candidate receives a majority, a runoff election is held between the top two finishers regardless of party affiliation.

---

[30] Crotty, pp. 205–34.
[31] This information can be found on the Federal Election Commission's website: www
.fec.gov/voteregis/primaryvoting.htm.

The rules can have a powerful influence on the types of voters who participate in primary elections and, therefore, the types of candidates who win them. However, despite these variations in rules, the nearly universal use of primary elections to choose party nominees has accomplished the major goal of the progressive reformers— shifting control of the nomination process from party leaders to ordinary voters.

The Initiative and Referendum

Along with primary elections, another legacy of the progressive reformers has enlarged the role of elections in American politics since the early twentieth century: **initiative** and **referendum** laws allow citizens to vote directly on public policy issues. Initiatives are proposed laws or constitutional amendments that are placed on the ballot through citizens' petitions; referenda are proposed laws or constitutional amendments that are placed on the ballot by state legislatures.

Initiatives, like primary elections, are unique to the United States, and although other democracies occasionally allow their citizens to vote on policy issues, referenda are far more common in the U.S. than anywhere else. Twenty-seven states and the District of Columbia allow citizens to vote on initiatives or referenda or both. In some states, such as California, it is not unusual for dozens of initiatives, including some containing contradictory provisions, to appear on the ballot simultaneously. The importance of the policy issues dealt with by these initiatives can be seen from the fact that interest groups frequently spend millions of dollars first trying to place initiatives on the ballot and then trying to get them either passed or defeated.[32]

Certainly, part of the explanation for the number, variety, and frequency of elections in the United States is simply the size and diversity of the nation and the federal structure of American government. Within the United States, there are 50 separate state governments and thousands of cities, counties, townships, and school districts, each spending public funds and each carrying out policies that affect the lives of their constituents. Beyond this structural explanation, however, we must look to the influence of American ideals, especially to the values of egalitarianism and populism. The importance of elections in the contemporary American political system is a direct reflection of the widely shared beliefs of Americans that all

[32]David B. Magleby, *Direct Legislation: Voting on Ballot Propositions in the United States* (Baltimore, MD: Johns Hopkins University Press, 1984).

citizens have an equal right to participate in the political process and that ordinary citizens, to the maximum extent possible, should exercise political power.

FROM ELITIST TO POPULAR DEMOCRACY

The role of elections in American politics has expanded along with the nation itself. In 225 years, the United States has evolved from a fragile confederation of former British colonies along the Atlantic seaboard with a population of less than 4 million to a continental nation with a racially, ethnically, and religiously diverse population of more than 280 million. Over those 225 years, American democracy has also undergone drastic change. A political system that was founded on the principles of **elitist democratic theory** has evolved into one whose operation is much more consistent with the principles of **popular democratic theory.**

The elitist theory of democracy assumes that ordinary citizens are poorly equipped to make political decisions. According to this theory, responsibility for policy making is best entrusted to an educated elite that is relatively insulated from popular influence. The purpose of elections is to allow voters periodically to hold political leaders accountable for their performance by either keeping them in office or replacing them with a different set of leaders, not to provide any specific policy directives for these leaders to follow.[33] As a corollary, many elitist thinkers, including such American founders as James Madison and John Adams, favored limiting the right to vote to those citizens with a stake in the social order—generally those who either owned land or paid taxes.[34]

The Constitutional Convention

The group of wealthy and educated white males who gathered in Philadelphia in the summer of 1787 to write the U.S. Constitution consisted largely of conservative politicians who had little faith in the ability of ordinary citizens to govern themselves. Most of the

[33]One of the most influential statements of the elitist theory of democracy is found in Joseph A. Schumpeter, *Capitalism, Socialism, and Democracy* (New York: Harper and Row, 1962). A critical analysis of the work of Schumpeter and other elitist theorists is found in Peter Bachrach, *The Theory of Democratic Elitism* (Boston: Little, Brown, 1967).
[34]Keyssar, *The Right to Vote,* chapter 1.

democratic leaders of the revolutionary era, including Thomas Jefferson, Patrick Henry, and Samuel Adams, were absent from the convention. Ten years earlier, the American revolutionaries had been inspired by the democratic ideals of the European Enlightenment—ideals that were embodied in the ringing phrases of the Declaration of Independence. But by 1787, the delegates to the Constitutional Convention were more concerned about feuding among the states over trade and other issues, a deteriorating economic situation, and the possibility of a British invasion. Moreover, some of the new state governments were being taken over by representatives of poor, uneducated farmers, threatening the interests of large landowners and creditors.

The delegates to the Philadelphia convention realized that the weak national government created by the Articles of Confederation was powerless to deal with these problems, so they set out to create a stronger union, giving the federal government much greater power to raise taxes and impose uniform laws across the entire nation.[35] Despite intense opposition in several of the larger states, especially New York and Virginia, within 2 years the necessary two-thirds of the states had ratified the new Constitution. However, to alleviate widespread concerns that the new, powerful federal government would threaten many of the rights that Americans had fought for in the Revolution, supporters of the Constitution agreed to accept a series of amendments designed to protect individual freedoms and preserve some of the traditional powers of the states. Ten such amendments were quickly adopted and later became known as the Bill of Rights.

The Right to Vote

Given the general hostility of most of the framers to popular democracy, it is not surprising that neither the original Constitution nor the Bill of Rights included any guarantee of a right to vote. Instead, the determination of who would be allowed to exercise the franchise was left to the discretion of the individual states, whose laws regarding the suffrage varied widely. During the 1790s, most of the states

---

[35] Wood, *The Creation of the American Republic,* chapters 12–13. See also Thornton Anderson, *Creating the Constitution: The Convention of 1787 and the First Congress* (University Park, PA: Pennsylvania State University Press, 1993). The arguments for the new Constitution were set forth by John Jay, Alexander Hamilton, and James Madison in *The Federalist Papers* (New York: New American Library, 1961).

imposed some landownership requirements for voting, although the amount of land varied considerably and several states, including Pennsylvania, Georgia, and New Hampshire, allowed citizens who were not landowners but who paid taxes to vote. During the first few decades of the nineteenth century, however, almost all of these landownership requirements, along with other economic restrictions on the franchise, were abandoned, and by the time of the Civil War, universal white male suffrage was the general rule throughout the nation.[36]

The Senate

The achievement of universal white male suffrage did nothing to alter the elitist provisions of the Constitution, however. Perhaps the most important restriction on popular democracy that was incorporated into the Constitution was the indirect election of both the Senate and the president. Under the original provisions of the Constitution, the House of Representatives was the only part of the national government directly elected by the people. From 1789 until the ratification of the Seventeenth Amendment in 1913, U.S. senators were chosen by the state legislatures. In addition, to this day each state, regardless of population, is entitled to choose two senators, making the U.S. Senate the most malapportioned legislature in the world. A senator from California represents more than 30 million people while a senator from Wyoming represents fewer than 500,000 people.

The Electoral College

The procedure devised by the framers for choosing the president was much more complicated than that for choosing senators. In fact, according to public opinion polls, until the events of the disputed 2000 election thrust the **Electoral College** into the news, most Americans had little or no idea of what it was or how it worked.[37] The Electoral College was created to insulate the presidency from direct popular control. According to the plan of the framers, every 4 years presi-

---

[36] Keyssar, *The Right to Vote,* chapters 1–2.
[37] In a 1955 Gallup Poll, only 35 percent of Americans were able to give a reasonably accurate explanation of the purpose of the Electoral College. For a general discussion of the level of political information in the American public, see Michael X. Delli Carpini and Scott Keeter, *What Americans Know About Politics and Why It Matters* (New Haven, CT: Yale University Press, 1996).

dential electors chosen by the state legislatures were to meet in each of the state capitols to deliberate and vote for a presidential candidate. The framers assumed that the electors would be drawn mainly from the educated, landowning elite, and would vote for presidential candidates who came from similar backgrounds.

The framers of the Constitution also assumed that after George Washington, the consensus choice to become the first president, divisions between the large and small states and among different regions of the country would make it very difficult for any candidate to obtain the majority of electoral votes necessary to become president. In this event, which the framers expected to be quite common, the president was to be chosen by the House of Representatives, with each state delegation, regardless of size, casting one vote.

During the first few decades of the nineteenth century, two developments fundamentally altered the elitist presidential selection process created by the framers—the advent of popular voting for presidential electors and the development of political parties. The emergence of competition for the presidency after Washington declined to seek a third term in 1796 led a number of states to pass laws giving their citizens the right to vote for presidential electors. By 1824, the large majority of states had adopted popular voting for presidential electors, and by the time of the Civil War, South Carolina was the only state whose electors were still chosen by the state legislature.[38]

The spread of popular voting for presidential electors coincided with another development that permanently changed the presidential election process and the role of the Electoral College—the emergence of a competitive, two-party system.[39] With the departure of Washington from the presidency in 1797, the intense disagreements that had arisen over the adoption of the Constitution quickly reemerged. Those who had supported and opposed the Constitution gravitated into two opposing political camps: **Federalists** who supported a strong national government and **Anti-Federalists,** also known as **Democratic-Republicans,** who favored states' rights and a

[38]For a description of the spread of popular voting for presidential electors, see Arthur M. Schlesinger, Jr., ed., *History of American Presidential Elections, 1789–1968,* Vol. 2 (New York: McGraw-Hill, 1971), p. 1244.

[39]For an account of the early development of the American party system, see William N. Chambers, *Political Parties in a New Nation: The American Experience* (New York: Oxford University Press, 1963). See also Everett C. Ladd, *American Political Parties: Social Change and Political Response* (New York: Norton, 1970).

limited role for the national government. The Federalists were led by John Adams and Alexander Hamilton; the Democratic-Republicans were led by Thomas Jefferson.

Along with popular voting, the development of a competitive two-party system produced a fundamental alteration in the role of the Electoral College. After 1796, each party began to nominate a slate of electors in each state who were committed to voting for its presidential candidate. As a result, voters were able to choose a slate of electors who were committed to their preferred candidate. The electors were no longer independent political actors exercising their own judgment, but agents of the political parties. In effect, the voters in each state, not the electors, were really choosing the president.

While the role of electors as autonomous political actors was eliminated after 1796 by the development of political parties, the Electoral College continues to play an important role in presidential elections, a fact that many Americans discovered for the first time in the aftermath of the 2000 election. The winner of the presidential election is still determined by the electoral vote, not the popular vote, with the number of electoral votes cast by each state based on the size of its House delegation plus its two senators. Because each state's two senators are included in determining its electoral votes, the less populated states carry disproportionate weight in the Electoral College. The results of the 2000 presidential election show that this is not a trivial fact. If electoral votes had been allocated only on the basis of representation in the House, Al Gore would have defeated George W. Bush.

The fact that the winner of the presidential election is determined by electoral votes has other important consequences. Since the early nineteenth century, almost every state has awarded its electoral votes on a winner-take-all basis. Today every state except Maine and Nebraska awards all of its electoral votes to the candidate who receives a plurality of the popular vote in the state. By awarding their electoral votes on a winner-take-all basis, states make these votes more valuable to the presidential candidates—a candidate who carries a state by a single ballot in the popular vote still receives all of the state's electoral votes.

The winner-take-all system of awarding electoral votes has important consequences for the strategies of presidential candidates and Chapter 6 will explore these consequences in much greater detail. For now, it will suffice to say that this system produces a powerful incentive for candidates to concentrate on campaigning in states that cast large blocs of electoral votes and are highly competitive. In these states, a small swing in the popular vote can shift a large bloc of electoral votes.

In the aftermath of the 2000 presidential election, most Americans now realize that the winner-take-all system of awarding electoral votes, in combination with the overrepresentation of less populous states in the Electoral College, makes it possible for a candidate to win a majority of the electoral vote while losing the popular vote. In the 2000 election, the Democratic candidate, Al Gore, received over 500,000 more votes than the Republican candidate, George W. Bush. However, Bush became president by winning the electoral vote by a razor-thin 271-267 margin after receiving 25 disputed electoral votes from the state of Florida. Thus, George W. Bush became the first president since Benjamin Harrison in 1888, and only the fourth president in American history, to win the presidency despite losing the popular vote.[40]

The Democratization of the Constitution

Since the adoption of the Bill of Rights, 17 additional amendments have been added to the U.S. Constitution. Several of these amendments have modified the elitist design of the original Constitution by extending the right to vote to previously disenfranchised groups such as African Americans (the Fifteenth Amendment in 1870), women (the Nineteenth Amendment in 1920), and 18–20 year olds (the **Twenty-sixth Amendment** in 1971). The **Twenty-third Amendment,** ratified in 1961, gave residents of the District of Columbia the right to vote in presidential elections. However, residents of the District, whose population exceeds that of several states, still lack voting representation in either the House of Representatives or the Senate.

Other amendments to the Constitution have eliminated barriers to voting and strengthened the connection between public officials and voters. The Seventeenth Amendment, ratified in 1913, provided for direct popular election of U.S. senators; the **Twentieth Amendment,** ratified in 1933, reduced the "lame duck" period between Election Day and the date when the new Congress and president assume

[40]For a thorough and unbiased account of the 2000 presidential election, see James W. Ceaser and Andrew E. Busch, *The Perfect Tie: The True Story of the 2000 Presidential Election* (Lanham, MD: Rowman and Littlefield, 2001). Two collections of insightful essays on various aspects of the 2000 election are provided by Michael Nelson, ed., *The Elections of 2000* (Washington, DC: Congressional Quarterly Press, 2001); and Gerald M. Pomper, ed., *The Election of 2000* (New York: Chatham House, 2001).

office; the **Twenty-fourth Amendment,** ratified in 1964, prohibited poll taxes; the **Twenty-seventh Amendment,** ratified in 1992, required that legislation increasing the salaries of members of Congress not take effect until after the next election. By modifying or eliminating many of the elitist provisions of the original Constitution, these amendments have moved the American political system dramatically in the direction of popular democracy.

RECENT DEVELOPMENTS

Some of the most significant developments that have increased the importance of elections in American politics have not involved changes in the Constitution itself. Since 1960, court decisions, legislation, and trends in American society have strengthened the electoral connection by equalizing citizens' representation in government, broadening access to the polls, and making political leaders more responsive to public opinion. These developments have included Supreme Court decisions requiring that state legislative and U.S. House districts within each state be approximately equal in population, passage of the federal Voting Rights Act of 1965, the spread of two-party competition to the South and other areas of the country previously dominated by one party, changes in the mass media, the growth of public opinion polling, and new laws aimed at reducing obstacles to registration and voting.

One Person, One Vote

The Constitution left it up to the individual states to determine how to conduct their own elections, including elections for representatives in the U.S. House. In many states, the voting systems that were used gave vastly more weight to some citizens than to others. Rural areas, for example, were frequently over represented in both state legislatures and the House of Representatives, compared with urban areas.

Historically, the courts in the United States had been very reluctant to accept cases dealing with "political issues" such as the populations and boundaries of legislative districts. However, in the 1960s that changed dramatically. In a series of decisions between 1962 and 1964, the U.S. Supreme Court found that differences in the value of a vote between one part of a state and another were unconstitutional.[41] First, in *Baker* **v.** *Carr* (1962), the Court ruled that the apportionment of Tennessee's state legislative seats could be challenged in the federal courts under the equal protection clause of the Fourteenth Amendment. Then, in *Gray* **v.** *Sanders* (1963), the Court struck down Georgia's county unit primary system on the grounds that it violated the equal protection clause by giving far more weight to voters in sparsely populated, rural counties than to voters in heavily populated, urban counties.

In 1964, the Supreme Court extended the logic of *Gray* v. *Sanders* to federal elections by ruling, in *Wesberry* **v.** *Sanders,* that the vast differences in population among Georgia's U.S. House districts violated both the equal protection clause and the requirement of article 1, section 2 of the Constitution that representatives be chosen "by the people." Later that year, in *Reynolds* **v.** *Sims,* the Court, again citing the equal protection clause, struck down Alabama's state legislative districting system because of substantial differences in population among districts.

In these decisions, the Supreme Court for the first time interpreted the right to vote to include not only the right to cast a ballot but also the right to have that ballot count as much as a ballot cast by any other citizen. In a democracy, the Court concluded, citizens were entitled not just to representation in government but to *equal* representation. From that point on, the rule in drawing legislative districts would be, in the words of Justice William O. Douglas, **"one person, one vote."**

The 1965 Voting Rights Act

Nearly a century after the ratification of the Fifteenth Amendment, the federal Voting Rights Act of 1965 finally transformed that Amendment's promise of equal voting rights for African Americans into a reality.[42] Following his landslide reelection victory in 1964, President Lyndon Johnson, the first southerner to occupy the White House since Woodrow Wilson, made voting rights a key part of his Great Society program. Johnson knew that his strong support for civil rights would alienate many white voters in the South and that the

---

[41] Keyssar, *The Right to Vote,* pp. 285–87.
[42] Earl Black and Merle Black, *Politics and Society in the South* (Cambridge, MA: Harvard University Press, 1987), pp. 112–25. See also Keyssar, *The Right to Vote,* pp. 257–67.

future of the Democratic Party in the region depended on mobilizing African American voters. Passage of the bill was also aided by public outrage over the highly publicized murders of three civil rights workers participating in a voter registration drive in Mississippi during the "freedom summer" of 1964.

Although it was opposed by some conservative Republicans and by a majority of southern Democrats, the Voting Rights Act passed the House and Senate with overwhelming majorities. The law immediately suspended the use of literacy tests and other discriminatory practices that had prevented large numbers of African Americans, along with some low-income whites, from voting in many parts of the South. Even more significantly, the law authorized the attorney general to send federal examiners into the southern states to observe voter registration procedures and, when necessary, to directly register voters.

The impact of the Voting Rights Act was immediate and dramatic.[43] In a few years, registration and voting among African Americans increased substantially throughout the South, and especially in the states of the Deep South. Between 1964 and 1968, the percentage of African Americans registered to vote rose from less than 10 percent to almost 60 percent in Mississippi and from 24 percent to 57 percent in Alabama. Throughout the South, approximately a million new voters were registered in fewer than 5 years. By the end of the decade, an estimated 62 percent of African American citizens were registered to vote across the region, a percentage only slightly lower than that for whites.

Although it resulted in a dramatic increase in African American registration and voting in the South, the Voting Rights Act did not end all forms of racial discrimination in the conduct of elections. Despite the requirement that governments covered by the Voting Rights Act obtain approval from the Justice Department before making any significant changes in their election procedures, states and cities with large concentrations of African American residents often sought to minimize the impact of the Voting Rights Act through the use of **at-large elections** or districting schemes that diluted the minority vote. By holding at-large elections or spreading minority voters across a large number of districts, states and cities could make it difficult or

---

[43] For an overview of the impact of the Voting Rights Act on southern politics, see Chandler Davidson and Bernard Grofman, eds., *Quiet Revolution in the South: The Impact of the Voting Rights Act, 1965–1990* (Princton, NJ: Princeton University Press, 1994).

impossible for African Americans to elect their own representatives to public office.

Since the 1960s, the attention of civil rights lawyers and the courts has shifted from the right to vote itself to the consequences of election laws and districting arrangements for minority representation in government.[44] This has led to a series of controversial, and sometimes contradictory, court decisions regarding the use of race as a factor in drawing district boundaries and the legality of weirdly shaped **majority-minority districts.** Most recently, in *Hunt* v. *Cromartie* (2001), the Supreme Court held that such majority-minority districts are constitutional if race was not the "predominant factor" in drawing the district boundaries.

Notwithstanding the controversy over racial districting, the Voting Rights Act has resulted in a dramatic increase in the number of African Americans holding elected office. Between 1970 and 1998, the total number of black elected officials in the United States increased sixfold—from fewer than 1,500 to almost 9,000—with the large majority of that increase occurring in the southern states. As of 1998, 63 percent of the black elected officials in the U.S. came from the 11 states of the old Confederacy.[45] Thus, whether it is judged in terms of its impact on African American voting or African American representation in government, the 1965 Voting Rights Act must be considered one of the most important civil rights laws ever enacted.

Two-Party Competition

One of the best-known features of American politics is the two-party system. Since the early nineteenth century, Democrats and Whigs, and later Democrats and Republicans, have battled for control of Congress and the presidency. Throughout much of American history, however, many states and regions within the United States have really had only a one-party system. From the end of Reconstruction in 1876 until the early 1960s, not a single Republican was elected to statewide office in the 11 states of the old Confederacy. During these years, Democrats controlled every state legislature in the South,

---

[44] For an analysis of the major court cases in this area, see Chandler Davidson, "The Recent Evolution of Voting Rights Law Affecting Racial and Language Minorities," in Davidson and Grofman, eds., *Quiet Revolution in the South*, pp. 21–37.
[45] U.S. Census Bureau, *Statistical Abstract of the United States*, p. 288.

almost all local elected offices, and all but a handful of the region's seats in the House of Representatives.[46]

Nor did Republicans fare much better in presidential elections. Between 1880 and 1952, the only Republican presidential candidate to win any electoral votes in the South was Herbert Hoover who carried four Rim South states in 1928 against Democratic Governor Al Smith of New York. Despite Smith's Catholicism and opposition to prohibition, which were anathema to most southern voters, the Democratic nominee still managed to win a majority of the South's electoral votes, sweeping the Deep South and receiving 82 percent of the vote in Mississippi and 91 percent of the vote in South Carolina. Four years later, Franklin Roosevelt restored Democratic hegemony in the South. Roosevelt carried all 11 states of the old Confederacy, winning 92 percent of the vote in Georgia, 93 percent in Louisiana, 96 percent in Mississippi, and 98 percent in South Carolina. In his four elections, Roosevelt never received less than 60 percent of the vote in any southern state.

During the late nineteenth and early twentieth centuries, the Democrats' domination of the South was nearly matched by the Republicans' domination of much of the Northeast and Midwest.[47] There were a few pockets of Democratic strength in the North in cities like New York, Chicago, and Boston where Democratic machines held sway by cultivating the support of poor, mostly Catholic, immigrants. Elsewhere, however, Republican candidates could generally count on victory by appealing to traditional party loyalties and stirring up memories of the terrible losses suffered during the Civil War, a tactic known as "waving the bloody shirt."

The New Deal realignment brought two-party competition to many parts of the North that had previously been dominated by the Republican Party. During the 1930s, President Roosevelt's policies and the effects of the Great Depression resulted in the mobilization of millions of new voters, including many recent immigrants and their children, and the conversion of millions of traditional Republican voters to the Democratic Party. By the 1950s, even though Re-

---

[46] The best account of the traditional one-party system in the South is found in Key, *Southern Politics in State and Nation.* For analyses of the emergence of two-party competition in the region, see Black and Black, *Politics and Society in the South;* and Alexander Lamis, *The Two-Party South* (New York: Oxford University Press, 1988).

[47] See James L. Sundquist, *Dynamics of the Party System: Alignment and Realignment of Political Parties in the United States,* rev. ed. (Washington, DC: Brookings Institution, 1983), chapters 7–9.

publicans were able to regain some of the ground that they had lost during the thirties, two-party competition was the rule in all of the large, industrial states of the North.[48]

Two-party competition was much slower to develop in the South, however. There the initial effect of the Depression and New Deal was to reinforce the region's loyalty to the Democrats. The South was the poorest part of the United States even before the 1930s, and it was hit harder by the Depression than any other region. It is not surprising, therefore, that the large majority of southerners strongly supported Roosevelt and the New Deal.

After the end of World War II, three developments began to gradually erode the South's loyalty to the Democratic Party: economic development and the rise of a new middle class, migration from the North, and the national Democratic Party's growing support for civil rights.[49] The growth of the middle class in many of the metropolitan areas of the South provided a natural base of support for the Republican Party. Relative affluence and economic security meant that many of these new voters were less concerned about the benefits that they received from government programs than about the taxes that they paid for these programs.

Many of the members of the new middle class were northern migrants who moved to the South to find jobs or retire. Since the 1950s, millions of these migrants have left the Northeast and Midwest for new homes in southern Florida, northern Virginia, Atlanta, Dallas, and other metropolitan areas of the South, bringing their political loyalties with them. Although extremely diverse in terms of religion, ethnicity, and political outlook, the northern migrants helped to transform southern politics by increasing the representation of two groups in the electorate—Republicans and liberal Democrats.

Economic development and migration were not the only forces undermining the South's one-party system in the postwar years, however. In his monumental treatise, *Southern Politics in State and Nation,* first published in 1949, the late V. O. Key observed, "In its grand outlines the politics of the South revolves around the position of the Negro."[50] Race, Key argued, was the major factor responsible for the one-party system in the South. From the end of Reconstruction until

[48]Sundquist, chapter 11.

[49]Earl Black and Merle Black, *The Rise of Southern Republicans* (Cambridge, MA: Harvard University Press, 2002). See also Black and Black, *Politics and Society in the South;* and Lamis, *The Two-Party South,* chapters 1–2.

[50]Key, *Southern Politics in State and Nation,* p. 5.

the 1960s, the Democratic Party was seen as the guardian of white supremacy in the region. Political unity served to maximize southern influence in Congress and minimize the temptation to build coalitions across racial lines. That unity was threatened, however, when the national Democratic Party, at first hesitatingly at its 1948 national convention, and then decisively in its 1964 party platform, embraced the cause of civil rights. Racial conservatives, a group that comprised a majority of the white electorate in the South, began to abandon the Democratic Party during the 1960s and 1970s. Some of these former conservative Democrats adopted the independent label for a time. By the 1980s and 1990s, however, most of them had moved into the Republican camp. By then the South's one-party system was little more than a relic of the past.[51]

Modern democratic theorists generally consider competition between political parties essential to the vitality of representative democracy.[52] Parties provide continuity in the electoral process. While individual politicians come and go, political parties usually endure for many election cycles. Moreover, parties tend to have fairly stable policy orientations. Even if they do not follow politics closely, citizens can learn to associate party labels with general policy orientations. Thus, political parties help voters to make rational decisions by reducing their information costs.

Competition between parties also helps citizens hold politicians accountable for their collective performance. If they are satisfied with the governing party's policies and the way it is managing the government, citizens can vote to keep it in office; if they are dissatisfied with the governing party's policies and managerial performance, they can vote for the opposition party. In this way, competition between parties allows voters to act as rational "gods" of vengeance and reward. Moreover, by enforcing collective accountability, citizens provide a powerful incentive for politicians to cooperate in fulfilling their party's campaign promises. This is especially important in a decentralized political system like that of the United States in which

---

[51] Black and Black, *The Rise of Southern Republicans.* See also Black and Black, *Politics and Society in the South,* chapters 11–14; Lamis, *The Two-Party South,* chapter 3; and Black and Black, *The Vital South: How Presidents Are Elected* (Cambridge, MA: Harvard University Press, 1992), chapters 6–7.

[52] For a classic statement of this idea, see E. E. Schattschneider, *Party Government* (New York: Farrar and Rinehart, 1942). See also Giovanni Sartori, *Democratic Theory* (Detroit: Wayne State University Press, 1962); and Key, *Politics, Parties, and Pressure Groups,* pp. 9–10.

any major policy change requires the support of numerous independently elected public officials representing diverse constituencies.

From the late nineteenth century until the middle of the twentieth century, electoral competition in much of the United States was limited to competition within the dominant party's primary—the Democratic primary in the South and the Republican primary in parts of the Northeast and Midwest. In many states and localities, winning that primary was tantamount to election. But, as V. O. Key forcefully argued in *Southern Politics*, intraparty competition was a poor substitute for interparty competition.[53] Without the assistance of party labels, voters often had a difficult time discerning candidates' issue positions or holding officeholders accountable for policy failures or mismanagement. The spread of two-party competition to every region of the United States since the 1950s has enhanced electoral accountability and strengthened the connection between elections and policy outcomes.

The Mass Media

Since the end of World War II, changes in the mass media and advances in communications technology have transformed political campaigning in the United States and altered the relationship between citizens and public officials. The most obvious effect that these developments have had on elections has been the growing use of television advertising in political campaigns. Since the first TV spots were aired by the Eisenhower presidential campaign in 1952, the use of television advertising has spread to candidates for state and local as well as national office. Today, 30-second **spot advertisements** are the most important way that most political candidates communicate with voters and television advertising is the largest budget item in most campaigns.[54]

Over the past 50 years, television news has gradually replaced newspapers as the main source of political information for most Americans.[55] More Americans watch the network evening news broadcasts than read news stories about government and politics in

---

[53] Key, *Southern Politics in State and Nation,* chapter 14.
[54] Stephen Ansolabehere, Roy Behr, and Shanto Iyengar, *The Media Game: American Politics in the Television Age,* chapter 4. See also Doris A. Graber, *Mass Media and American Politics* (Washington, DC: Congressional Quarterly Press, 1997).
[55] Ansolabehere, Behr, and Iyengar, *The Media Game,* chapter 3.

the newspaper. Furthermore, despite frequent allegations of bias on the part of network journalists, Americans generally have more confidence in the accuracy and fairness of the network news broadcasts than they do in their daily newspapers.

The development of radio and television has also allowed politicians, and especially presidents, to communicate directly with the public, bypassing traditional intermediaries such as journalists and party leaders. Since the nineteenth century, presidents have recognized the importance of using the bully pulpit provided by the White House to publicize their ideas, but until the development of the electronic media, they had to rely on newspapers or surrogates to get their message out to the public. By the 1930s, however, Franklin Roosevelt was able to use the new medium of radio to speak directly to millions of Americans about his policies for dealing with the Depression in his famous **fireside chats.** Since the 1950s, presidents have made extensive use of televised press conferences, speeches, and events to build support for their policies through both words and visual images. The ability to communicate effectively on television has become an important qualification for the presidency and other public offices.[56]

From the end of World War II until the 1970s, the news media provided government officials, and especially presidents, with an effective tool for influencing public opinion. During the cold war era, the three major networks—CBS, NBC, and ABC—dominated television news coverage of national politics. During this era, network news executives and journalists, along with their counterparts in the print media, could generally be counted on to provide sympathetic coverage of the president and other high-ranking government officials.[57] Since then, however, two important developments have dramatically altered the role of the media in American politics: the changing attitude of journalists toward government officials in the aftermath of the Vietnam War and the Watergate scandal, and the proliferation of media outlets since 1980.

The discovery during the late 1960s and early 1970s that the Johnson and Nixon administrations had deliberately misled the American people about the war in Vietnam led to a serious erosion of trust in political leaders among both journalists and the public. Later revelations that President Nixon and many of his top advisors had been deeply involved in the planning and cover-up of the Watergate break-

[56] Ibid., chapter 5.
[57] Ibid., chapter 1.

in reinforced this distrust and caused journalists to adopt a much more critical tone in their coverage of the president and other high-ranking government officials. In the post-Vietnam, post-Watergate era, national political leaders could no longer count on receiving sympathetic coverage from journalists. Increasingly, as Thomas Patterson has argued, they found their motives, as well as their policies, questioned. Instead of merely reporting politicians' statements and actions, journalists now are much more inclined to analyze the behavior of politicians in strategic terms. Moreover, mainstream media outlets now routinely cover activities that were once considered private and off-limits, such as extramarital relationships.[58]

Along with this change in journalistic attitudes, the 1980s and 1990s produced a tremendous proliferation of media outlets.[59] The development of cable and satellite television and, more recently, the explosive growth of the Internet, have provided citizens with a far greater number and variety of political information sources to choose from than in the past. Instead of one or two daily newspapers and three network news broadcasts, citizens can now choose from hundreds of news and opinion programs on cable and satellite TV along with thousands of websites offering political news, information, and a wide range of opinions. Moreover, unlike the newspapers and network news broadcasts, these programs and websites supply political information 24 hours per day, 7 days per week.

The fact that citizens now have far more options when it comes to political news and information does not necessarily mean that they are better informed. The quality of information available on cable TV and the Internet varies tremendously and the number of viewers who watch C-SPAN regularly or tune in to more serious, in-depth news broadcasts remains quite small. Nevertheless, the proliferation of media outlets and the development of a continuous news cycle, along with the more cynical attitude of journalists toward politicians, have altered the relationship between political leaders and citizens. Elected officials and candidates now have much less control over the information about their actions and positions that is available to the public. The result is that politicians feel less secure than in

[58] Thomas E. Patterson, *Out of Order* (New York: Vintage Books, 1994). See also Larry Sabato, *Feeding Frenzy: How Attack Journalism has Transformed American Politics* (New York: Free Press, 1991).

[59] Jerry Yeric, *Mass Media and the Politics of Change* (Itasca, IL: F. E. Peacock Publishers, 2001), chapter 2. See also, Richard Davis and Diana Owen, *New Media and American Politics* (New York: Oxford University Press, 1998).

the past and are more inclined to tailor their actions and positions to what they perceive to be the wishes of their constituents, or at least their attentive constituents.

Public Opinion Polling

Heightened sensitivity to public opinion has been reinforced by another trend that has affected American politics since the 1960s—the growing use of public opinion polling by elected officials, candidates, and the media. Given the populist ethos of American society, it is not surprising that the first attempts to systematically measure public opinion took place in the United States. George Gallup, Sr., the founder of the Gallup Poll, conducted the first "scientific" public opinion polls during the 1930s. Since 1960, every major party presidential candidate has made extensive use of public opinion polling in shaping his campaign strategy. It was not until the 1970s, however, that advances in computer technology and the development of relatively inexpensive telephone polling techniques made it possible for candidates for state and local office as well as many newspapers and television stations to conduct their own polls.[60]

In recent years, Americans have been subjected to a barrage of poll results, especially during election campaigns. Candidates, party organizations, and interest groups all conduct polls and release their results, often selectively, to the public. Of course, the quality and accuracy of these polls vary tremendously. Candidates and interest groups are often more interested in influencing public opinion than in accurately measuring it. Survey questions are frequently written to produce a desired result, rather than to measure accurately the opinions of those being questioned. In addition, legitimate polling organizations have become increasingly concerned in recent years about the growing use of so-called push polls by political campaigns. These are pseudo-polls whose real purpose is not to measure public opinion but to spread negative information about a candidate's

---

[60] For a description of the development of modern public opinion polling, see Daniel J. Robinson, *The Measure of Democracy: Polling, Market Research, and Public Life, 1930–1945*. An excellent discussion of the various types of polls and their uses and misuses is found in Herbert B. Asher, *Polling and the Public: What Every Citizen Should Know*, 5th ed. (Washington, DC: Congressional Quarterly Press, 2001). See also Paul J. Lavrakas and Michael W. Traugott, eds., *Election Polls, the News Media, and Democracy* (New York: Chatham House, 2000).

opponent.[61] Such abuses, along with the explosive growth of tele-marketing, have contributed to a rising level of cynicism among Americans about public opinion polls and a declining willingness to participate in legitimate surveys.[62]

Politicians in the U.S. were concerned about the opinions of their constituents long before public opinion polls existed; however, they had to rely on sources such as letters to the editor or constituent mail for information about these opinions. Despite all of their problems and limitations, polls provide candidates and elected officials with a much more accurate gauge of the opinions of ordinary citizens than such sources. The availability of polling data has made it much easier for political leaders to take public opinion into account in formulating both campaign strategy and public policy. For example, Newt Gingrich and other Republican leaders in the House of Representatives made extensive use of polling data in deciding what policy proposals to include in their 1994 campaign manifesto, the "Contract with America." After the Republicans won control of the House for the first time in 40 years, the Contract supplied much of their agenda during the 104th Congress.[63]

The Motor Voter Law and Other Recent Legislation

Since the passage of the landmark Voting Rights Act in 1965, the federal government and many states have passed additional laws aimed at lowering barriers to registration and voting. The Voting Rights Act itself was amended during the 1970s to apply to states outside the South and to minority groups, such as American Indians and Latinos, that have experienced discrimination in gaining access to the ballot. In addition, counties with high concentrations of citizens who

---

[61] Michael W. Traugott and Mee-Eun Kang, "Push Polls as Negative Persuasive Strategies," in Lavrakas and Traugott, eds., *Election Polls, the News Media, and Democracy,* pp. 281–300.

[62] Paul J. Lavrakas and Michael W. Traugott, "Election Polling in the Twenty-first Century: Challenges and Opportunities," in Lavrakas and Traugott, eds., *Election Polls, the News Media, and Democracy,* pp. 321–34.

[63] Clyde Wilcox, *The Latest American Revolution? The 1994 Elections and Their Implications for Governance* (New York: St. Martin's Press, 1995). See also Michael W. Traugott and Elizabeth C. Powers, "Did Public Opinion Support the Contract with America?" in Lavrakas and Traugott, eds., *Election Polls, the News Media, and Democracy,* pp. 93–112.

speak a particular foreign language are now required to provide ballots printed in that language as well as poll workers who speak the language.[64]

In response to the increasing mobility of the American population, in recent years many states have liberalized their registration laws by reducing the length of their residency requirement and moving their registration deadline closer to Election Day. In addition, to ease overcrowding at the polls and assist those who are traveling or have physical infirmities, a number of states have made it easier for citizens to vote by absentee ballot and Tennessee and Texas allow registered voters to cast their ballots at special polling stations up to 2 weeks before Election Day. In 2000, Oregon became the first state to conduct its elections entirely by mail and Washington allowed its citizens to vote either by mail or in person. Although these reforms have undoubtedly made it more convenient for many citizens to vote, to date none of them has had any measurable impact on voter turnout.

Perhaps the most ambitious attempt since the 1960s to increase voter registration and turnout in the United States has been the **National Voter Registration Act of 1993**. This act has become known as the **Motor Voter Law** because it requires states to offer citizens the opportunity to register to vote when they apply for a driver's license or visit other government agencies, including public assistance offices. By lowering the cost of registration to near zero, the sponsors of the law hoped to greatly increase the proportion of Americans registered to vote and, ultimately, the proportion who actually voted.[65] The assumption was that once you got people over the hurdle of registration, most of them would come out to vote on Election Day. The evidence from the 1996 election, however, raises serious doubts about the validity of that assumption.

Between January 1995, when the Motor Voter Law took effect, and November 1996, more than 18,000,000 Americans registered to vote at government offices under the provisions of the law. However, according to a study conducted by Raymond Wolfinger and Jonathan Hoffman of the University of California at Berkeley, the proportion of American citizens who were registered to vote did not in-

---

[64] Davidson, "The Recent Evolution of the Voting Rights Law Affecting Racial and Language Minorities," in Davidson and Grofman, eds., *Quiet Revolution in the South*, pp. 21–37.

[65] Keyssar, *The Right to Vote*, pp. 311–15.

crease between 1992 and 1996 and voter turnout actually declined.[66] Based on Wolfinger and Hoffman's research, it appears that the large majority of citizens who registered at government agencies during 1995 and 1996 would have registered by traditional means and the Motor Voter Law had very little impact on either registration levels or turnout.

It remains to be seen whether the Motor Voter Law contributed to the rather modest increase in voter turnout in the 2000 election, but so far the results have clearly been disappointing to the law's sponsors. Despite the Motor Voter Law and other recent attempts to reduce the cost of voting, voter turnout in recent U.S. elections has remained well below the level of the 1950s and 1960s and among the lowest of any industrial democracy.

SUMMARY

American politics has come a long way since 1787. Much of the original constitutional framework, including the three branches of government with their mutual checks and balances, remains in place. What has changed dramatically is the relationship between political leaders and citizens, and this change is largely a result of the growing importance of elections. Many of the original provisions of the Constitution that were intended to insulate leaders from public pressure, such as the indirect election of the president and U.S. senators, have been eliminated by constitutional amendment or modified by political practice. The franchise has been extended to women, African Americans, and members of other racial and linguistic minority groups. Barriers to voting such as literacy tests and poll taxes have been eliminated and registration requirements have been eased. Primary elections allow voters to choose party nominees, and in many states, initiatives and referenda allow them to decide important public policy issues. Finally, competition between the two major parties for control of Congress and the presidency has never been more intense.

As a result of these changes, elections now have a greater influence on the actions of political leaders and more citizens have an opportunity to participate in the electoral process than at any time in

[66]Raymond E. Wolfinger and Jonathan Hoffman, "Registering and Voting with Motor Voter," *PS: Political Science and Politics* 34 (March 2001), pp. 85–92.

American history. Yet close to half of the American people choose not to participate in that electoral process and many contests for local, state, and federal office lack meaningful competition. The remainder of this book will examine elections and voting in the contemporary American political system. Our purpose is to understand why Americans choose to participate or not participate in the electoral process, how those who do participate decide which candidates to support, and how those decisions are affected by the rules of the electoral game and the strategies of party leaders and candidates.

THE PLAN OF THIS BOOK

Elections do not take place in a vacuum. They are strongly influenced by the strategic environment in which they occur. We therefore continue our examination of elections and voting behavior in Chapter 2 by describing first the legal-institutional environment and then the social-cultural environment in which campaigns and elections take place. We will show how changes in both of these aspects of the political environment in the past 30 years have had important consequences for the electoral process in the United States.

The U.S. electoral system, with its emphasis on single-member districts and winner-take-all contests, has changed little in recent decades, but the regulations governing campaign finance have become much looser since the 1980s, allowing party organizations and interest groups to greatly increase their influence in the electoral process. At the same time, American society has become increasingly diverse socially and culturally as a result of immigration, changes in family structure, and shifting religious beliefs and practices. We will explore the ways in which these trends have created a more complex environment for politicians trying to build electoral coalitions.

Within the boundaries set by the legal-institutional and social-cultural environments, two major types of actors, voters and politicians, attempt to achieve their goals. In Chapters 3 and 4 we will focus our attention on the first type of actor—voters. We will begin by examining Americans' attitudes toward the Democratic and Republican parties in Chapter 3 before turning our attention to their participation in the electoral process in Chapter 4. Our treatment of political attitudes will focus on perceptions and evaluations of the two major political parties because partisan attitudes play a central role in the formation of voting decisions and because they have undergone considerable change in recent years.

In Chapter 4 we will examine the extent, causes, and consequences of participation in electoral politics among U.S. citizens. We recognize that voting is only one of several ways in which citizens participate in the electoral process in the United States. We will also examine activities such as contributing money, displaying buttons and bumper stickers, attending campaign rallies, working for a party or candidate, and simply trying to persuade someone you know to support your candidate.

The presidency is the grand prize of American politics. Control of the White House brings with it not only control of the executive branch of government but also unmatched access to the mass media in the crucial battle for public opinion. In addition, the outcome of a presidential election can affect the results of contests for the House and Senate and even state and local offices. While presidential coattails may not be as important as they once were, there is still, to quote James E. Campbell, a "presidential pulse" to congressional elections.[67] We will therefore devote Chapters 5 and 6 to presidential campaigns and elections. We will first examine the presidential nominating process and then turn our attention to the general election campaign.

To become president of the United States, a candidate must first win the nomination of one of the two major parties and then win the November election. What makes this two-stage process especially challenging is that the rules and participants involved in each stage are very different. Moreover, the rules and participants involved in the nomination process have undergone dramatic changes over the past 40 years. In Chapter 5 we will examine these changes and their consequences for the candidates who seek the presidency, their strategies, and the results of the nomination process.

As the battle for control of the White House shifts from the nomination to the general election phase, there are major differences in both the participants and the rules of the game. In addition to a larger and more diverse electorate, the candidates' campaign strategies in the general election are shaped by an institution left over from the eighteenth century—the Electoral College. Chapter 6 will examine these differences and their consequences for the strategies of the candidates and the outcomes of presidential elections.

Congressional elections are simultaneously local and national. Chapter 7 will therefore be divided into two major sections. In the

---

[67]James E. Campbell, *The Presidential Pulse of Congressional Elections,* 2nd ed. (Lexington, KY: University of Kentucky Press, 1997).

first section, we will examine House and Senate elections from the local perspective by focusing on the candidates and their constituencies. This will allow us to examine one of the most important phe-
nomena in congressional elections—the advantage of incumbency.
We will then turn our attention to the influence of national electoral
forces such as economic conditions and presidential coattails on congressional elections. We will then discuss the interaction of these
forces and the local factors discussed in the previous section.

In our concluding chapter we will discuss the consequences of
recent changes in the electoral process for the performance of the
political system and the quality of representative democracy in the
United States. We will also evaluate several popular ideas for reforming the electoral process, including public financing of campaigns and Election Day voter registration, in terms of their desir-
ability and feasibility. We will see that contemporary debates about
electoral reform continue to be shaped by the conflicting values of
populism and egalitarianism on the one hand and personal freedom
and self-reliance on the other. Our goal is not to resolve this conflict
but to help students evaluate reform proposals in light of their own
values and political goals.

KEY TERMS AND CONCEPTS

Anti-Federalists (Democratic-
    Republicans)
at-large elections
Baker v. *Carr*
Bipartisan Campaign Reform
    Act of 2002 (McCain-Feingold
    Law)
blanket primary
Buckley v. *Valeo*
closed primary
direct primary
egalitarianism
Electoral College
elitist democratic theory
Federal Election Campaign Act
Federal Election Commission
Federalists
Fifteenth Amendment

fireside chats
Gray v. *Sanders*
Hunt v. *Cromartie*
initiative
majority-minority districts
National Voter Registration Act
    of 1993 (Motor Voter Law)
Nineteenth Amendment
one person, one vote
open primary
party registration
personal freedom
political culture
popular democratic theory
populism
progressive movement
referendum
Reynolds v. *Sims*

self-reliance
Seventeenth Amendment
spot advertisements
Twentieth Amendment
Twenty-fourth Amendment

Twenty-seventh Amendment
Twenty-third Amendment
Twenty-sixth Amendment
Voting Rights Act of 1965
Wesberry v. *Sanders*

DISCUSSION QUESTIONS

1. What is the American creed and how has it affected the development of democracy in the United States? To what extent do Americans support these ideas today and what role do they play in the political process?
2. How did racism, sexism, and ethnocentrism affect the development of democracy in the United States? How prevalent are such attitudes today and what consequences do they have for elections and voting behavior?
3. How have the elitist principles of the original Constitution been modified since 1787? What safeguards against popular democracy remain in the Constitution and how do they affect American politics today?
4. Why has voter turnout in the United States remained very low in comparison with other democracies despite the Motor Voter Law and other recent reforms aimed at making registration and voting more convenient?

SUGGESTED READINGS

Brown, Dee. *Bury My Heart at Wounded Knee: An Indian History of the American West.* New York: Henry Holt and Company, 2001. Brown examines the westward expansion from the American Indian perspective and it is not a pretty picture.

de Tocqueville, Alexis. *Democracy in America.* Chicago: University of Chicago Press, 2000. The diaries of French aristocrat Alexis de Tocqueville provide many insights into American society and culture in the early nineteenth century and even today.

Flexner, Eleanor. *Century of Struggle: The Woman's Rights Movement in the United States.* rev. ed. Cambridge, MA: Harvard University Press, 1975. Flexner provides a comprehensive history of the women's rights movement in the nineteenth and early twentieth centuries with special emphasis on the struggle for the right to vote.

Handlin, Oscar. *The Uprooted.* 2nd ed. Boston: Little, Brown, 1990. This is the revised and updated edition of the classic study of the immigrant experience in the United States. Handlin was one of the pioneers in applying social science methods to the study of American history.

Jay, John; Alexander Hamilton; and James Madison. *The Federalist Papers.* New York: New American Library, 1961. Jay, Hamilton, and Madison present the arguments for the new Constitution to their fellow citizens. These essays offer many insights into the political struggles of the late eighteenth century and are considered among the most important American contributions to democratic theory.

Keyssar, Alexander. *The Right to Vote: The Contested History of Democracy in the United States.* New York: Basic Books, 2000. In this comprehensive history of the franchise in the United States, Keyssar demonstrates that the struggle for universal suffrage has been hard fought and marked by frequent setbacks.

Schuman, Howard; Charlotte Steeh; and Lawrence Bobo. *Racial Attitudes in America: Trends and Interpretations,* rev. ed. Cambridge, MA: Harvard University Press, 1997. The authors describe contemporary racial attitudes in the United States and argue that while overt racism has declined dramatically, more subtle forms of racial prejudice remain widespread among white Americans.

Verba, Sidney, and Gary Orren. *Equality in America.* Cambridge, MA: Harvard University Press, 1985. Verba and Orren analyze popular attitudes toward equality in the United States and offer explanations for the apparent conflict in Americans' opinions toward procedural and substantive equality.

Wood, Gordon S. *The Creation of the American Republic, 1776–1787.* Chapel Hill, NC: University of North Carolina Press, 1969. Wood chronicles not just the events of this crucial period but also the evolution of American political ideas from the idealism of the Declaration of Independence to the realism of the Constitution.

CHAPTER 2

The Strategic Environment of Elections

A LOOK BACK AT THE 2000 ELECTION

It was one of the closest, one of the most contentious, and, in some ways, one of the strangest elections in American history. After almost a year of nonstop campaigning, three televised debates, and millions of dollars spent on television advertising, the outcome of the 2000 presidential election came down to a battle over hand recounts in three south Florida counties. The presidential contest was not decided until December 12, more than 4 weeks after Election Day, when a divided U.S. Supreme Court issued its ruling in the case of *Bush v. Gore.* By blocking additional recounts in Florida, the Court effectively awarded the state's 25 electoral votes and the presidency to George W. Bush. Thus, Mr. Bush became the first person since Benjamin Harrison in 1888 to win the presidency while losing the popular vote.[1]

The presidential contest was not the only race that went right down to the wire in 2000. The congressional elections also produced a photo finish.[2] In the House of Representatives, Republicans

---

[1]For a thorough and balanced account of the 2000 presidential election and its aftermath, see James W. Ceaser and Andrew E. Busch, *The Perfect Tie: The True Story of the 2000 Presidential Election* (New York: Rowman and Littlefield, 2001). Other scholarly analyses of the 2000 election can be found in Michael Nelson, ed., *The Elections of 2000* (Washington, DC: Congressional Quarterly Press, 2001); and Gerald M. Pomper, ed., *The Election of 2000* (New York: Chatham House, 2001).

[2]For in-depth analyses of the 2000 congressional elections, see Paul Herrnson, "The Congressional Elections," in Pomper, ed., *The Election of 2000*; and Gary C. Jacobson, "Congress: Elections and Stalemate," in Nelson, ed., *The Elections of 2000.*

maintained control but saw their majority reduced for the third consecutive election as Democrats scored a net gain of two seats. The new House would have 221 Republicans, 212 Democrats, and two independents—the closest party division in almost 50 years. In the Senate elections, Democrats picked up 4 seats, giving each party 50 seats—the first tie in over 100 years.

At first glance, the 2000 election might appear to be an aberration from the normal patterns of American political life. Certainly no one could have predicted that George W. Bush would win the presidential election despite losing the popular vote, that the outcome of the presidential race would be decided by a 5-4 vote of the Supreme Court, or that the Senate elections would produce a 50-50 tie. Despite these extraordinary events, however, the conditions that shaped the behavior of candidates and voters in 2000 were very similar to those at work in previous elections. Among the most important of these conditions were the laws and regulations governing elections in the United States and the major social and cultural divisions within American society. These constituted the **strategic environment** within which the 2000 campaign and election took place. In the remainder of this chapter, we will examine the strategic environment of elections in the United States, describe some of the ways in which it is changing, and show how that strategic environment influenced the behavior of candidates and voters in an election whose results were quite extraordinary.

THE RULES OF THE GAME: THE LEGAL-INSTITUTIONAL ENVIRONMENT

One of the most important aspects of the strategic environment in any democracy is the system of laws and regulations under which elections are contested. These laws and regulations constitute the rules of the electoral game. They define when elections take place, who can participate, how money can be raised and spent and, most important, how votes are counted and winners and losers determined. Moreover, the rules of the electoral game are not neutral. They help some players and hurt others. As a result, the rules themselves sometimes become the subject of intense conflict among the parties and candidates and their supporters.

The American Electoral System

Most Americans probably take it for granted when they go to their polling places on Election Day that they will be asked to vote for a single candidate for each office on the ballot and that the candidate who receives a plurality of the votes cast for each office will be elected. However, the American **single-member, simple plurality (SMSP) electoral system** is actually rather unusual among the major democracies of the world. Most of the other industrial democracies utilize electoral systems based partially or entirely on proportional representation.

Under a **proportional representation, or PR,** system, several candidates are elected within a single electoral district. This district can be either the entire nation, or some smaller geographical unit. Instead of voting for individual candidates, voters choose a preferred party. Seats are then allocated among the parties based on their shares of the overall vote. For example, a party that receives 30 percent of the vote receives 30 percent of the seats. To discourage fringe parties, the rules sometimes require parties to obtain above some minimum share of the vote in order to win any seats. In Germany, for example, a party must receive at least 5 percent of the vote to win any seats. The determination of which candidates are elected from each party is usually based on the candidates' positions on a list prepared by party leaders.

There is no provision in the U.S. Constitution that requires the use of single-member districts and plurality voting. The Constitution allows each state to choose its own rules for conducting elections. A few states have used multimember districts in one or both chambers of their legislatures and many localities utilize multimember districts or at-large elections in which two or more candidates are elected simultaneously from an entire city or county. In contrast to electoral systems based on PR, however, winners in these elections are determined by votes cast for individual candidates. In addition, several southern states require runoff elections in party primaries when no candidate wins an outright majority in the first round of voting and the state of Georgia requires a runoff in general elections when no candidate receives more than 45 percent of the vote in the first round of voting.[3]

---

[3] The use of runoff elections in Democratic primaries in the South has been criticized by civil rights organizations on the grounds that it discriminates against minority candidates. For a discussion of this issue, see Chandler Davidson, "The Recent Evolution

A few municipalities in the United States have experimented with elections based on proportional representation. Almost all of these experiments were quickly abandoned, however, once their consequences became clear. In New York City, for example, a PR system was adopted for city council elections after World War II. The results were dramatic—the old city council made up almost entirely of Democrats was replaced by one with a much smaller Democratic majority, a much larger number of Republicans, several members of the socialist-leaning American Labor Party, and one Communist. The Democratic majority on the council soon decided to abandon PR and return to an electoral system based on individual districts.[4]

The results of New York City's experiment with proportional representation illustrate why winner-take-all elections are so popular in the United States—they generally work to the advantage of the two major parties by making it very difficult for minor party candidates to win elections. In areas where there is a single dominant party, like New York City, winner-take-all elections also make it very difficult for candidates from the minority party to win elections.

In general, there is a strong relationship between the type of electoral system that a country uses and the type of party system that is likely to exist in that country. The French political scientist, Maurice Duverger, first described this relationship in the early 1950s and it has been found to hold so consistently since that time that it has become known as **Duverger's Law.**[5] Duverger's Law states very simply that countries with electoral systems based on winner-take-all elections will generally develop two-party systems while countries with electoral systems based on proportional representation will generally develop multiparty systems. This is because, under the winner-take-all system, only the candidate who finishes first in each district is elected and very few minor party candidates are able to finish first. As a result, the winner-take-all system discourages minor party candidates from running and discourages voters from supporting minor party candidates out of fear of wasting their votes on candidates who have no chance of winning.

---

of Voting Rights Law Affecting Racial and Language Minorities," in Chandler Davidson and Bernard Grofman, eds., *Quiet Revolution in the South: The Impact of the Voting Rights Act, 1965–1990* (Princeton, NJ: Princeton University Press, 1994).

[4] For an account of this period, see Wallace S. Sayre and Herbert Kaufman, *Governing New York City: Politics in the Metropolis* (New York: Russell Sage Foundation, 1960).

[5] Maurice Duverger, *Political Parties: Their Organization and Activity in the Modern State* (New York: John Wiley and Sons, 1954). For more recent analyses of the effects of electoral systems on political parties, see Grofman, Bernard, and Arend Lijphart, eds., *Electoral Laws and their Political Consequences* (New York: Agathon Press, 1986).

In addition to discouraging voters from supporting minor party candidates, the winner-take-all system can result in the election of a candidate who is the first choice of fewer voters than another candidate on the ballot. This can occur in a close election if most voters supporting a third-party candidate prefer the candidate who finished second to the candidate who finished first. Such situations are not unusual in American politics. In the 2000 presidential election, for example, exit polls indicate that most of those who voted for Green Party candidate Ralph Nader preferred Al Gore to George W. Bush. Given the number of votes for Nader and the closeness of the presidential election in Florida, it is very likely that a majority of Florida voters (even among those whose votes were counted) preferred Al Gore to George W. Bush.

One potential solution to the wasted vote problem in winner-take-all elections is the **single transferable vote (STV)** or "instant runoff" system. Under STV, which has been used in some elections in Australia and Ireland, voters rank all of the candidates running for a given office. After all of the first-choice votes have been tabulated, the candidate finishing last is eliminated and the second-choice votes of those who supported that candidate are allocated to the remaining candidates. This process of elimination and redistribution of votes continues until only two candidates remain and the one with a majority of votes is elected. Since it removes a powerful disincentive for voting for minor party candidates, some supporters of third parties in the U.S. have advocated the STV system. Thus far, however, they have had almost no success in getting this system adopted.[6]

Under the PR system, a party that wins a small share of the vote can still elect some of its candidates to office. As a result, minor parties have a strong incentive to contest elections and voters have much less reason to be concerned about wasting their votes by supporting a minor party. Because of the proliferation of minor parties, however, proportional representation also makes it much more difficult for any single party to win an outright majority. As a result, coalition governments involving two or more parties are quite common in countries that use PR electoral systems. In contrast, electoral systems based on single-member districts with plurality voting almost always produce a clear majority winner.

[6] For a detailed discussion of STV and other more esoteric electoral systems, see Douglas J. Amy, *Behind the Ballot Box: A Citizen's Guide to Voting Systems* (Westport, CT: Praeger, 2000). The relative merits of the American single-member plurality electoral system and alternative systems such as PR are debated in Mark E. Rush and Richard L. Engstrom, *Fair and Effective Representation? Debating Electoral Reform and Minority Rights* (New York: Rowman and Littlefield, 2001).

Political leaders generally have a stake in preserving whatever electoral system got them into office. For this reason, electoral systems are highly resistant to change. In the case of the United States, leaders of both major parties have a vested interest in preserving the system of winner-take-all elections and other rules that make it difficult for minor parties to challenge the dominant position of the two major parties.

In addition to discouraging minor parties, the American electoral system has important consequences for the relationships between elected representatives and both citizens and party leaders. In an electoral system based on single-member districts, a representative is accountable only to the voters in his or her own constituency. As a result, there is a strong incentive for representatives to cultivate their districts by providing personal services, obtaining public works projects, and taking popular stands on key issues. In contrast, in a PR system, every representative is accountable to the same national or regional constituency. Since candidates are elected based on their party's overall performance and their position on a party list, there is little incentive for representatives to engage in activities aimed at cultivating the support of constituents.

To maintain the support of the voters in their districts, elected representatives in the United States sometimes have to take positions that conflict with those of their party's leaders. This is especially important for representatives whose constituencies are atypical for their party such as Democrats who represent rural districts in the South and Republicans who represent urban districts in the Northeast. Building a personal base of support in their districts can also help representatives to survive when the national electoral tide is running against their party. In contrast, under PR, a politician's chance of being elected depends entirely on his or her position on a party list. This gives party leaders almost complete control over the electoral prospects of office seekers. Not surprisingly, party loyalty is much stronger in countries with electoral systems based on PR than in the United States.

Drawing the Lines

In an electoral system based on single-member districts, the process of drawing district boundaries is of critical importance to current and would-be officeholders. In some other democracies that utilize district-based electoral systems, such as Great Britain, the responsibility for drawing district boundaries is given to a special commission of nonpartisan experts. In the United States, however, except for a few states such as Iowa that use nonpartisan commissions, partisan elected officials draw the lines. Every 10 years, following the completion of the Census, state legislatures in the United States are required to redraw all of their congressional and state legislative districts in a manner consistent with the Supreme Court's one-person, one-vote rule. Not surprisingly, given the enormous personal stakes that the legislators and other political leaders have in this process, **redistricting** is often one of the most contentious issues dealt with by state legislatures and redistricting plans are frequently challenged in the courts.

Most redistricting plans seek to accomplish one of two basic goals—maximizing the number of seats held by the majority party or protecting incumbents of both parties.[7] Partisan redistricting plans generally seek to maximize majority party seats by concentrating minority party voters in a limited number of districts and/or placing two or more minority party incumbents in the same district, ensuring that only one will survive. Bipartisan plans generally seek to protect incumbents of both parties by creating safe districts for as many of them as possible. Mixed plans may seek to protect most incumbents while allowing the majority party to make limited gains. In addition, political mapmakers are often constrained by the need to preserve majority-minority districts. The end result is often the creation of oddly shaped districts that zigzag across the political landscape to capture voters of a particular race or party affiliation—a process sometimes referred to as **gerrymandering** in honor of one of the early practitioners of the art of political mapmaking, eighteenth-century Massachusetts Governor Elbridge Gerry.

Whatever the specific goals of political mapmakers, one of the main consequences of redistricting is that most state legislative and U.S. House districts are relatively safe for one party or the other. This fact, in combination with the personal popularity of most incumbents and the weakness of most challengers, means that in any given election, only a small fraction of seats are really in play. In 2000, for example, out of the 435 U.S. House seats at stake in the election, there were fewer than 40 where both parties had a realistic chance of winning. Because of the extraordinary closeness of the overall battle for control of the House, both parties poured enormous amounts of money and effort into these few highly competitive races while

[7]David Butler and Bruce Cain, *Congressional Redistricting: Comparative and Theoretical Perspectives* (New York: Macmillan, 1992).

virtually ignoring the large majority of races that were not considered competitive. As a result, despite the intensity of the battle for control of the House, most voters in the United States heard little or nothing about the House contest in their own district.

Primary Elections

Winning elected office in the United States is a two-stage process. To have a realistic chance of being elected to almost any state or national office, a candidate must first win his or her party's nomination in a primary election. Primary elections are conducted under a different set of rules from general elections. One of the most important differences is that not all registered voters are allowed to vote in primary elections. Like many other election rules, the rules governing who is eligible to vote in primary elections vary considerably from state to state. About half of the states hold **closed primaries** in which only voters who declare in advance that they support a particular party are allowed to participate in that party's primary. A few states, including New Hampshire, also allow registered independents to participate in a party's primary. Most of the remaining states hold **open primaries** in which any registered voter can participate in a party's primary simply by showing up at the polling place and requesting a primary ballot for that party. Finally, three states—Washington, Alaska, and California—utilize a special type of open primary known as a **blanket primary.** Sometimes referred to by its critics as a "free love" primary, a blanket primary allows registered voters to participate in different parties' primaries for different offices. For example, a voter can participate in the Democratic primary for governor and the Republican primary for lieutenant governor.

The rules concerning who is allowed to vote in a party's primary election can have a dramatic impact on the composition of the primary electorate and, ultimately, the kinds of candidates who are nominated. In general, independents and crossover voters—Republicans and Democrats who vote in the opposing party's primary—make up a larger proportion of the electorate in open primaries than in closed primaries. As a result, most Democratic and Republican party leaders strongly prefer closed primaries to open primaries. Their main objection to open primaries is that they allow members of the opposing party to engage in **raiding**—voting for the candidate who would make the weakest opponent in the general election.

Political scientists who have studied voting in primary elections have found almost no evidence of this sort of raiding. Instead, the large majority of **crossover voters** seem to be motivated by a clear preference for one of the candidates in the opposing party's primary.[8] In 2000, for example, exit poll data from New Hampshire and other states showed that the reason many Democrats voted for John Mc-Cain in the Republican presidential primaries was not, as some GOP strategists alleged, because they thought he would make a weaker opponent for Al Gore, but because they preferred McCain to George W. Bush. A large proportion of these Democratic crossover voters also preferred McCain to either of the Democratic presidential candidates, Al Gore or Bill Bradley.

Even in open primaries, the proportions of independents and crossover voters are usually fairly small. Democratic identifiers make up the large majority of voters in most Democratic primaries and Republican identifiers make up the large majority of voters in most Republican primaries. For this reason, as John McCain discovered, it is usually very difficult for a candidate who appeals mainly to independents and crossover voters to win a primary election. Primary elections, and especially closed primary elections, usually favor candidates who appeal to a party's core supporters. This generally means that successful candidates in Republican primaries must appeal to conservative Republican voters and successful candidates in Democratic primaries must appeal to liberal Democratic voters. In the 2000 presidential primaries, the candidate with the strongest appeal among conservative Republican voters was George W. Bush while the candidate with the strongest appeal among liberal Democratic voters was Al Gore.

Counting the Votes

Some of the most important rules affecting elections involve how ballots are actually cast, counted and, when necessary, recounted. In the aftermath of the 2000 presidential election and the battle over Florida's electoral votes, many Americans discovered for the first time what election officials have long known—that in every national election, clerical errors, confusing ballot forms, overcrowded and understaffed polling places, and equipment breakdowns deprive millions of citizens of the right to vote and the right to have their vote accurately counted. A study by a group of social scientists and engineers

[8]See for example Alan I. Abramowitz, John J. McGlennon, and Ronald B. Rapoport, "A Note on Strategic Voting in a Primary Election," *Journal of Politics* 43 (August 1981), pp. 899–904.

at the California Institute of Technology and the Massachusetts Institute of Technology recently estimated that between 4 and 6 million votes were lost throughout the country in the 2000 election due to a combination of registration problems, overcrowded polling places, poorly designed ballots, and faulty voting equipment.[9] This study found that the problems that occurred in Florida were not at all unusual. In fact, several other states had higher percentages of lost votes. It was only the extraordinary closeness of the presidential race that caused the media to focus so much attention on the problems in Florida.

Many of the problems that occurred in Florida and other states in 2000 reflected two crucial and highly unusual characteristics of the way elections are administered in the United States—partisanship and decentralization. The United States, unlike almost every other democracy in the world, places the responsibility for administering elections in the hands of partisan elected officials. In Florida, for example, the official in charge of overseeing the presidential recount in 2000 was Republican Secretary of State Katherine Harris who was also the co-chair of the Bush campaign in the state. During the post-election battle for Florida, Ms. Harris made several crucial decisions that benefited the Bush campaign, most notably refusing to extend the deadline for counties to complete hand recounts. While Ms. Harris justified her decision on the grounds that she was following the letter of the law, it seems highly unlikely that a Democratic official in her position would have made the same decision.

Unlike almost every other democracy in the world, the United States has no uniform national standards for record keeping, ballot design, or voting equipment. Each state makes up its own rules for administering elections. Many states, including Florida, give individual counties considerable discretion in designing ballots and choosing voting equipment. The consequences of this extremely decentralized voting system were clearly evident in the 2000 election. Different counties used different procedures for checking registration records, different ballot designs, and different voting equipment, even within a single state. In some counties, poll workers were able to check registration information instantly by computer; in other counties, workers had to call county or state offices on the telephone and were sometimes kept on hold for hours. In some counties, voters were given clear instructions on how to mark their ballots; in other

[9]Guy Gugliotta, "Study Finds Millions of Votes Lost," *Washington Post*, July 16, 2001, p. A-1. The full report, "Voting: What Is, What Could Be," can be found on the website of the Cal Tech/MIT Technology Project: web.mit.edu/voting.

counties, voters were given confusing or contradictory information. In some counties, voters used optical scanning equipment that alerted them if they skipped an office or voted for two different candidates for the same office; in other counties, voters used punch-card machines that provided no feedback and sometimes became jammed with excess bits of paper.

As a result of these variations in election procedures, the proportion of votes lost due to clerical errors, poorly designed ballots, and equipment problems varied tremendously from state to state, and from county to county within a single state. Within the state of Florida, for example, the proportion of ballots without a valid presidential vote ranged from less than 1 percent in some counties that used optical scanning equipment to more than 6 percent in some counties that used punch-card machines.

Problems caused by confusing ballots and outmoded voting equipment had a disproportionate impact on low-income and minority voters in the 2000 election. This was due to a combination of two factors. First, these voters were more likely to live in counties that used outmoded voting equipment such as punch-card machines. In addition, because of poor education and inexperience, low-income and minority voters were more likely than higher-income white voters to have difficulty understanding complicated ballots and following instructions for using the voting equipment properly. As a result, low-income and minority voters were much more likely to have their votes invalidated than higher-income white voters. In Duval County, Florida, for example, which used punch-card machines and a confusing two-page presidential ballot, the percentage of invalid presidential votes averaged less than 2 percent in upper-income white precincts compared with more than 10 percent in low-income African American precincts.

In response to the 2000 election controversy, and after considerable partisan wrangling, in October 2002 Congress passed and President Bush signed into law the **Help America Vote Act.** This law will provide $3.9 billion in federal aid to the states to replace punch-card and lever machines, train poll workers, and improve voter education. The law also calls for safeguards such as allowing citizens to cast a provisional ballot if no record of registration can be found at their polling place and requires states to create computerized statewide voter registration lists in time for the 2006 election.[10] None of the provisions had any effect on the 2002 midterm election and some

[10]See Robert Pear, "Bush Signs Legislation Intended to End Voting Disputes," *The New York Times*, October 30, 2002, p. A22.

will take several years to implement. However, a few states, most notably Florida and Georgia, have already implemented reforms aimed
at reducing errors in recording and tabulating votes.[11]

Campaign Finance

It has been said that money is the mother's milk of politics, and this
statement certainly applies to American political campaigns.[12] Far
more money is spent on elections in the United States than in any
other democracy. Moreover, despite stricter regulations imposed
by the **Federal Election Campaign Act Amendments of 1974,** the
amount of money spent on elections in the U.S. has risen dramatically over the past 30 years. During the 1999–2000 election cycle, according to data compiled by the Federal Election Commission, about
$2.7 billion were spent on the presidential and congressional elec-
tions. This total included almost $500 million in spending by the
presidential candidates, over a billion dollars in spending by House
and Senate candidates, and almost $1.2 billion in spending by vari-
ous party committees. By way of contrast, in the 2001 election in
Great Britain, each party was limited to about $24 million in total
spending while individual candidates for the House of Commons
were limited to about $36,000 each. The total amount spent by all of
the parties and candidates in Britain was about $100 million or less
than 4 percent of the amount spent on the 2000 U.S. election.[13]

Three characteristics of the electoral process in the United States
help to explain the enormous sums of money spent on political campaigns. First, the American district-based electoral system encourages individual candidates to run their own campaigns appealing to
the voters in their constituencies rather than relying on party leaders

---

[11] In the aftermath of the 2002 election controversy, Florida passed legislation banning
punch-card voting machines and providing additional funds for training local election officials. However, the state continued to permit counties to use a wide variety of
methods for tabulating votes including optical scanning, paper ballots, and touch-
screen machines. The state of Georgia implemented a more ambitious program requiring all counties in the state to use identical touch-screen voting machines in 2002.
These machines do not permit voters to choose more than one candidate for the same
office and they warn voters when they have skipped any office on the ballot. For a description of the new Georgia voting system, see www.georgiacounts.com.

[12] The quotation is from the late Jesse Unruh, who served as Treasurer of the State of
California and chaired the California Democratic Party during the 1970s.

[13] T. R. Reid, "Pound for Pound, British Campaign is a Bargain," *Washington Post,* June 7,
2001, p. A25.

to conduct a single national campaign. This means that each candidate must pay for his or her own staff, office space, consultants, polling, advertising, phone banks, and all of the other costs of running a political campaign. Second, candidates in the United States have to run two separate campaigns—they have to run for their party's nomination in a primary election before they can run in the general election. They must therefore pay for the cost of the primary campaign as well as the cost of the general election campaign, and sometimes the primary campaign can be more expensive than the general election campaign. Third, and most important, in comparison with other democracies, the laws and regulations governing campaign finance in the United States are extraordinarily weak. Except for presidential candidates who accept public financing, there are no limits on how much money candidates or party organizations can raise and spend.

The fundamental law governing campaign finance in presidential and congressional elections is the Federal Election Campaign Act.[14] This law was passed in 1971 and substantially amended in 1974. Its most important provisions include limits on how much money **political action committees (PACs),** individuals, and political parties can contribute to federal candidates, a requirement that candidates report all expenditures and contributions of more than $100, and public financing of presidential nomination and general election campaigns. The 1974 amendments originally included limits on the total amount of money that congressional candidates could spend, the amount that candidates could contribute to their own campaigns, and the amount that outside individuals and groups could spend to support or oppose federal candidates. However, none of these provisions was implemented because the U.S. Supreme Court, in *Buckley v. Valeo* (1976), ruled that mandatory spending limits violated the First Amendment's guarantee of freedom of speech.

By equating campaign spending with constitutionally protected speech, the *Buckley* decision made it almost impossible for Congress or the states to limit the influence of money in political campaigns. For spending limits to be constitutional, according to the Court, they have to be voluntary. But the only way that has been found to get candidates to voluntarily limit their spending is by tying spending limits to public financing, and so far Congress has shown little interest

[14]For an analysis of changes in campaign finance laws and regulations in the United States since 1971, see Anthony Gierzynski, *Money Rules: Financing Elections in America* (Boulder, CO: Westview Press, 2000).

in extending public financing beyond presidential elections and only four states have adopted voluntary public financing systems for state elections.

Between 1974 and 2002, there was only one major change in federal campaign law, but it has had far-reaching consequences. In 1979, Congress amended the Federal Election Campaign Act to allow state party organizations to spend money on grassroots activities, such as voter registration and get-out-the-vote drives, without counting any of that spending as contributions to federal candidates. Shortly thereafter, the **Federal Election Commission** ruled that national party committees could accept unlimited contributions from individuals, corporations, and labor unions to pay for nonfederal campaign activities and could transfer these funds to state party organizations as long as the contributions were allowed under state law. This ruling, in combination with the 1979 amendment to the Federal Election Campaign Act, created a huge loophole in federal election law—a loophole that led to the explosion of **soft money** during the 1990s.[15]

Soft money refers to unregulated money that is raised and spent by party organizations. Unlike **hard money**, which is regulated, soft money is supposed to be used only for party-building activities such as voter registration and get-out-the-vote drives. In addition to these grassroots activities, however, national and state party organizations have increasingly used soft money to pay for issue ads that clearly target individual races. The only difference between these ads and those paid for with hard money is that the issue ads do not directly ask viewers to vote for or against specific candidates.

The amount of soft money raised by the two major parties has increased dramatically over the past three presidential elections, according to data compiled by the Federal Election Commission (see Figure 2.1). While hard money raised by Democratic and Republican committees rose from $422 million in 1992 to $617 million in 1996 and $741 million in 2000, soft money rose from $85 million in 1992 to $263 million in 1996 and $495 million in 2000. In percentage terms, the share of party funds made up of soft money rose from 17 percent in 1992 to 30 percent in 1996 and 40 percent in 2000.

Soft money has been especially important to the Democratic Party in recent years. During the 2000 election cycle, soft money contributions made up 47 percent of funds raised by Democratic committees compared with only 35 percent of funds raised by Republi-

---

[15] For an explanation of the soft money loophole, see Gierzynski, p. 45.

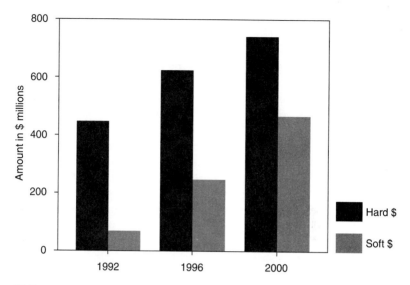

FIGURE 2.1 Sources of Party Funds, 1992–2000
Source: Federal Election Commission.

can committees. Republican committees had a huge advantage in hard money during 2000, raising $466 million compared with only $275 million for Democratic committees. However, Democratic committees raised almost as much soft money as Republican committees—$245 million compared with $250 million. Based on these figures, it is easy to understand why some Democrats have had second thoughts recently about reforms aimed at reducing or eliminating the role of soft money in political campaigns.

The explosive growth of soft money has been largely responsible for one of the most important recent trends in campaign finance— the increasing role played by party organizations vis-à-vis individual candidates, especially in congressional elections. During the 1970s and 1980s, party organizations played a relatively minor role in financing House and Senate campaigns. Individual candidates raised the overwhelming majority of their own campaign funds. During 1996 and 2000, however, Democratic and Republican committees raised more money than all of the parties' House and Senate candidates combined.

The party organizations have become major players in the campaign finance game. Candidates, especially those involved in competitive races, now expect the party organizations to provide a substantial share of the funding for their campaigns through direct, hard money contributions, and indirect, soft money support. In return, of course, the party organizations expect the candidates to demonstrate a high level of loyalty to the party and its positions.

The consequences of the American campaign finance system, with its lax regulations and overwhelming reliance on private funding, were clearly evident in the 2000 election. The parties and candidates spent a record $2.7 billion in 2000. Independent groups like the National Organization for Women and the Christian Coalition spent millions more. But that spending was very unequally distributed. In the Republican primaries, for example, Texas Governor George W. Bush enjoyed an overwhelming financial advantage over his main opponent, Arizona Senator John McCain. Even though McCain was able to quickly raise several million dollars in small donations—much of it through the Internet—following his upset victory in the New Hampshire Primary, Bush still outspent McCain by a 2-1 margin overall: $89.1 million to $44.6 million. In addition, because he was able to turn down federal matching funds, Bush did not have to abide by the same spending limits in each state as his Republican rivals, including McCain, who accepted public financing. Finally, Bush benefited from several million dollars in "independent" spending by conservative individuals and groups in key primary states. While Bush had other advantages in the Republican primaries besides money, there is no question that his vast financial resources helped him to survive John McCain's challenge after McCain's early victories in New Hampshire and Michigan.

The effects of one-sided campaign spending were also evident in the 2000 congressional elections, most notably in the overwhelming reelection rate of House incumbents. Out of 398 House incumbents who ran in the general election, 392, or 98.5 percent, were successful. As usual, money played a major role in the electoral success of these incumbents. The vast majority of incumbents were able to overwhelm their challenger financially. According to data compiled by the Federal Election Commission, the average House incumbent spent $804,000 compared with $305,000 for the average House challenger. These figures are misleading, however, because a few challengers in competitive races spent far more than the average, several million dollars in some cases, thereby pulling up the overall average. A more revealing statistic with regard to the typical spending levels of House incumbents and challengers is the median. In the 2000 election, the median spending figures were $550,000 for Democratic incumbents and $703,000 for Republican incumbents compared with

$68,000 for Democratic challengers and $36,000 for Republican challengers. This means that half of all Democratic challengers spent less than $68,000 and half of all Republican challengers spent less than $36,000—not enough to make any impression on the electorate. It is easy to understand why members of the House of Representatives have been reluctant to reform a campaign finance system that works so clearly to the advantage of incumbents.

THE SOCIAL AND CULTURAL ENVIRONMENT

The American electoral system and the laws governing campaigns and elections set the ground rules under which parties and candidates compete for votes. However, to understand how parties and candidates appeal to the electorate and how voters respond to these appeals, we must also consider the social characteristics and values of the American people.

Since its founding, the United States has been one of the most dynamic societies in the world. This is as true today as it was in the nineteenth and twentieth centuries. The population of the United States, which grew from just over 150 million in 1950 to more than 280 million in 2000, is expected to grow to over 400 million by 2050.[16] Immigration, internal migration, economic upheaval, and technological change continue to transform American society and shape electoral competition. In this section, we will examine several major demographic and cultural trends, as summarized in Table 2.1, that are producing a new American electorate in the twenty-first century— an electorate that is increasingly diverse in its social composition, lifestyles, and religious beliefs.

The Aging of American Society

One of the most fundamental characteristics of any society is its age distribution and the population of the United States, like the populations of most advanced industrial societies, is getting older.

---

[16]The source for most of the census and other data cited in this chapter is the *Statistical Abstract of the United States: 2000* published in 2000 by the U.S. Census Bureau. Some data on long-term historical trends are taken from *Historical Statistics of the United States, Colonial Times to 1970*, published in 1974 by the U.S. Department of Commerce.

TABLE 2.1 The Changing American Population

	1950	2000
Median age	30.2	35.8
Place of residence		
% Living in Sun Belt	44	58
% Living in suburbs	32	50
Workforce		
% White collar	37	59
% Female	29	46
% Unionized	32	14
Families		
% Households with married couple and children	43	24
% Single-parent families	7	27
% married working mothers of children under age 6	12	63
Race and ethnicity		
% Non-Hispanic white	88	71
% Black	10	12
% Asian	*	4
% American Indian	*	1
% Hispanic	1	12
Religious affiliation		
% Mainline Protestant	45	22
% Evangelical Protestant	29	33
% Catholic	20	26
% Jewish	3	2
% Other or none	3	16

Note: For race and ethnicity, data are for 1940 and 2000 because comparable data were not available for 1950. For religious affiliation, data are for 1960 and 1996.

*denotes less than 0.5 percent.

Sources: U.S. Census Bureau, U.S. Bureau of Labor Statistics, American National Election Studies.

According to data compiled by the U.S. Census Bureau, the median age of the American population increased from 28.0 years in 1970 to 30.0 in 1980, 32.8 in 1990, and 35.8 in 2000. This was the largest increase in the median age of the population for any 30-year period in U.S. history and the increase would have been even greater if not for the impact of immigration. Moreover, this trend is expected to continue for the foreseeable future, although at a somewhat slower rate, with the median age of the population expected to reach 38.5 years in 2025 and 38.8 years in 2050. By way of contrast, the median age of the U.S. population was 18.9 years in 1850 and 22.9 years in 1900.

The recent increase in the median age of the U.S. population is attributable to three factors: the aging of the post–World War II **baby**

boom generation, decreasing birth rates, and increasing longevity due to improvements in medical care. As a result of these trends, the proportion of the population that is 65 years of age and older, which rose from 11.3 percent in 1980 to 12.7 percent in 2000, is expected to reach 18.5 percent by 2010.

The aging of the U.S. population, and especially the dramatic increase in the elderly proportion of that population, has important implications for many aspects of American politics including the electoral process. This is especially true because the elderly are well organized and turn out to vote at a higher rate than younger citizens. In the 2000 election, Americans aged 65 and older made up 14 percent of the electorate according to the Voter News Service national exit poll and this percentage should increase substantially over the next decade. In addition, many younger voters are concerned about the problems of older Americans because they have elderly parents or grandparents. This means that politicians in the United States will have to be even more sensitive in the future to the needs and concerns of senior citizens, who depend more on federal programs than any other age group in the population. Issues such as the financial solvency of Social Security and the quantity and quality of benefits provided by Medicare will probably receive increased attention from candidates and officeholders.

Internal Migration

The United States has one of the most mobile populations of any nation in the world. According to data compiled by the Census Bureau, during 1998–1999, 15 percent of Americans changed their place of residence. This percentage was fairly typical for the entire decade of the 1990s. Most of these moves were local in nature—about 60 percent of movers stayed in the same county. During this 2-year period, however, 20 percent of those who changed their residence, about 3 percent of the American population, moved to a different state.

Since the end of World War II, millions of people have moved within the United States, and this movement has substantially changed the geographical distribution of the American population. Two of the most important consequences of internal migration have been the rise of the **Sun Belt** and the growing **suburbanization** of American society. Americans have been moving westward since the arrival of the first European setters. In recent decades, however, millions of Americans have left the Northeast and Midwest (the **Frost Belt**) in search of economic opportunity or a comfortable retirement in the warmer climates of the South and West. Moreover, based on the findings of the 2000 Census, this trend seems likely to continue for the foreseeable future.

According to Census Bureau data, between 1950 and 2000, the proportion of Americans living in the Northeast declined from 26 percent to 19 percent, and the proportion living in the Midwest fell from 29 percent to 23 percent. During the same time period, the proportion of Americans living in the South increased from 31 percent to 35 percent, and the proportion living in the West rose from 13 percent to 22 percent. Largely as a result of migration within the United States, California and Texas are now the two most populous states in the union and, by 2020, Florida is expected to pass New York as the third most populous state. California alone had 33.9 million residents in 2000, more than 12 percent of the entire population of the United States.[17]

The other major result of migration within the United States has been the growth of the suburbs. Since the end of World War II, millions of American families have left the nation's central cities, small towns, and rural areas in search of better jobs, housing, and schools in the suburbs. Between 1950 and 2000, according to Census Bureau data, the proportion of Americans living in suburbs increased from 32 percent to 50 percent while the proportion living in central cities declined from 32 percent to 30 percent and the proportion living in small towns and rural areas fell from 36 percent to 20 percent.[18] Although suburban growth has slowed considerably since 1970 in the older metropolitan areas of the Northeast and Midwest, it has accelerated in Sun Belt states like Florida, Georgia, and Texas, where suburban development has been rapidly expanding outward into previously rural areas.

In a democracy, political power is based on population. Since the end of World War II, the movement of millions of Americans from the Frost Belt to the Sun Belt and from the central cities and rural areas to the suburbs has produced a corresponding shift in the locus of political power. This shift can be seen most clearly in the changing geographical distribution of seats in the U.S. House of Representatives and votes in the Electoral College. Between 1950 and 2000, the

---

[17] During the 1990s, however, California experienced a net loss of more than 2 million residents due to domestic migration, reversing a longstanding trend. The state's growth during this decade was due entirely to natural increase and immigration from abroad.
[18] The definition of the suburban population was somewhat different in 2000 (residents of metropolitan areas not living in central cities) from 1950 (residents of urbanized areas not living in cities).

number of House seats from the Northeast and Midwest fell from 272 to 211 while the number of seats from the South and West increased from 163 to 224. Because states receive one electoral vote for each Senator and Representative, there was a corresponding shift in electoral votes from the Frost Belt to the Sun Belt. In 2002, as a result of the 2000 Census, the Northeast and Midwest lost an additional 11 House seats, and 11 electoral votes, to the South and the West, and this trend is likely to continue for many years to come.

Some observers of American politics have argued that the continuing shift of population from the Frost Belt to the Sun Belt is providing a growing electoral advantage for the Republican Party.[19] As a result of the 2000 Census, for example, there was a net shift of seven House seats and electoral votes from states that were carried by Al Gore in the 2000 presidential election to states that were carried by George W. Bush. Certain traditionally Democratic voting groups such as union members and Jews are found disproportionately in the older metropolitan areas of the Northeast and Midwest. In addition, since 1980, the South and the Mountain West have been the most conservative and Republican regions of the nation in presidential and congressional elections. In the 2000 election, every state in the South and every state in the Mountain West except New Mexico supported George W. Bush. Following the 2000 election, Republicans held 30 of the 42 Senate seats and 94 of the 154 seats in the House of Representatives from the South and Mountain West.

The partisan implications of the growth of the Sun Belt are not entirely one-sided, however. African Americans make up a large and growing segment of the population of many Sun Belt states, and African American voters have been extraordinarily loyal to the Democratic Party in recent elections, supporting Al Gore over George W. Bush by a 10-1 margin in 2000. The Pacific Coast states of California, Oregon, Washington, and Hawaii, which together cast 76 of the West's 119 electoral votes in 2000, have been trending Democratic since the 1980s. All four states supported Bill Clinton in 1992 and 1996 and Al Gore in 2000. Following the 2000 election, Democrats held 7 of the 8 Senate seats and 44 of the 68 seats in the House of Representatives from the Pacific Coast states. In addition, in recent years one of the major sources of population growth in many of the Sun Belt states has been immigration, especially immigration from Mexico and other parts of Latin America. Hispanics, who have traditionally

[19]See, for example, Kevin Phillips, *The Emerging Republican Majority* (New Rochelle, NY: Arlington House, 1969).

voted Democratic and who supported Al Gore over George W. Bush by a better than 2-1 margin in 2000, comprise a large and growing segment of the electorate in the three largest Sun Belt states—California, Texas, and Florida. But the effects of immigration are by no means confined to the Sun Belt. Throughout the United States, immigration is changing the face of the American population and, more gradually, the American electorate.

Immigration

Between 1990 and 2000, the population of the United States grew from 248.7 million to 281.4 million, an increase of 32.7 million. This was the largest population increase for any decade in American history, breaking the record of 28 million that was set between 1950 and 1960 during the post–World War II baby boom. A large part of the explanation for this surge in population growth, which greatly exceeded the expectations of most demographers as well as the Census Bureau's own forecasts, was immigration.

During the 1990s, as a result of liberalized immigration laws and a booming economy, legal and illegal immigration to the United States reached its highest level since the turn of the twentieth century—the heyday of American immigration. Between 1991 and 2000, the Immigration and Naturalization Service estimated that almost 1 million immigrants per year entered the United States, of whom about 300,000 were undocumented. Based on these figures, about one-third of the overall increase in the U.S. population during the 1990s was due to legal and illegal immigration.

The sources of immigration today are very different from what they were a hundred years ago. During the late nineteenth and early twentieth centuries, when the United States received the largest immigration in its history, most of the new arrivals came from southern and eastern Europe. More recently, however, the largest numbers of immigrants have come from Asia and Latin America. According to the Immigration and Naturalization Service, out of 6.1 million immigrants who arrived in the United States between 1991 and 1996, about 900,000 came from Europe, 200,000 from Africa, 1.9 million from Asia, and just over 3 million from Latin America, including over 1.6 million from Mexico. As a result of increased immigration, the number of foreign-born residents in the United States reached an all-time record of 26.4 million in 1999, almost 10 percent of the entire population. Over one-fourth of those foreign-born residents, some 7.2 million, were from Mexico.

Despite the large numbers of immigrants arriving during the 1990s, the impact of immigration has been very uneven across the United States because the large majority of immigrants have settled in a few states. During 1998, for example, six states—California, New York, Texas, Florida, Illinois, and New Jersey—received about two-thirds of the 660,000 immigrants who arrived in the United States. California alone received more than 170,000 immigrants during 1998, more than one-fourth of the national total.

Largely as a result of immigration, the racial and ethnic makeup of the United States has been undergoing a gradual metamorphosis. According to the Census Bureau, between 1980 and 2000, the share of the American population made up of non-Hispanic whites fell from 80 percent to 71 percent. During this same time period, the proportion of African Americans in the U.S. population increased from 11.5 percent to 12.2 percent, the proportion of native Americans increased from 0.6 percent to 0.7 percent, and the proportion of Asians and Pacific Islanders increased from 1.6 percent to 3.9 percent. However, by far the fastest growing ethnic or racial group in the United States during this 20-year span was Hispanics. Between 1980 and 2000, the Hispanic share of the U.S. population rose from 6.4 percent to 11.8 percent.

Over the next several decades, the American population is expected to become much more diverse in its ethnic and racial composition. By 2050, according to Census Bureau projections, only 53 percent of the U.S. population will be made up of non-Hispanic whites. By that year, the Census Bureau projects that 24 percent of the American population will be Hispanic, 13 percent will be black, 9 percent will be Asian, and 1 percent will be native American.

The American electorate, like the overall population, is becoming increasingly diverse as a result of immigration. However, the changes in the composition of the electorate are occurring more slowly than the changes in the composition of the population. It takes at least 5 years for newly arrived legal immigrants to become naturalized citizens and the Immigration and Naturalization Service estimates that only about half of all legal immigrants eventually obtain citizenship and with it the right to vote. In addition, of course, most illegal immigrants never become American citizens.

According to the Census Bureau, of the 26.4 million foreign-born residents of the United States in 1999, only about 9.9 million, or 38 percent, were citizens. The citizenship gap was especially large among immigrants from Mexico because a large percentage of them entered the country illegally and many did not plan on staying in the United

States permanently. Of the estimated 7.2 million U.S. residents in 1999 who were born in Mexico, only about 1.5 million, or 20 percent, were citizens. Largely as a result of the **citizenship gap** among immigrants from Mexico and other parts of Latin America, the Census Bureau found that only 27 percent of Hispanics reported voting in the 2000 presidential election compared with 53 percent of African Americans and 62 percent of non-Hispanic whites.[20]

Despite the citizenship gap, immigration along with higher birth rates among Hispanics and other minority groups are gradually transforming the American electorate. In the 2000 presidential election, according to the Voter News Service exit poll, the national electorate was 81 percent white, 10 percent black, 7 percent Hispanic, and 2 percent Asian. This was the smallest percentage of whites and the highest percentage of Hispanics since the advent of exit polling in 1976. Moreover, racial and ethnic minorities made up an even larger proportion of the electorate in the four most populous states that together cast more than one-fourth of the votes in the Electoral College—California, Texas, New York, and Florida. In California, the most populous state and the one that has received the largest number of immigrants since World War II, citizens of Hispanic and Asian descent comprised one-fifth of the electorate in 2000.

During the nineteenth and early twentieth centuries, hostility to immigrants, especially to those belonging to racial or religious minority groups, was a common theme in American political campaigns. Despite the large numbers of immigrants arriving in the United States in recent years, however, there has been relatively little evidence of any political backlash against immigration. Indeed, Reform Party candidate Patrick Buchanan's attempt to appeal to anti-immigration sentiment in his 2000 presidential campaign fell completely flat. Despite spending over $13 million in public funds on his campaign, much of it to pay for anti-immigration television ads, Buchanan received less than 1 percent of the national popular vote.

Two factors help to explain the absence of any significant political backlash against immigration during the 1990s. One is prosperity—a high rate of economic growth and low unemployment reduced concern about immigrants taking jobs away from American citizens. The second factor is the growing clout of Hispanic voters. Hispanics are already a sizable voting bloc in several key states, including California where they made up 14 percent of the electorate

[20]U.S. Census Bureau, "Voting and Registration in the Election of November 2000," *Current Population Reports,* February 2002, Table C.

in 2000. Over the next several decades, as millions of immigrants and their children become eligible to vote, the national electorate will come to look more and more like the California electorate today.

Already, Democratic and Republican politicians are working hard to court the Hispanic vote. During the 2000 campaign, both parties ran radio and television advertisements in Spanish in states with large Hispanic populations. George W. Bush emphasized his strong support among Hispanic voters in Texas and even occasionally spoke Spanish on the campaign trail. Bush was able to increase the Republican share of the Hispanic vote from 21 percent in 1996 to 31 percent in 2000, including 43 percent in Texas. Following up on this success, the first foreign leader that President-elect Bush met with after the election was newly elected Mexican President Vicente Fox. A few months later, a task force including several high-ranking members of the Bush Cabinet announced that it was considering recommending legislation that would allow more than a million undocumented Mexican immigrants to obtain legal residency status in the United States. All of these developments indicate that Republican as well as Democratic strategists now see the Hispanic vote as crucial to their future success.

The New Economy and the Changing Structure of the American Workforce

Since the end of World War II, the American economy has undergone a dramatic transformation. The manufacturing-based economy of the mid-twentieth century has been replaced by the service- and information-based economy of the early twenty-first century. In the process, the American workforce has also been transformed. Today's workforce differs dramatically from the workforce of the 1950s. It is much better educated, it is much more female, and it includes a much higher ratio of white-collar workers to blue-collar workers. According to data compiled by the Bureau of Labor Statistics, between 1950 and 1999, the proportion of American workers employed in white-collar occupations rose from 37 percent to 59 percent while the proportion employed in blue-collar occupations fell from 41 percent to 25 percent. During these same years, the female share of the workforce increased from 29 percent to 46 percent and the proportion of workers with at least a high school degree rose from less than 40 percent to over 90 percent.

Partially because of structural changes that have taken place in the economy, the American workforce today includes a much smaller proportion of labor union members than it did in the mid-twentieth century. Manufacturing and mining, traditionally the most heavily unionized sectors of the economy, have been losing jobs for decades while the service sector, where unions have been much weaker, has been expanding. As a result, the proportion of American workers belonging to labor unions has been declining steadily since reaching an all-time high of 35 percent in 1954. In 1999, only 14 percent of all wage and salary workers in the United States, and only 9 percent of workers in the private sector, were members of labor unions. Only the growth of public sector jobs, where union members still constituted 37 percent of the workforce in 1999, prevented an even steeper decline in overall union membership.

The changing composition of the American workforce has had important consequences for the electoral strategies of the two major parties, especially the Democratic Party. The electoral coalition forged by Franklin Roosevelt during the 1930s that made the Democrats the dominant party in the United States for the next 30 years rested on a foundation of blue-collar workers and union members. Today, however, that foundation has shrunk considerably. In the 2000 election, according to the VNS national exit poll, only 16 percent of all voters and only 21 percent of Democratic voters were union members despite a strong get-out-the-vote effort by **organized labor.** Although the exit poll did not include any questions about occupation, it is revealing that when voters were asked for their class identification, 74 percent of all voters and 70 percent of Democratic voters described themselves as middle class; only 18 percent of all voters and only 21 percent of Democratic voters described themselves as working class.

Class conflict was never as salient a theme in American politics as it was in some other Western democracies. From the 1930s through the 1950s, however, Democratic candidates and office holders frequently utilized class-based appeals to mobilize their party's working-class supporters. As a result, social class was a prominent feature of the public's images of the two major parties during these years. The Democrats were generally seen as the party of the poor and the working class while the Republicans were seen as the party of big business and the wealthy.[21]

In recent elections, the decline of organized labor and the changing American occupational structure have caused Democratic politi-

[21] See Angus Campbell, Philip E. Converse, Warren E. Miller, and Donald E. Stokes, *The American Voter* (New York: John Wiley and Sons, 1960), pp. 234–40.

cians to de-emphasize class-based rhetoric to appeal to an increasingly middle-class electorate. As a result, class differences in voting, which were never very large in the United States, have diminished further. In the 2000 presidential election, for example, according to the VNS national exit poll, voters who identified themselves as working class favored Al Gore over George W. Bush by a narrow 51 to 46 percent margin while voters who identified themselves as middle class favored Bush over Gore by an equally narrow 51 to 46 percent margin. Similarly, voters in the lowest income category, those earning less than $15,000 per year, favored Gore over Bush by a 57 to 37 percent margin while voters in the highest income category, those earning over $100,000 per year, favored Bush over Gore by a 54 to 43 percent margin. The 14-point difference in support for the Democratic candidate between the lowest and highest income groups was the smallest such difference since the advent of national exit polls in 1976.

The Changing American Family

In the twenty-first century, the traditional politics of class is giving way to a new politics based on values and lifestyles. This shift in the basis of political conflict is being fueled by the changing structure of the American economy and by the changing structure of the American family. That family has changed dramatically since the 1950s.[22] Fewer American families today consist of a married couple and their children. More families consist of unmarried or divorced individuals, single parents and their children, and unmarried opposite-sex or same-sex partners.

Even during the 1950s and 1960s, the **traditional nuclear family** with its working dad, stay-at-home mom, and two or more children, as depicted by television programs such as "Father Knows Best," "Ozzie and Harriet," and "Leave It to Beaver," was far from universal.[23] In 1950, according to the Census Bureau, 43 percent of the nation's 43.6 million households consisted of a married couple with children; in 2000, only 24 percent of the nation's 104.7 million households consisted of a married couple with children. In 1950, only 11 percent of American households consisted of one or more unmarried adults

---

[22] See Scott J. South and Stewart E. Tolnay, eds., *The Changing American Family: Sociological and Demographic Perspectives* (Boulder , CO: Westview Press, 1992).
[23] We assume that Ozzie had a job outside the home, although this was never clearly established.

without children; in 2000, 31 percent of households consisted of one or more unmarried adults without children. In 1950, only 7 percent of families with children under the age of 18 were headed by a single parent; in 2000, 27 percent of families with children under the age of 18 were headed by a single parent.

Among today's married couples, far more wives are working outside the home than in the past. According to data compiled by the Bureau of Labor Statistics, between 1960 and 1999, the workforce participation rate of married women nearly doubled, from 32 percent to 61 percent, while the rate for single women rose from 59 percent to 69 percent. During this same period, the workforce participation rate of married men fell from 89 percent to 78 percent while the rate for single men rose slightly, from 70 percent to 73 percent. Even among married couples with very young children, far fewer mothers are staying at home to take care of the kids. The proportion of married women with children younger than 6 who worked outside the home rose from 12 percent in 1950 to 30 percent in 1975 to 63 percent in 2000.

The increasing workforce participation of women and the growing diversity of American families have important implications for electoral politics in the twenty-first century. Among both women and men, nontraditional lifestyles are associated with liberal attitudes on social issues and Democratic voting tendencies. In the 2000 presidential election, for example, women working outside the home favored Al Gore over George W. Bush by a margin of 58 percent to 39 percent, but women who did not work outside the home favored Bush over Gore by a margin of 52 percent to 44 percent. Similarly, single women favored Gore over Bush by an overwhelming 63 to 32 percent margin but married women favored Bush over Gore by a 49 to 48 percent margin. Single men favored Gore over Bush by a narrow 48 to 46 percent margin but married men favored Bush over Gore by a decisive 58 to 38 percent margin. The 15-point **marriage gap** between single and married women was even larger than the 12-point **gender gap** between women and men. However, both were dwarfed in size by the 20-point **sexual preference gap** between gays and straights. According to the VNS exit poll, gays and lesbians, who made up approximately 4 percent of the national electorate, supported Al Gore over George W. Bush by an overwhelming 70 to 25 percent margin while straight men and women supported Bush over Gore by a much narrower 50 to 47 percent margin.

The changing American family structure is creating challenges for leaders of both major parties. Democrats have done well recently among working women, single parents, and gays, but the party's increasingly liberal image has hurt it among some traditional supporters, especially socially conservative **white southerners.** In the 2000 presidential election, Al Gore, a native southerner, received only 31 percent of the vote among southern white voters—the worst showing for a Democratic presidential candidate since Walter Mondale in 1984. Republicans, meanwhile, find their party's base of white voters in traditional families shrinking in size with every election. To appeal to the growing segment of the electorate made up of voters with nontraditional lifestyles, however, Republican leaders would have to risk offending what has become one of their party's largest and strongest support groups—**religious conservatives.**

The Religious Factor

As early as the 1830s, the French writer Alexis de Tocqueville noted the importance of religion in American life in his accounts of his travels across the United States.[24] Today, Americans remain among the most religious people in the Western world in terms of both beliefs and practices.[25] Compared with residents of Western Europe, Americans are more likely to profess belief in God and an afterlife, belong to a church or synagogue, attend religious services, and pray on a regular basis. But Americans' religious beliefs and practices have been evolving as a result of forces such as immigration and changing lifestyles. While traditional beliefs and practices remain strong among a large segment of the population, a growing proportion of Americans have been opting out of organized religion or seeking less traditional ways to satisfy their spiritual needs.

One sign of the changing role of religion in American life is the shift that has taken place in religious affiliation. Between the 1950s and the 1990s, according to National Election Study (NES) surveys, the proportion of Americans describing themselves as Protestant declined from 73 percent to 57 percent, the proportion describing themselves as Catholic increased from 21 percent to 26 percent, and the proportion describing themselves as Jewish fell from 3 percent to 2 percent. However, the most dramatic change during these five decades was the increase in the proportion of Americans with no

[24] Alexis de Tocqueville, *Democracy in America* (Chicago: University of Chicago Press, 2000). Originally published in 1841.
[25] See George Gallup, Jr., and D. Michael Lindsay, *Surveying the Religious Landscape: Trends in U.S. Beliefs* (Harrisburg, PA: Morehouse Publishing, 1999).

religious affiliation or an affiliation other than Protestant, Catholic, or Jewish. Between the 1950s and the 1990s, this group nearly tripled in size from 6 percent of the population to 17 percent.

Despite these changes, Protestants remained by far the largest religious group in the United States at the beginning of the twenty-first century. Within Protestantism, however, there has been a dramatic shift in affiliation since the 1950s. Mainline Protestant denominations—Methodists, Lutherans, Presbyterians, and Episcopalians—have been shrinking in size while evangelical denominations have been growing. Between 1960 and 1996, according to NES data, the proportion of Americans affiliated with mainline Protestant denominations fell from 45 percent to 22 percent while the proportion affiliated with evangelical denominations increased from 29 percent to 33 percent.

The steady decline in membership in mainline Protestant denominations over the past 4 years suggests that religious moderates have been losing influence in the United States. The American public appears to be increasingly divided into two opposing camps—the strongly religious and the nonreligious. This division is clearly reflected in statistics on church attendance. According to NES data, since the 1950s the proportion of Americans who attend church regularly (every week or almost every week) has remained fairly steady at around 40 percent while the proportion who have no religious preference or never attend church has climbed from less than 10 percent in the 1950s to around 30 percent in the 1990s. The biggest decline has been in the ranks of the occasional churchgoers—those who attend services anywhere from a few times a year to once or twice a month. This group has fallen in size from over half the population in the 1950s to less than a third in the 1990s.

The growing polarization in religious beliefs and practices in the United States has important implications for electoral politics because religious beliefs are strongly related to attitudes toward issues such as abortion, gay rights, and government assistance to religious schools and organizations—issues that have divided the two major parties in recent elections. For this reason, the most politically important religious division in the United States is no longer between Catholics and Protestants, but between the religious and the nonreligious. In the 2000 presidential election, for example, frequency of church attendance was a much stronger predictor of candidate preference among white voters than Protestant versus Catholic affiliation. According to the VNS exit poll, support for George W. Bush among white voters ranged from 34 percent among those who said that they never attend church services to 79 percent among those who said that they attend services every week—a difference of 45 points. In contrast, the difference in support for Bush between white Catholics and Protestants was only 11 points (52 percent versus 63 percent).

SUMMARY

The laws and regulations governing elections and the social and cultural divisions within American society form the strategic environment within which campaigns and elections take place. That strategic environment at the beginning of the twenty-first century is very different from that of the mid-twentieth century. Many of the basic features of the American electoral process—winner-take-all elections, decentralized election administration, and the use of primary elections to choose party nominees—have changed very little since the end of World War II. However, the amount of money spent on political campaigns has increased dramatically in the television era. In the aftermath of the Watergate scandal, the laws governing campaign finance in federal elections were strengthened considerably in 1974. However, largely as a result of the Supreme Court's 1976 ruling that limits on campaign spending are unconstitutional, the 1974 reforms have been ineffective in limiting the influence of money in federal elections.

The basic electoral institutions of the United States have been fairly stable for the past 50 years. However, American society and culture have changed dramatically during these years and these changes have altered the way politicians appeal for votes and the way voters respond to those appeals.

- The population has gotten older due to the aging of the baby boom generation, declining birth rates, and increased longevity. Senior citizens make up a growing proportion of the electorate.
- The manufacturing-based economy of the mid-twentieth century has given way to a service- and information-based economy with a workforce that is much better educated, much more female, and much less unionized than the workforce of the 1950s and 1960s.
- Families are more diverse with fewer households consisting of married couples with children and more households consisting of unmarried or divorced individuals, single parents with children, and unmarried opposite-sex or same-sex partners.
- More Americans are living in the Sun Belt and the suburbs and fewer are living in the Frost Belt, the central cities, and rural areas.

- There are 33 million more Americans than there were in 1990 and about one-third of these new Americans are immigrants.
- Religion continues to exert a strong influence on American life, but Americans' religious beliefs are becoming increasingly diverse.

Taken together, these changes in American society and culture are producing a new electorate in the twenty-first century—an electorate that is increasingly diverse in its racial and ethnic composition, its lifestyles, and its religious beliefs. What makes this growing diversity significant politically is that racial and ethnic characteristics, lifestyle choices, and religious beliefs are strongly related to political attitudes, including attitudes toward the two major political parties.

KEY TERMS AND CONCEPTS

baby boom generation
blanket primaries
Buckley v. *Valeo*
Bush v. *Gore*
citizenship gap
closed primaries
crossover voters
Duverger's Law
Federal Election Campaign Act
   Amendments of 1974
Federal Election Commission
Frost Belt
gender gap
gerrymandering
hard money
Help America Vote Act
marriage gap
open primaries

organized labor
political action committees
   (PACs)
proportional representation (PR)
raiding
redistricting
religious conservatives
sexual preference gap
single transferable vote (STV)
   system
single-member, simple plurality
   (SMSP) electoral system
soft money
strategic environment
suburbanization
Sun Belt
traditional nuclear family
white southerners

DISCUSSION QUESTIONS

1. What are the major advantages and disadvantages of electoral systems based on single-member districts versus those based on proportional representation? What would happen to American politics if the United States switched to an electoral system based on proportional representation?

2. How has the Supreme Court's decision in *Buckley* v. *Valeo* (1976) affected efforts to regulate campaign spending in the United States? Do America's current campaign finance laws promote or stifle electoral competition?
3. How will the McCain-Feingold Law banning soft money affect presidential and congressional elections? What new laws and regulations, if any, are needed to regulate campaign finance?
4. What are the most important demographic and cultural trends affecting American society today? What groups are gaining and losing influence as a result of these trends and how will this affect political parties and elections in the future?

SUGGESTED READINGS

Amy, Douglas J. *Behind the Ballot Box: A Citizen's Guide to Voting Systems.* Westport, CT: Praeger, 2000. Amy provides a clear explanation of the workings of different electoral systems, including winner-take-all plurality voting, proportional representation, and single transferable vote.

Ceaser, James W., and Andrew E. Busch. *The Perfect Tie: The True Story of the 2000 Presidential Election.* Lanham, MD: Rowman and Littlefield, 2001. This is a balanced account of the very strange events of the 2000 presidential election, including the lengthy postelection struggle for Florida's electoral votes.

Gallup, George, Jr., and D. Michael Lindsay. *Surveying the Religious Landscape: Trends in U.S. Beliefs.* Harrisburg, PA: Morehouse Publishing, 1999. Gallup and Lindsay use Gallup Poll data to describe trends in American religious beliefs and practices.

Gierzynski, Anthony. *Money Rules: Financing Elections in America.* Boulder, CO: Westview Press, 2000. Gierzynski provides a brief but thorough examination of the current system of campaign finance in the United States and its consequences for electoral competition.

Handlin, Oscar. *The Uprooted.* Boston: Little, Brown, 1990. This is the most recent edition of the classic study of the immigrant experience in the United States.

Rush, Mark E., and Richard L. Engstrom. *Fair and Effective Representation? Debating Electoral Reform and Minority Rights.* New York: Rowman and Littlefield, 2001. Rush and Engstrom debate the advantages and disadvantages of the American single-member plurality-voting electoral system versus alternative systems such as proportional representation.

South, Scott J., and Stewart E. Tolnay, eds. *The Changing American Family: Sociological and Demographic Perspectives.* Boulder, CO: Westview Press, 1992. This is a diverse collection of scholarly papers on the causes and consequences of change in the American family.

United States Census Bureau, *Statistical Abstract of the United States: 2002.* Washington, DC: 2002. The latest edition of this invaluable reference work includes an enormous variety of statistical data on the political, economic, and social characteristics of the American population.

INFORMATION SOURCES ON THE INTERNET

American National Election Studies: www.umich.edu/~nes/nesguide/ nesguide.htm. This is the website for the NES Guide to Public Opinion and Electoral Behavior. The guide provides a wide range of information about the social characteristics, political attitudes, and voting behavior of the American electorate since 1952.

Federal Election Commission: www.fec.gov. The FEC is the agency responsible for enforcing the nation's campaign finance laws. Although it is sometimes considered a toothless tiger by reformers, the agency's website provides valuable information about federal election laws and regulations, election results, and campaign spending.

United States Census Bureau: www.census.gov. This site provides a wide variety of data from the U.S. Census, including the 2000 Census, along with special reports on population-related topics.

United States Government: www.fedstats.gov. This site provides access to statistical data from many different federal agencies.

CHAPTER 3

The Parties
in the Electorate

PARTY IDENTIFICATION

Since the publication of *The American Voter* in 1960, political scientists have generally divided the factors that influence individual voting decisions and election outcomes into two types: **short-term forces** and **long-term forces.**[1] Short-term forces include the candidates, issues, and conditions specific to a particular election. In U.S. presidential elections these short-term forces, especially the popular appeal of the candidates, can vary dramatically from one election to the next. In 1956, for example, the Republican incumbent, World War II hero Dwight D. Eisenhower, was much more popular than his Democratic challenger, Illinois Senator Adlai Stevenson. Eisenhower was reelected in a landslide. In 1960, however, voters rated the Republican candidate, Vice President Richard M. Nixon, and his Democratic opponent, Massachusetts Senator John F. Kennedy, about evenly and Kennedy was able to squeak past Nixon in one of the closest presidential elections in the twentieth century. The outcomes of the 1956 and 1960 presidential elections were very different because of differences in voters' reactions to the presidential candidates. However, there was almost no change in voters' party loyalties between 1956 and 1960.

---

[1] Angus Campbell, Philip E. Converse, Warren E. Miller, and Donald E. Stokes, *The American Voter* (New York: John Wiley and Sons, 1966). See also Philip E. Converse, "The Concept of a Normal Vote," in Campbell, Converse, Miller, and Stokes, eds., *Elections and the Political Order* (New York: John Wiley and Sons, 1966).

The most important long-term force in American elections is **party identification:** the psychological attachment of most American citizens to one of the two major parties. The authors of *The American Voter* found that the large majority of Americans thought of themselves as Republicans or Democrats and that this partisan identification was far more stable, both at the individual level and in the aggregate, than attitudes toward either issues or candidates. Party identification exerted a strong influence on individual voting decisions and election results, especially in elections below the presidential level, by shaping attitudes toward the candidates and issues. Between the election of Franklin Roosevelt in 1932 and the election of Ronald Reagan in 1980, the Democratic Party dominated elections below the presidential level in the United States, including congressional elections, because there were far more Democratic than Republican identifiers in the American electorate. During these 48 years, Republicans controlled the White House for 16 years, but they controlled Congress for only 4 years.

More recent research has confirmed the findings of *The American Voter* that party identification is more stable than attitudes toward candidates and issues and exerts a much stronger influence on these attitudes than they exert on party identification during the course of a single election campaign.[2] Moreover, when voters know little or nothing about the candidates for a particular office, which is a common occurrence because of the large number of elected offices in the United States, party identification provides them with a simple cue for selecting a candidate.[3]

[2] Philip E. Converse and Gregory B. Markus, "Plus Ca Change: The New CPS Election Study Panel," *American Political Science Review* 73 (March 1979), pp. 32–49. See also Morris Fiorina, *Retrospective Voting in American National Elections* (New Haven, CT: Yale University Press, 1981); M. Kent Jennings and Richard G. Niemi, *Generations and Politics* (Princeton, NJ: Princeton University Press, 1981); M. Kent Jennings and Gregory B. Markus, "Partisan Orientations Over the Long Haul: Results from the Three-Wave Political Socialization Panel Study," *American Political Science Review* 78 (December 1984), pp. 1000–18; William G. Jacoby, "The Impact of Party Identification on Issue Attitudes," *American Journal of Political Science* 32 (August 1988), pp. 643–61; Dee Allsop and Herbert F. Weisberg, "Measuring Change in Party Identification in an Election Campaign," *American Journal of Political Science* 32 (November 1988), pp. 996–1017; Paul R. Abramson and Charles W. Ostrom, "Macropartisanship: An Empirical Reassessment," *American Political Science Review* 85 (March 1991), pp. 181–92; Donald P. Green and Bradley Palmquist, "Of Artifacts and Partisan Instability," *American Journal of Political Science* 34 (August 1990), pp. 872–901; and Green and Palmquist, "How Stable Is Party Identification?" *Political Behavior* 16 (1994), pp. 437–66.

[3] Of course this is only true if the candidates' party affiliations are printed on the ballot. However, many local elections in the United States are nonpartisan. Without party

Party identification remains a key influence on voter decision-making and election outcomes in the United States. In the 2000 presidential election, for example, 89 percent of Democratic identifiers and 92 percent of Republican identifiers voted for their own party's presidential candidate. As a result, George W. Bush carried every state with a plurality of Republican identifiers and Al Gore carried every state outside the southern and border region with a plurality of Democratic identifiers. Similarly, the outcomes of the large majority of Senate and House contests in the 2000 election reflected the partisan orientations of the voters: states and districts with Democratic electorates generally elected Democrats to Congress and states and districts with Republican electorates generally elected Republicans to Congress.

MEASURING PARTY IDENTIFICATION

The authors of *The American Voter* developed a two-part question to measure party identification and, despite some controversy about its reliability and validity,[4] this measure of party identification has been used in every subsequent National Election Study (NES) survey, and in many other surveys of the American electorate since 1952. The first party identification question is, "Generally speaking, do you usually think of yourself as a Republican, a Democrat, an independent, or

---

labels on the ballot, voters are sometimes influenced by factors such as ballot position or the ethnic characteristics of the candidates' names.

[4]For alternative approaches to conceptualizing and measuring party identification, see Herbert F. Weisberg, "A Multidimensional Conceptualization of Party Identification," in Richard G. Niemi and Herbert F. Weisberg, eds., *Controversies in Voting Behavior*, 2nd ed. (Washington, DC: Congressional Quarterly Press, 1984); Stephen C. Craig, "Partisanship, Independence, and No Preference: Another Look at the Measurement of Party Identification," *American Journal of Political Science* 29 (May 1985), pp. 274–90; Arthur H. Miller and Martin P. Wattenberg, "Measuring Party Identification: Independent or No Partisan Preference?" *American Journal of Political Science*, 27 (February 1983) pp. 106–21; Richard G. Niemi, Stephen Wright, and Lynda W. Powell, "Multiple Party Identifiers and the Measurement of Party Identification," *Journal of Politics* 49 (November 1987), pp. 1093–103; Patrick J. Kenney and Tom W. Rice, "The Evaporating Independents: Removing the 'Independent' Option From the NES Party Identification Question," *Public Opinion Quarterly* 52 (Summer 1988), pp. 231–39; Charles H. Franklin, "Measurement and the Dynamics of Party Identification," *Political Behavior* 14 (1992), pp. 297–310; and Donald P. Green and Eric Schickler, "Multiple-Measure Assessment of Party Identification," *Public Opinion Quarterly* 57 (Winter 1993), pp. 503–35.

what?" Those who answer either "Republican" or "Democrat" to this question are then asked, "Do you consider yourself a strong (Democrat, Republican) or not too strong?" This follow-up question makes it possible to classify respondents as either strong identifiers or weak identifiers. Those who answer "independent" are asked, "Do you usually feel closer to the Republican Party or to the Democratic Party?" This follow-up question makes it possible to classify respondents as either leaning independents or pure independents.

Based on their answers to the first question and the follow-up questions, respondents are placed on a seven-point party identification scale ranging from "Strong Democrat" at one end to "Strong Republican" at the other end. In the 2000 National Election Study, for example, 19 percent of respondents were classified as strong Democrats, 15 percent as weak Democrats, 15 percent as independents closer to the Democratic Party, 12 percent as independents with no party preference, 13 percent as independents closer to the Republican Party, 12 percent as weak Republicans, and 12 percent as strong Republicans.[5]

Since the two-part party identification question was first used in 1952, the large majority of persons classifying themselves as independents in NES surveys have responded to the follow-up question by indicating that they usually feel closer to one of the two major parties. One of the main issues concerning the seven-point party identification scale has been whether these **independent leaners** should be treated as independents or as partisans for analytical purposes. While there has been some disagreement about this question, most students of voting behavior now classify independent leaners as party identifiers rather than independents.[6] That is because independent leaners turn out to vote at a rate that is similar to that of weak party identifiers and much higher than that of **pure independents** and, when they do vote, they are usually at least as loyal to their preferred party as weak party identifiers. In the remainder of this book we will therefore treat independent leaners as partisans rather than as true independents.

---

[5] An additional 1 percent of respondents in the 2000 NES survey were classified as "apolitical," because they had too little interest in politics to respond in a meaningful way to the party identification questions. The seven party identification categories plus the apoliticals add up to a total of 99 percent due to rounding error.
[6] See the discussion of these issues in Niemi and Weisberg, eds., *Controversies in Voting Behavior*, 2nd ed.

CRITICAL ELECTIONS AND
PARTY REALIGNMENTS

Political scientists have long recognized that party identification has a dynamic component. Major shifts in the partisan orientation of the electorate, or realignments, have occurred periodically throughout American history and these **party realignments** have been extensively described and analyzed by electoral scholars.[7] Some scholars have argued that realignments primarily involve the conversion of voters' party loyalties in response to changes in the issue context or the social and economic environment.[8] Other scholars have argued that realignments mainly involve the disproportionate mobilization of new or previously disenfranchised voters.[9] In either case, **critical elections** are sometimes seen as harbingers of a partisan realignment. These critical elections, characterized by severe stresses to the political system resulting from some cataclysmic event such as the Civil War or the Great Depression, can set off a realignment of party loyalties that continues for several election cycles.

In light of this theory, however, it is difficult to explain the outcomes of recent elections in the United States. The outcome of the 1994 midterm election seemed to reflect more than normal voter dissatisfaction with the performance of the incumbent president. The Republican Party picked up 54 seats in the House of Representatives and 8 seats in the Senate to gain control of both chambers of Congress for the first time in 40 years. In winning majorities in both the House

[7] V. O. Key, Jr., "A Theory of Critical Elections," *Journal of Politics* 17 (February 1955), pp. 3–18; V. O. Key, Jr., "Secular Realignment and the Party System," *Journal of Politics* 21 (February 1959), pp. 198–210; Walter D. Burnham, *Critical Elections and the Mainsprings of American Politics* (New York: W. W. Norton, 1970); Jerome M. Clubb, William H. Flanigan, and Nancy H. Zingale, *Partisan Realignment: Voters, Parties, and Government in American History* (Beverly Hills, CA: Sage Publications, 1980); and James L. Sundquist, *Dynamics of the Party System: Alignment and Realignment of Political Parties in the United States* (Washington, DC: The Brookings Institution, 1983).

[8] Everett C. Ladd with Charles Hadley, *Transformations of the American Party System*, 2nd ed. (New York: W. W. Norton, 1978).

[9] Paul A. Beck, "Youth and the Politics of Realignment," in Edward C. Dreyer and Walter A. Rosenbaum, eds., *Political Opinion and Behavior* (Belmont, CA: Wadsworth Publishing, 1976); Kristi Anderson, *The Creation of a Democratic Majority, 1928–1936* (Chicago: University of Chicago Press, 1979); James E. Campbell, "Sources of the New Deal Realignment: The Contributions of Conversion and Mobilization to Partisan Change," *Western Political Quarterly* 38 (September 1985), pp. 357–76; and Edward G. Carmines and James A. Stimson, *Issue Evolution: Race and the Transformation of American Politics* (Princeton, NJ: Princeton University Press, 1989).

and Senate for the first time since the Eisenhower Administration, Republicans won majorities of Senate and House seats from the South for the first time since the end of Reconstruction.[10] Two years later, Republicans retained control of both chambers, winning consecutive terms as the majority party for the first time since 1928 and 1930.[11] Meanwhile, Republicans made substantial gains in state and local elections throughout the United States. Between 1993 and 1997, the number of states with Republican governors increased from 18 to 32 and the number of state legislative chambers controlled by Republicans increased from 32 to 47 out of 98.[12] Yet none of the conditions usually associated with a critical election was present. There seemed to be no crisis or cataclysmic event that could have triggered such a dramatic change in party fortunes.

IDEOLOGICAL REALIGNMENT

In the absence of a national crisis, how can we explain the dramatic Republican gains in the 1994 election and subsequent Republican victories in the 1996, 1998, and 2000 elections? The explanation is that 1994 was not a critical election in the traditional sense. Rather, the GOP takeover of Congress and gains in state and local elections were the culmination of an **ideological realignment** that had been occurring for more than a decade prior to the momentous Republican victory. This realignment reflected the increased ideological polarization of the two major parties and changes in public perceptions of the parties during this period. These developments show that even without a cataclysmic event or crisis, changes in the parties' issue positions can produce substantial changes in the party loyalties of the electorate over the course of several elections.

[10] For an in-depth analysis of the 1994 election and its consequences for American politics, see Clyde Wilcox, *The Latest American Revolution? The 1994 Elections and Their Implications for Governance* (New York: St. Martin's Press, 1995).
[11] For analyses of the 1996 presidential and congressional elections, see Paul R. Abramson, John H. Aldrich, and David W. Rohde, *Change and Continuity in the 1996 Elections* (Washington, DC: Congressional Quarterly Press, 1998); Larry J. Sabato, ed., *Toward the Millennium: The Elections of 1996* (Boston: Allyn and Bacon, 1997); and Gerald R. Pomper, ed., *The Election of 1996: Reports and Interpretations* (Chatham, NJ: Chatham House, 1997).
[12] Information on party control of governorships and state legislatures was taken from the 2000 edition of the *Statistical Abstract of the United States*. One state, Nebraska, has a nonpartisan, unicameral legislature.

Political scientists have discovered that partisan identification can itself be affected by a variety of short-term factors. This research has demonstrated that party identification at the individual level can be influenced by presidential vote choice[13] as well as retrospective evaluations of party performance.[14] However, neither of these factors would seem to offer a satisfactory explanation for long-term shifts in the distribution of partisan identification within the electorate, as neither has consistently favored one party or the other.

The inability of either retrospective evaluations or presidential vote choice to explain long-term shifts in the party loyalties of the electorate leads us to consider a third explanatory variable: policy preferences. A considerable body of research has demonstrated that party identification can be influenced by policy preferences.[15] Although these studies did not attempt to explain long-term shifts in the distribution of partisanship, their findings imply that changes in the parties' policy stands or the salience of these policy stands could, over the course of several election cycles, alter the distribution of party loyalties in the electorate as individuals respond to these changes by bringing their party loyalties into line with their policy preferences.

The remainder of this chapter will present evidence that the Republican takeover of Congress and gains in state and local elections

[13]Gregory B. Markus and Philip E. Converse, "A Dynamic Simultaneous Equation Model of Electoral Choice," *American Political Science Review* 83 (December 1979), pp. 1055–70.

[14]Fiorina, *Retrospective Voting in American National Elections*. See also Michael B. MacKuen, Robert S. Erikson, and James A. Stimson, "Macropartisanship," *American Political Science Review* 83 (December 1989), pp. 1125–42.

[15]The most important studies include Benjamin I. Page and Calvin C. Jones, "Reciprocal Effects of Policy Preferences, Party Loyalties, and the Vote," *American Political Science Review* 73 (December 1979), pp. 1071–89; Charles H. Franklin and John E. Jackson, "The Dynamics of Party Identification," *American Political Science Review* 77 (December 1983), pp. 957–73; Charles H. Franklin, "Issue Preferences, Socialization, and the Evolution of Party Identification," *American Journal of Political Science* 28 (August 1984), pp. 459–78; Edward G. Carmines, John P. McIver, and James A. Stimson, "Unrealized Partisanship: A Theory of Dealignment," *Journal of Politics* 49 (May 1987), pp. 376–400; Robert C. Luskin, John P. McIver, and Edward G. Carmines, "Issues and the Transmission of Partisanship," *American Journal of Political Science* 33 (May 1989), pp. 440–58; Charles H. Franklin, "Measurement and the Dynamics of Party Identification," *Political Behavior* 14 (1992), pp. 297–310; and Greg D. Adams, "Abortion: Evidence of an Issue Evolution, *American Journal of Political Science* 41 (July 1997), pp. 718–37. A much earlier study indicating that policy preferences have important effects on voting behavior is V. O. Key, Jr., *The Responsible Electorate: Rationality in Presidential Voting, 1936–1960* (Cambridge, MA: Harvard University Press, 1966).

during the 1990s reflected a long-term shift in the relative strength and bases of support of the two major parties and that this shift in the party loyalties of the electorate was in turn based on the increased **ideological polarization** of the Democratic and Republican parties during the Reagan and post-Reagan eras. Clearer differences between the parties' ideological positions made it easier for Americans to choose a party identification based on their policy preferences. The result has been a gradual shift, or **secular realignment,** of party loyalties along ideological lines.

The election of Ronald Reagan, the most prominent leader of the American conservative movement, resulted in a marked increase in ideological polarization among party leaders and activists in the United States.[16] Reagan's program of tax cuts, increased military expenditures, and reductions in domestic social programs divided the nation along ideological lines and produced the highest levels of party unity in Congress in decades. Liberal Republicans and conservative Democrats found themselves under increasing pressure to follow the party line on key votes. Some went along with their party's leadership at the risk of losing support in their own constituencies. Others switched parties or retired. The result was an increasingly liberal Democratic Party and an increasingly conservative Republican Party.[17]

The results of the 1992 elections accelerated the movement toward ideological polarization. Although he campaigned as a "new Democrat" rather than a traditional liberal, Bill Clinton moved quickly to reward liberal interest groups that had supported his candidacy by announcing policies such as permitting gays and lesbians to serve in the military and ending the ban on abortion counseling in federally funded health care clinics. The President further antagonized conservatives with his proposals to raise taxes on middle-and upper-income Americans and dramatically expand the role of the federal government in providing health insurance.[18]

[16] Walter J. Stone, Ronald B. Rapoport, and Alan I. Abramowitz, "The Reagan Revolution and Party Polarization in the 1980s," in L. Sandy Maisel, ed., *The Parties Respond* (Boulder, CO: Westview Press, 1990).

[17] For evidence of the increasing ideological polarization in Congress during the Reagan years, see David W. Rohde, *Parties and Leaders in the Postreform House* (Chicago: University of Chicago Press, 1991).

[18] For an insightful analysis of these events, see Paul J. Quirk and Joseph Hinchcliffe, "Domestic Policy: The Trials of a Centrist Democrat," in Colin Campbell and Bert A. Rockman, eds., *The Clinton Presidency: First Appraisals* (Chatham, NJ: Chatham House, 1996).

The actions of the Republican Party in the House of Representatives may have contributed even more to ideological polarization in the 1990s than the President's policies. At the beginning of the 103rd Congress (1993–1995), House Republicans chose Representative Newt Gingrich of Georgia as their minority whip, the second highest leadership position in the party. The election of Gingrich as the minority whip and heir apparent to minority leader Robert Michel (R-Illinois) reflected a long-term shift in the distribution of power within the House GOP. The older, relatively moderate wing of the party, based in the Midwest and the Northeast and represented by accommodationist leaders such as Michel, was gradually losing influence to a younger, more conservative wing, based in the South and represented by leaders such as Gingrich who preferred confrontation to accommodation in dealing with the Democrats.[19]

The 1994 election campaign was a direct result of the Republican leadership changes in the 103rd Congress. The Contract with America, a compendium of conservative issue positions chosen for maximum public appeal, was the brainchild of Newt Gingrich and Richard Armey (R-Texas), another hard-line conservative and Gingrich's top lieutenant. They decided what issues to include in the Contract and they persuaded the overwhelming majority of Republican House candidates in 1994 to publicly endorse its contents. The result was one of the most unified and ideological campaigns in the history of U.S. midterm elections: Republican candidates across the country ran as members of a party team committed to enacting a broad legislative program.

One of the conditions for a party realignment is the emergence of party leaders who take sharply contrasting positions on the realigning issue or issues.[20] To choose a party based on issue positions, voters must recognize the differences between the parties' positions. The increased ideological polarization of Democratic and Republican party leaders and activists since 1980, and especially since 1992, has made it easier for voters to recognize the differences between the parties' positions and to choose a party based on its proximity to their own ideological position. The result has been an ideological

---

[19] For an in-depth description and analysis of these events, see Wilcox, *The Latest American Revolution?* For a discussion of the consequences of the Contract with America for governance, see James G. Gimpel, *Fulfilling the Contract: The First 100 Days* (Boston: Allyn and Bacon, 1996).

[20] For an analysis of the emergence of realigning issues and their consequences for the party system, see Sundquist, *Dynamics of the Party System,* chapter 3.

realignment of party loyalties within the electorate—a realignment that contributed to the Republican takeover of Congress and GOP gains in state and local elections during the 1990s.

In the remainder of this chapter we will examine evidence showing that:

1. Since 1980, there has been an increase in the proportion of Republican identifiers and a corresponding decrease in the proportion of Democratic identifiers in the American electorate. This shift in party loyalties has resulted in a substantial reduction in the size of the Democratic advantage in party identification. However, Republican gains have been very uneven among different groups of voters. The largest gains have occurred among groups with conservative policy preferences such as white males and southerners.

2. There has been a substantial intergenerational shift in party identification in favor of the GOP—today's voters are considerably more Republican and less Democratic than were their parents. The largest intergenerational differences are found among those groups with conservative policy preferences such as white males and southerners and among voters of relatively high socioeconomic status.

3. Since 1980, voters have become more aware of differences between the parties' ideological positions. Because of this increased awareness, voters in the 1980s and 1990s were more likely to choose a party identification based on ideology than voters before 1980. As a result, there is now a closer correspondence between ideology and party identification in the American electorate.

TRENDS IN PARTISANSHIP

For 50 years following the Great Depression and the New Deal, the Democratic Party enjoyed a major electoral advantage over the Republican Party because far more Americans identified with the Democrats than with the Republicans. Table 3.1 shows the distribution of party identification in the U.S. electorate from the 1950s through the 1990s. During the 1950s and 1960s, according to the data in Table 3.1, between 45 and 50 percent of Americans identified with the Democratic Party, between 25 and 30 percent identified with the Republican Party, and approximately 25 percent were independents.

During the late 1960s and 1970s, in response to racial strife, the war in Vietnam, and the Watergate scandal, many Americans be-

TABLE 3.1 Party Identification in the U.S. Electorate by Decade

	1952–1960	1962–1970	1972–1980	1982–1990	1992–2000
Strong Democrat	23%	22%	16%	19%	18%
Weak Democrat	25	25	24	21	18
Lean Democrat	8	9	13	12	14
Pure Independent	8	10	14	11	11
Lean Republican	7	7	10	12	12
Weak Republican	15	15	14	15	14
Strong Republican	14	11	9	12	13
(Total cases)	(8108)	(7057)	(11,716)	(9635)	(8944)

Source: American National Election Studies, 1952–2000.

came dissatisfied with both major parties. During these years, the proportion of independents in the electorate rose and the proportions of strong Republican and Democratic identifiers declined. The most dramatic decline in party identification during this period occurred among young people whose opinions about the political parties were influenced more by the events of the sixties and seventies than were the opinions of older voters.[21]

Some analysts have argued that the American electorate was undergoing a **party dealignment** during the 1960s and 1970s and that the influence of party identification in U.S. elections would continue to diminish as new voters with weak or nonexistent party loyalties replaced older voters with stronger ties to the parties.[22] However, more recent developments do not appear to support this conclusion. Since the late 1970s, the percentage of party identifiers in the American electorate has remained fairly stable or increased slightly. Moreover, even during the sixties and seventies, most independents, when pressed, leaned toward one party or the other and these independent leaners were just as likely or more likely to vote for their party's candidates as weak party identifiers.

While the percentage of party identifiers in the U.S. electorate has remained fairly stable since 1980, the Democratic advantage in party identification has been shrinking. Despite the Democrats' victories in the 1992 and 1996 presidential elections, the data in Table 3.1

---

[21] For evidence of generational differences in response to the political events of the 1970s, see M. Kent Jennings and Richard G. Niemi, *Generations and Politics* (Princeton, NJ: Princeton University Press, 1981).

[22] See for example Martin P. Wattenberg, *The Decline of American Political Parties, 1952–1996* (Cambridge, MA: Harvard University Press, 1998).

show that the gap between the percentage of Democratic identifiers and the percentage of Republican identifiers in the U.S. electorate declined from 20 points in the 1970s to 13 points in the 1980s and 11 points in the 1990s. Because of the normal Republican advantage in turnout, this decline in Democratic identification means that the proportions of Democratic and Republican identifiers among actual voters have been very close in recent elections. In the 2000 election, for example, according to the Voter News Service national **exit poll,** Democratic identifiers only outnumbered Republican identifiers by a 39 to 35 percent margin.

The data in Table 3.1 show that there was a substantial decrease in the overall Democratic advantage in party identification between the 1970s and the 1990s. However, these data conceal considerable variability in the timing and magnitude of this shift across subgroups. Therefore, Table 3.2 presents data on the party loyalties of key subgroups within the American electorate from the 1950s through the 1990s. The percentages in this table represent the Democratic proportion of Democratic and Republican identifiers, including leaning independents, during each decade.

The data in Table 3.2 show that both timing and the magnitude of the decline in Democratic identification varied across subgroups. The decline in Democratic identification among southern whites actually began long before the election of Ronald Reagan. Between the 1950s and the 1970s, Democratic identification declined by 19 points among white southern males and by 9 points among white southern females. During this period, which coincided with the rise of the civil rights movement and the enfranchisement of southern blacks, Republican presidential candidates enjoyed considerable success in the region and Republican candidates began to make inroads in state and local elections. It was not until the 1990s, however, that the decline in Democratic identification among whites reached the point that the Republican Party began to dominate state and local politics in much of the South.[23]

In the electorate as a whole, most of the decline in Democratic identification took place in the first decade after Ronald Reagan's election as president. Every demographic group included in Table 3.2, including groups with liberal policy views as well as those with conservative policy views, showed a decline in Democratic identification

---

[23]See Earl Black and Merle Black, *The Rise of Southern Republicans* (Cambridge, MA: Harvard University Press, 2002).

TABLE 3.2 Democratic Percentage of Party Identifiers
Among Subgroups by Decade

	1952– 1960	1962– 1970	1972– 1980	1982– 1990	1992– 2000	Change, 70s to 90s
Overall electorate	61%	63%	62%	57%	56%	−6%
Blacks	74	91	92	90	91	−1
Whites	59	60	58	51	50	−8
Northern males	56	58	55	46	47	−8
Northern females	52	57	56	51	56	0
Southern males	81	69	62	52	39	−23
Southern females	76	71	67	59	52	−15
Protestants	54	54	50	45	42	−8
Religious	NA	NA	44	40	34	−10
Less religious	NA	NA	54	48	49	−5
Catholics	74	74	71	59	56	−15
Religious	NA	NA	69	63	51	−18
Less religious	NA	NA	73	56	60	−13
Jews	83	90	83	74	87	+4
Other, no religion	64	70	68	58	63	−5
College	47	49	50	45	45	−5
No college	63	64	62	56	58	−4
Upper income	56	56	50	44	42	−8
Middle income	62	63	61	51	51	−10
Lower income	62	63	63	59	61	−2
Union household	71	73	70	62	62	−8
Married	60	60	56	48	46	−10
Unmarried	52	60	61	55	56	−5

Source: American National Election Studies, 1952–2000.

Note: Percentages are based on Democratic identifiers, including independent Democrats, divided by combined total of Democratic and Republican identifiers. South includes the 11 states of the old Confederacy.

NA = Not available: question not asked.

between the 1970s and the 1980s. Between the 1980s and 1990s, however, the pattern of change in party identification was much more variable. Groups with conservative views, such as white southerners and religious white Catholics and Protestants, experienced a continued decline in Democratic identification. However, among groups with moderate to liberal policy views such as northern white women, the nonreligious, and Jews, Democratic identification stabilized or rebounded during the 1990s.

The consequences of these trends included the emergence of a **gender gap** and a reversal of the traditional regional gap in party identification. During the 1970s, white males and females supported the Democratic Party at almost identical rates. By the 1990s, however, northern white females were 9 points more Democratic than northern white males and southern white females were 13 points more Democratic than southern white males. During the 1970s and even during the 1980s, southern white males and females still identified with the Democratic Party at a higher rate than northern white males and females. By the 1990s, however, southern white females were four points more Republican than northern white females and southern white males were eight points more Republican than northern white males.

These shifts in party identification within the electorate, along with changes in the demographic characteristics of the American population, have produced dramatic changes in the social composition of the **party coalitions** in the past half-century. Table 3.3 presents data on the social characteristics of Democratic and Republican identifiers who voted during the 1950s, 1970s, and 1990s. The entries in this table represent a group's percentage of all Democratic or Republican identifiers who reported voting in presidential and midterm elections during each decade. For example, blacks made up 6 percent of all Democratic identifiers who reported voting in presidential and midterm elections during the 1950s.

According to the data in Table 3.3, there were major shifts in the racial, regional, and gender characteristics of the Democratic and Republican coalitions between the 1950s and the 1990s. During the 1950s, blacks made up only 6 percent of the Democratic electoral coalition while white southerners made up 24 percent. The relatively small proportion of blacks reflected the fact that very few blacks were able to vote in the South before the 1965 Voting Rights Act. By the 1990s, however, blacks made up 19 percent of the Democratic electoral coalition while white southerners made up only 16 percent. On the Republican side, the contribution of blacks declined slightly from 3 percent in the 1950s to 2 percent in the 1990s while the contribution of white southerners rose from 8 percent in the 1950s to 26 percent in the 1990s. The contribution of white males to the Republican electoral coalition rose slightly from 45 percent in the 1950s to 48 percent in the 1990s while their contribution to the Democratic electoral coalition fell sharply from 48 percent in the 1950s to only 30 percent in the 1990s.

TABLE 3.3 A Comparison of the Party Coalitions
in the 1950s, 1970s, and 1990s

	Democratic Voters			Republican Voters		
	1950s	1970s	1990s	1950s	1970s	1990s
Blacks	6%	14%	19%	3%	1%	2%
Other nonwhites	1	4	10	0	2	7
Whites	93	82	71	97	97	91
Southerners	24	20	16	8	17	26
Northerners	69	62	55	89	80	66
Males	48	36	30	45	44	48
Females	45	46	41	52	54	44
College	19	36	56	30	48	68
No college	81	64	44	70	52	32
Upper income	40	32	32	46	47	48
Middle income	30	35	34	26	32	32
Lower income	31	33	34	28	21	20
Union household	33	30	22	19	18	13
Protestant	61	58	53	83	75	66
Catholic	31	30	27	14	18	24
Jewish	6	4	4	2	2	1
Other, no religion	2	7	15	2	5	9
Religious	NA	41	39	NA	48	51
Nonreligious	NA	18	31	NA	14	22
Married	82	65	47	79	72	66
Unmarried	18	35	53	21	28	34
Ages 18–34	26	33	22	22	28	23
Ages 35–64	62	50	55	62	53	56
Ages 65+	12	17	23	16	19	21

Source: American National Election Studies for 1952–1960, 1972–1980, and 1992–2000.

Note: Other nonwhites includes Hispanics, Asian Americans, and native Americans.

NA = Not available: question not asked.

There were also substantial changes in the educational and religious characteristics of the party coalitions. As a result of rising education levels in the population, the proportions of Democrats and Republicans with a college education increased dramatically between the 1950s and the 1990s. During the 1950s, Catholics made up more than twice as large a proportion of Democratic voters as Republican voters. By the 1990s, however, Catholics were almost as well represented among Republican voters as among Democratic voters. Meanwhile, voters with no religious affiliation or an affiliation other that Protestant, Catholic, or Jewish, increased from 2 percent to 9 percent of Republicans and from 2 percent to 15 percent of Democrats.

The data in Table 3.3 show that there were also important changes in the marital and age composition of the party coalitions between the 1950s and the 1990s. The proportion of unmarried voters increased substantially in both parties, but especially in the Democratic Party. During the 1950s, unmarried voters made up about one-fifth of both parties' electoral coalitions. By the 1990s, however, unmarried voters made up about a third of the Republican electoral coalition and more than half of the Democratic electoral coalition. At the same time, both parties' electoral coalitions were growing older along with the American population. As a result of the post–World War II baby boom, the proportions of Democratic and Republican voters under the age of 35 increased between the 1950s and 1970s and then declined between the 1970s and 1990s. Meanwhile, the proportions of Democratic and Republican voters over the age of 65 increased steadily. By the 1990s, seniors made up more than one-fifth of Republican voters and almost one-fourth of Democratic voters. Once the postwar baby boomers begin to reach retirement age in 2010, these proportions will grow substantially.

Despite these changes, important elements of continuity in the composition of the party coalitions are clearly evident in Table 3.3. The lasting effects of the **New Deal realignment** can be seen in the class differences between Democratic and Republican voters. In fact, the gap in family income between Democratic and Republican voters actually increased between the 1950s and the 1990s. During the 1990s, upper-income Americans made up almost half of Republican voters but less than a third of Democratic voters while lower-income Americans made up a third of Democratic voters but only a fifth of Republican voters. And while the proportion of Americans belonging to labor unions declined substantially between 1952 and 2000, members of union households were still concentrated disproportionately among the ranks of Democratic voters during the 1990s.

INTERGENERATIONAL CHANGE

According to studies of **political socialization** in the United States, Americans generally learn their party identification from their parents during their preteen and adolescent years. Moreover, once formed, this party affiliation is usually resistant to change. The result is a high degree of continuity in party affiliation between generations.[24] During a realigning era, however, this intergenerational continuity may be interrupted.[25] To the extent that citizens choose their party identification on the basis of current issues, the influence of parental partisanship should be attenuated.

One way of testing for the occurrence of a partisan realignment since the 1970s is to compare the party identification of voters in the 1990s with the recalled party identification of their parents when the voters were growing up. If realignment has been occurring, then we should find that the current generation of voters is more Republican than were their parents. Furthermore, the largest intergenerational shifts in party identification should be found among groups known to have conservative policy views such as white males, southerners, and those of higher **socioeconomic status (SES)**.

Table 3.4 presents data on intergenerational change in party identification from the 1992–1994 NES panel survey. This was the most recent NES survey in which respondents were asked to recall which party their father supported and which party their mother supported when the respondents were growing up. We can use the answers to these questions to construct a measure of parental partisanship that allows us to compare the party identification of survey respondents with the recalled party identification of their parents.

The data in Table 3.4 provide strong evidence of an intergenerational shift in party identification. The magnitude of the shift toward the Republican Party is especially impressive considering that this sort of recall data is likely to underestimate the actual extent of change.[26] There was a net gain of 13 points in Republican identification in the overall electorate, representing a major shift toward the

[24]Campbell, Converse, Miller, and Stokes, *The American Voter;* See also M. Kent Jennings and Richard G. Niemi, *The Political Character of Adolescence* (Princeton, NJ: Princeton University Press, 1974); and Jennings and Niemi, *Generations and Politics* (Princeton, NJ: Princeton University Press, 1981).

[25]Paul A. Beck, "Youth and the Politics of Realignment," in Edward C. Dreyer and Walter A. Rosenbaum, eds., *Political Opinion and Behavior* (Belmont, CA: Wadsworth, 1976).

[26]Studies have found that survey respondents tend to overestimate agreement between themselves and their parents with regard to party identification and other questions. Therefore, the extent of intergenerational change is probably even larger than these data indicate. For evidence on this point, see Richard G. Niemi, Richard S. Katz, and David Newman, "Reconstructing Past Partisanship: The Failure of the Party Identification Recall Questions," *American Journal of Political Science* 24 (November 1980), pp. 633–51.

Republican Party between generations. However, the pro-Republican shift was much larger among several subgroups: 22 points among upper-income whites, 24 points among white males, and 27 points among white southerners.

White males were just as likely to report growing up in Democratic families as white females. In 1994, however, white males were 16 points more Republican than white females. Two-thirds of southern whites reported growing up in Democratic families. In 1994, however, three-fifths of these southern whites identified with the Republican Party. Thus, even though southern whites were much more likely to report growing up in Democratic families than northern whites, by 1994 they were more Republican in their party loyalties than northern whites.

Table 3.5 presents additional data on the intergenerational shift toward the Republican Party by crosstabulating respondent partisan identification with recalled parental partisan identification in 1978 and 1994. In comparing the results from 1978 with those from 1994, we find little change among respondents raised in Republican families. These respondents were about as likely to maintain their par-

TABLE 3.4 Intergenerational Difference in Party Identification by Subgroups in 1994

Group	Support for Democratic Party (%)			
	Parents	Respondents	Difference	(Total cases)
Overall	65%	52%	−13%	(723)
Blacks	95	91	−4	(85)
Whites	61	46	−15	(597)
Northern	57	49	−8	(420)
Southern	68	41	−27	(177)
Male	62	38	−24	(294)
Female	60	54	−6	(303)
No college	63	54	−9	(261)
College	59	42	−17	(318)
Lower income	65	67	+2	(122)
Middle income	58	43	−15	(281)
Upper income	59	37	−22	(160)

Source: Americal National Election Study Panel Survey, 1992–94.

Note: Support for Democratic Party is based on Democratic identifiers, including independent Democrats, divided by combined total of Democratic and Republican identifiers.

TABLE 3.5 Party Identification by Parental Party Identification in 1978 and 1994

Respondent Party Identification	Parental Party Identification					
	Democratic		None or Independent		Republican	
	1978	1994	1978	1994	1978	1994
Democratic	73%	65%	44%	38%	23%	23%
Independent	10	6	24	15	12	7
Republican	17	29	32	47	65	70
Total	100%	100%	100%	100%	100%	100%
(Total cases)	(1136)	(353)	(559)	(179)	(549)	(191)

Sources: American National Election Study, 1978; and American National Election Study Panel Survey, 1992–94.

ents' party affiliation in 1994 as in 1978. However, respondents raised in Democratic families were less likely to maintain their parents' party affiliation in 1994 than in 1978. In 1978, 73 percent of respondents from Democratic families identified themselves as Democrats and only 17 percent identified themselves as Republicans. In 1994, however, only 65 percent of respondents from Democratic families identified themselves as Democrats and 29 percent identified themselves as Republicans. Thus, among voters raised in Democratic families, the link between parental partisanship and party identification was considerably weaker in 1994 than in 1978.

AWARENESS OF PARTY DIFFERENCES

One of the key arguments advanced in this chapter is that the connection between parental partisanship and party identification has weakened since the 1970s because of the increasing importance of ideology in American politics. According to this line of reasoning, the growing polarization of the parties in the Reagan and post-Reagan eras made it easier for voters to recognize the differences between the parties' policy positions and, therefore, to choose a party identification based on their own policy preferences. The major consequence of this was that many conservative voters who were raised as Democrats moved into the Republican camp during the 1980s and 1990s.

To test for growing awareness of policy differences between the parties, we can compare public awareness of party differences on four issues (overall liberalism-conservatism, government responsibility

TABLE 3.6 Awareness of Party Issue Differences
in 1978, 1988, and 1994

Awareness of Party Issue Differences	1978	1988	1994
Low (0–1)	59%	49%	37%
Moderate (2–3)	25	30	32
High (4)	16	21	32
Total	100%	100%	101%
(Total cases)	(2304)	(2040)	(1795)

Source: American National Election Studies for 1978, 1988, and 1994.

for jobs and living standards, private versus government health
insurance, and government aid to blacks) in 1978, 1988, and 1994.
These were the only NES surveys in which respondents were asked
to place the Democratic and Republican parties on all four issues.
Table 3.6 presents data on the percentage of respondents who placed
the Democratic Party to the left of the Republican Party on these four
issues in each year.

The data in Table 3.6 provide clear evidence of increasing public
awareness of party differences between the late 1970s and the 1990s.
Respondents in the 1994 NES survey were much more likely to recognize the differences between the parties' positions on these four issues than respondents in the 1978 NES survey.[27] Respondents in the
1988 NES survey fell between the 1978 and 1994 respondents on our
measure of ideological awareness. In 1978, 59 percent of respondents
were unable to differentiate between the parties' positions on more
than one of the four issues; by 1994, only 37 percent of respondents
displayed this level of ignorance of ideological differences. At the
same time, the proportion of respondents who achieved a perfect
score (4) doubled, from 16 percent in 1978 to 32 percent in 1994.

The results in Table 3.6 show that Americans were more aware of
differences between the parties' issue positions in 1994 than in 1978.
But did this increased awareness of party differences lead to a closer
connection between ideology and party identification? To address
this question, we can compare the correlations between party identification and ideology in 1978 and 1994 while controlling for awareness of party differences. The results of this comparison are presented in Table 3.7.

---

[27] This increase in awareness of party differences occurred across all four issues.

TABLE 3.7 Correlations Between Party Identification
and Ideology by Awareness of Party Differences
in 1978 and 1994

Awareness of Party Differences	1978	1994	(Total cases)
Low (0–1)	.06	.06	(1295/579)
Moderate (2–3)	.37	.40	(568/544)
High (4)	.48	.67	(361/589)
All respondents	.23	.42	(2224/1712)

Source: American National Election Studies, 1978 and 1994.

Note: Correlation coefficients are Kendall's tau-b.

The data in Table 3.7 show that among all respondents the correlation between ideology and party identification increased from .23 to .42 between 1978 and 1994. Furthermore, much of this increase was due to heightened awareness of ideological differences between the parties. Among respondents with little or no awareness of party differences, there was no relationship between ideology and party identification in either year. However, this group made up a much smaller proportion of the entire electorate in 1994 than in 1978.

IDEOLOGY AND PARTISAN CHANGE

The findings presented in Table 3.7 show that Americans were more aware of differences between the parties' issue positions in 1994 than in 1978 and that the relationship between ideology and party identification was much stronger among those who were aware of these differences. As a result, the relationship between ideology and party identification was considerably stronger in 1994 than in 1978. These findings suggest that during the 1980s and 1990s many Americans abandoned the party affiliation that they learned from their parents in favor of one based on their own policy preferences. To see the significance of this trend, examine Table 3.8, which shows the relationship between ideology and party identification while controlling for parental partisanship in both 1978 and 1994. If an ideological realignment was occurring between 1978 and 1994, then we should find a stronger relationship between ideology and party identification in 1994 than in 1978, regardless of parental partisanship.

The results in Table 3.8 are consistent with our expectations. After controlling for parental partisanship, the relationship between

TABLE 3.8 Party Identification by Ideology and Parental Partisanship in 1978 and 1944

Year	Party Id of Parents	Ideology of Respondent			Correlation (tau-b)
		Liberal	Moderate	Conservative	
1978	Democratic	94%	87%	59%	.28
	Independent	78	74	21	.39
	Republican	68	24	12	.38
1994	Democratic	95	72	35	.50
	Independent	79	44	10	.58
	Republican	75	27	4	.59

Sources: American National Election Study, 1978; and American National Election Study Panel Survey, 1992–94.

Note: Entries shown are Democratic percentages of party identifiers based on Democratic identifiers, including independent Democrats, divided by total number of Democratic and Republican identifiers. Correlation (Kendall's tau-b), between party identification and ideology is based on three-category party identification variable and three-category ideology variable. All correlations are statistically significant at .001 level.

ideology and party identification was much stronger in 1994 than in 1978. Liberals raised in Democratic families were just as loyal to the Democratic Party in 1994 as in 1978. For conservatives, however, the story was very different. In 1978, the large majority of conservatives raised by Democratic parents continued to identify with the Democratic Party. In 1994, however, only about a third of conservatives raised by Democratic parents still considered themselves Democrats. These results indicate that the intergenerational shift toward the Republican Party was based largely on ideology. Conservatives raised in Democratic families were abandoning the party of their parents and moving into the Republican camp.

The results in Table 3.8 show that liberals raised by Republican parents were also abandoning the party of their fathers and mothers. By 1994, three-fourths of these individuals indicated a preference for the Democratic Party. However, this group was only about half the size of the group of conservatives raised by Democratic parents. Therefore, the net result of this intergenerational movement in party identification was a noticeable increase in Republican identification in the American electorate.

Table 3.9 presents additional evidence regarding the changing influence of ideology on party identification in the American electorate. This table displays the relationship between ideology and party identification for blacks, whites, and several white subgroups in NES surveys during the 1970s, 1980s, and 1990s. The percentages

TABLE 3.9 Party Identification by Ideology for Blacks, Whites, and White Subgroups in Specified Time Periods

Group	Time Period	Liberals	Moderates	Conservatives	Correlation (tau-b)
Blacks	1972–1980	97	94	85	.08*
	1982–1990	95	91	84	.14
	1992–2000	97	94	85	.15
All whites	1972–1980	80	62	34	.32
	1982–1990	78	56	26	.38
	1992–2000	86	57	21	.47
High school– educated whites	1972–1980	79	65	43	.23
	1982–1990	72	60	36	.25
	1992–2000	80	63	36	.29
College- educated whites	1972–1980	80	55	24	.43
	1982–1990	81	51	19	.47
	1992–2000	88	51	14	.58
Southern whites	1972–1980	81	70	46	.24
	1982–1990	76	63	33	.32
	1992–2000	83	54	19	.47
Northern whites	1972–1980	80	60	30	.35
	1982–1990	78	54	24	.39
	1992–2000	86	58	22	.47

Source: American National Election Studies, 1972–2000.

Note: Entries shown are Democratic percentages of party identifiers based on Democratic identifiers, including independent Democrats, divided by total number of Democratic and Republican identifiers. Correlation (Kendall's tau-b) between party identification and ideology is based on three-category party identification variable and three-category ideology variable.

*$p < .05$. For all other correlations, $p < .001$.

in this table are based on Democratic identifiers, including independent Democrats, divided by Democratic and Republican identifiers.

The results in Table 3.9 indicate that ideology had very little influence on party identification among African Americans during any of these three decades. While the proportion of blacks describing themselves as liberal decreased and the proportion describing themselves as either moderate or conservative increased between the 1970s and 1990s, this ideological shift did not benefit the Republican Party. The overwhelming majority of African Americans, regardless of ideology, continued to identify with the Democratic Party. Among white respondents, however, the relationship between ideology and party identification became considerably stronger over time. Between the 1970s and 1990s, the percentage of conservative whites identifying with the Democratic Party decreased from 34 percent to 21 percent while the percentage of liberal whites identifying with the Democratic Party increased from 80 percent to 86 percent. As a result the correlation between ideology and party identification among whites increased from .32 during the 1970s to .47 during the 1990s.

The increase in the correlation between ideology and party identification among whites was not just a by-product of rising education levels during these three decades. The relationship between ideology and party identification became stronger among both high school and college-educated whites although the increase was larger among the college educated. Nor was this change entirely a result of party realignment in the South. The correlation between ideology and party identification increased among northern whites as well as southern whites although the increase was larger among southern whites.

The results examined thus far indicate that ideology became an increasingly important influence on party identification among white Americans during the Reagan and post-Reagan years. During the 1980s and 1990s, many conservative whites raised in Democratic families abandoned their parents' party affiliation and moved into the Republican camp; meanwhile, a smaller group of liberal whites raised in Republican families moved in the opposite direction. The net result of this ideological realignment was a substantial increase in the proportion of Republican identifiers within the white electorate, especially in the South.

To provide a more definitive test of the occurrence of an ideological realignment among white Americans, we can perform multiple regression analyses of party identification by using data from NES surveys conducted during the 1970s, 1980s, and 1990s. The dependent variable that we are trying to explain in these regression analyses is the seven-point party identification scale. The independent variables that we are using to explain party identification include ideology, measured by the seven-point liberal-conservative scale, gender, education, family income, age, region (South versus non-South), union membership, and religious affiliation. The results of the regression analyses for the years 1972–1980, 1982–1990, and 1992–2000 are presented in Table 3.10.

The most important conclusion that can be drawn from the results in Table 3.10 is that the effect of ideology on party identification became considerably stronger between the 1970s and the 1990s. In fact, by the 1990s, the influence of ideology dwarfed that of all of the other explanatory variables included in the regression analysis. Dur-

TABLE 3.10 Results of Regression Analyses of Party Identification Among Whites by Decade

Independent Variable	1972–1980		1982–1990		1992–2000	
	B	(S.E.)	B	(S.E.)	B	(S.E.)
Ideology	.483***	(.017)	.661***	(.021)	.787***	(.019)
Gender (Female)	−.006	(.044)	−.063	(.053)	−.127**	(.052)
Education	.222***	(.029)	.128***	(.034)	.227***	(.032)
Family income	.159***	(.022)	.183***	(.026)	.170***	(.025)
Age	.002*	(.001)	−.009***	(.002)	−.011***	(.002)
South/ non-South	.766***	(.054)	.540***	(.065)	.103*	(.059)
Nonunion household	.627***	(.053)	.676***	(.066)	.547***	(.070)
Religion Catholic	−.774***	(.053)	−.579***	(.064)	−.498***	(.062)
Jewish	−1.354***	(.122)	−.987***	(.164)	−1.081***	(.157)
Other/None	−.346***	(.083)	−.275***	(.089)	−.262***	(.075)
Constant	−1.583		−1.245		−.792	
Adjusted R^2	.21		.23		.34	
(Total cases)	(6429)		(4958)		(4486)	

Source: American National Election Studies, 1972–2000.

Note: Entries shown are unstandardized regression coefficients with accompanying standard errors. Dependent variable is seven-point party identification scale, ranging from 1 (Strong Democrat to 7 (Strong Republican). Ideology is measured by seven-point liberal-conservative scale ranging from 1 (Very Liberal to 7 (Very Conservative).

***$p < .001$.

**$p < .01$.

*$p < .05$.

ing the 1970s, ideology alone explained 12 percent of the variation in party identification among white Americans while all of the demographic variables explained 11 percent. By the 1990s, however, ideology alone explained 28 percent of the variation in party identification among white Americans while all of the demographic variables explained only 10 percent.

Among the demographic variables predicting the party identification of white Americans, the effects of region and religion became less important over time. During the 1970s, and even during the 1980s, southern whites remained significantly more Democratic in party identification than northern whites with similar ideological views. By the 1990s, however, this regional disparity in party affiliation had almost disappeared as more and more conservative southern whites abandoned their traditional party and moved into the Republican camp.

The results in Table 3.10 show that the difference in party identification between white Catholics and Protestants also became smaller during the 1980s and 1990s as conservative Catholics shifted their allegiance to the Republican Party. This movement did not completely eliminate the traditional Democratic allegiance of Catholic voters, however. Even during the 1990s, white Catholics remained significantly more Democratic in their party identification than white Protestants with similar ideological views.

The results in Table 3.10 show that the **New Deal coalition** forged by Franklin D. Roosevelt during the 1930s continued to play an important role in American politics as the twentieth century came to a close. Education, family income, and household union membership remained important predictors of party identification among white voters during the 1990s. Even after controlling for ideology, persons of lower socioeconomic status and members of union households were significantly more Democratic in party identification than persons of higher socioeconomic status and those who were not members of union households. These findings indicate that social context and economic self-interest continued to shape Americans' partisan orientations during the final decade of the twentieth century.

Along with these traditional differences between the parties, the results in Table 3.10 also point to the emergence of two new demographic correlates of party affiliation among white Americans during the 1980s and 1990s: age and gender. During the 1970s, older Americans tended to be slightly more Republican in party identification than younger Americans. By the 1980s and 1990s, however, older citizens were significantly more Democratic than younger citizens. This change probably reflects the fact that older citizens had stronger party loyalties than younger citizens and were therefore less likely to change their party identification in response to current issues during the 1980s and 1990s. In addition, it is possible that older voters viewed the Democrats as more likely than the Republicans to protect their Social Security and Medicare benefits.

The results in Table 3.10 also show that during the 1990s, for the first time, white women were significantly more Democratic in party identification than white men even after controlling for ideology. While this difference was relatively small—the estimated effect of gender was only about one-eighth of a point on the seven-point party identification scale—it does indicate that at the end of the twentieth century the gender gap in party identification was no longer just a by-product of differences in ideology and socioeconomic status between men and women. Each party seems to have developed a gender-specific appeal based on its image and policies.

SUMMARY

For almost five decades following the election of Franklin Roosevelt in 1932, the Democratic Party dominated elections below the presidential level in the United States, including congressional elections, because far more Americans considered themselves Democrats than Republicans. However, the era of Democratic domination of Congress and of state and local politics in much of the United States came to an end in 1994. The dramatic Republican victory in the 1994 midterm election, the reelection of Republican Congresses in 1996 and 1998 and a Republican House of Representatives in 2000, and Republican gains in state and local elections reflected a shift in the party loyalties of a substantial segment of the U.S. electorate.

Since 1980, the American electorate has undergone a secular realignment. As a result of this realignment, the advantage in party identification that the Democratic Party enjoyed from the 1930s through the 1970s has been significantly reduced. Today's voters are less inclined to identify with the Democratic Party than were voters during the 1960s and 1970s. They are also considerably less likely to identify with the Democratic Party than were their own parents.

Republican gains in party identification since the late 1970s have varied widely across subgroups of the electorate. In general, GOP gains have been greatest among members of groups with conservative policy preferences such as white males and southerners. Southern whites, whose parents overwhelmingly supported the Democratic Party, are now one of the most Republican segments of the electorate. College-educated and upper-income whites are also much more Republican than were their parents. Republican gains have been much smaller among blacks and northern whites. Among some groups with moderate-to-liberal policy views, such as white women outside the South, the GOP actually lost ground during the 1990s.

The secular realignment of the electorate since the late 1970s was based largely on ideology. Although past research by political scientists has shown that individuals can shift their party identification based on their policy preferences, the overall distribution of partisanship in the electorate has been seen as highly stable except during periods of extreme social or economic distress such as the 1930s. However, the evidence presented in this chapter shows that even without a cataclysmic precipitating event, changes in the parties' issue stances can alter the distribution of party loyalties in the electorate over the course of several election cycles.

The increasing ideological polarization of the Democratic and Republican parties in the Reagan and post-Reagan eras has made it easier for citizens to recognize the differences between the parties' policy stands. As a result, more Americans have been choosing their party identification on the basis of their policy preferences rather than maintaining the party allegiance that they inherited from their parents. There is now a greater correspondence between ideology and party identification within the American electorate than at any time in the recent past. As a result, fewer Democratic and Republican identifiers have been defecting in presidential and congressional elections due to dissatisfaction with the policy stands of their party's candidates.

The net result of ideological realignment within the U.S. electorate has been a narrowing of the overall Democratic advantage in party identification. This change has been most dramatic in the South. The era of Democratic domination of Congress and of state and local politics in much of the United States is over. A new era of intense party competition for control of Congress, state and local governments, and the presidency has begun.

KEY TERMS AND CONCEPTS

critical election	party coalitions
exit poll	party dealignment
gender gap	party identification
ideological polarization	party realignment
ideological realignment	political socialization
independent leaners	pure independents
long-term forces	secular realignment
New Deal coalition	short-term forces
New Deal realignment	socioeconomic status (SES)

DISCUSSION QUESTIONS

1. What is party identification and what role does it play in voter decision-making? In what types of elections is party identification most important and least important?
2. What is a party realignment? Why do party realignments occur and what consequences do they have for American politics?
3. Why did party identification decline in the U.S. electorate during the 1960s and 1970s? How significant was this party dealignment?
4. How have the Democratic and Republican electoral coalitions changed since the 1950s? What consequences have these changes had for the parties' electoral strategies and their policies?
5. Has the United States experienced a party realignment since 1980 or a continuation of party dealignment? Is party identification becoming more important or less important in American politics?

SUGGESTED READINGS

Black, Earl, and Merle Black. *The Rise of Southern Republicans.* Cambridge, MA: Harvard University Press, 2002. Black and Black provide an in-depth analysis of the transformation of southern politics and the realignment of the southern electorate in the past half-century.

Campbell, Angus; Philip E. Converse; Warren E. Miller; and Donald E. Stokes. *The American Voter.* New York: John Wiley and Sons, 1960. This is the first major study of American voting behavior based on national survey data. Campbell, Converse, Miller, and Stokes developed the measure of party identification that is still used by many election analysts.

Sundquist, James L. *Dynamics of the Party System: Alignment and Realignment of Political Parties in the United States.* Washington, DC: The Brookings Institution, 1983. Sundquist develops a policy-based theory of party realignment and uses this theory to explain party change in the United States from the Civil War through the 1970s.

Wattenberg, Martin P. *The Decline of American Political Parties, 1952–1996.* Cambridge, MA: Harvard University Press, 1998. Wattenberg argues that party identification has been declining in importance since the end of World War II due to the rise of candidate-centered politics. Although recent developments have called Wattenberg's thesis into question, his book still provides a wealth of information on trends in party identification in the American electorate.

INFORMATION SOURCES ON THE INTERNET

Political party websites generally provide statements of party philosophy,
   biographical information about party leaders, positions on major issues,
   recent press releases, and appeals to contribute money or volunteer:
Democratic National Committee: www.democrats.org.
Republican National Committe: www.rnc.org.
Libertarian Party: www.lp.org.
Green Party: www.greenparty.org.
National Election Studies: www.umich.edu/~nes. The official website of the
   American National Election Studies provides access to NES datasets
   and summary information on the results of NES surveys since 1948.
Take an ideological test: www.politopia.com. This website, sponsored by the
   Institute of Humane Studies at George Mason University, will locate
   your political views in a two-dimensional ideological space based on
   your answers to a series of questions on current issues. Then you can see
   how close your ideological views are to those of George W. Bush, Al
   Gore, and other well-known political leaders.

CHAPTER 4

Participation in the Electoral Process

THE ACTIVE MINORITY

Americans take great pride in their country's democratic form of government. They strongly support the right of ordinary citizens to participate in the political process, to choose their political leaders, and to hold those leaders accountable for their performance.[1] Yet many Americans choose not to exercise their most fundamental right as citizens of a democracy—the right to vote. Only 52 percent of Americans over the age of 18 bothered to vote in the 2000 presidential election, one of the closest and hardest fought elections in American history. Two years later, with control of both the Senate and House of Representatives at stake along with many governorships and other state and local offices, only 38 percent of the voting-age population turned out to vote in the midterm election.

Despite the easing of registration requirements and the elimination of such barriers to voting as poll taxes and literacy tests, today's generation of Americans is less likely to vote than their parents and

[1] For evidence concerning support for democracy in the American public, see Gabriel A. Almond and Sidney Verba, *The Civic Culture: Political Attitudes and Democracy in Five Nations* (Princeton, NJ: Princeton University Press, 1963), chapter 4. For more recent evidence, see Alan I. Abramowitz, "The United States: Political Culture Under Stress," in Almond and Verba, eds., *The Civic Culture Revisited* (Boston: Little, Brown and Company, 1980); and Russell J. Dalton, *Citizen Politics: Public Opinion and Political Parties in Advanced Industrial Democracies,* 3rd ed. (New York: Chatham House Publishers, 2002), pp. 247–50.

grandparents were 40 or 50 years ago. And despite the pride that they take in their country's democratic institutions, Americans are less likely to vote in national elections than citizens in almost any other industrial democracy in the world.[2] Moreover, those who do vote are not representative of the entire population. Voters tend to be older, wealthier, and better educated than nonvoters. As a result, their concerns and their policy views as well as their party and candidate preferences may differ from those of nonvoters.[3]

While many citizens fail to exercise their franchise, voting is by far the most common form of political participation in the United States. A majority of eligible voters generally turns out in presidential elections; however, only a minority tries to influence the votes of friends or neighbors and only a small minority engages in more intensive campaign-related activities. According to the American National Election Study, during the 2000 election campaign, 34 percent of citizens tried to persuade a friend or neighbor to support a political candidate, 10 percent displayed a campaign button or sign, 9 percent gave money to a party or candidate, 5 percent attended a campaign meeting or rally, and 3 percent worked for a party or candidate.

Despite their limited numbers, the members of the **active minority** are extremely important to candidates and officeholders. They help to shape the opinions of the less active majority of citizens and they provide much of the labor and money that are essential to the conduct of modern political campaigns.[4] We will present evidence in

[2] According to data compiled by Russell J. Dalton, between the 1950s and the 1990s, turnout in U.S. presidential elections was consistently lower than turnout in national elections in 19 of 20 other industrialized democracies. The only democracy with a lower turnout in national elections than the United States in recent years was Switzerland. According to these figures, during the 1990s, the United States had an average turnout rate of 53 percent compared with an average of 76 percent for all 21 democracies. See Dalton, *Citizen Politics*, p. 36. See also Mark N. Franklin, "Electoral Participation," in Lawrence LeDuc, Richard G. Niemi, and Pippa Norris, eds., *Comparing Democracies: Elections and Voting in Comparative Perspective* (New York: Sage Publications, 1996), pp. 216–35.

[3] See Ruy Teixeira, *The Disappearing American Voter* (Washington, DC: Brookings Institution, 1992). For additional evidence concerning class differences in voting and other forms of electoral participation, see Steven J. Rosenstone and John M. Hansen, *Mobilization, Participation, and Democracy in America* (New York: Longman, 2003), pp. 133–45; and Sidney Verba, Kay L. Schlozman, and Henry E. Brady, *Voice and Equality: Civic Voluntarism in American Politics* (Cambridge, MA: Harvard University Press, 1995).

[4] For a discussion of the growing influence of activists in contemporary party politics, see Nelson W. Polsby and Aaron Wildavsky, *Presidential Elections*, 9th ed. (Chatham,

this chapter that the active minority is in many respects even less representative of the characteristics and beliefs of the American population than the voters. Opinion leaders and activists are generally wealthier and better educated than rank-and-file voters. They are also somewhat more Republican in their party identification and somewhat more conservative on economic issues than the overall electorate. However, when we examine the active minority within each party separately, we find that active Democrats are much more liberal than other Democratic identifiers while active Republicans are much more conservative than other Republican identifiers.

Before examining the characteristics and beliefs of the active minority, we will explore some of the reasons for the low level of participation among a majority of the electorate. These include legal barriers to voting, structural characteristics of the American electoral and party systems, and the costs of registration and voting.

LEGAL BARRIERS TO VOTING

Part of the explanation for the relatively low level of participation in the electoral process among the adult population of the United States is the continued existence of certain legal barriers to voting. During the nineteenth and twentieth centuries, the right to vote, which was once the exclusive domain of white male property holders, was gradually extended through constitutional amendments and legislation to all Americans over the age of 18 with two major exceptions: noncitizens and, in the large majority of states, persons convicted of certain criminal offenses.

Citizenship

There is no constitutional requirement of citizenship for voting and, during the first half of the nineteenth century, noncitizens were allowed to vote in certain states and territories that were anxious to attract immigration. Since the mid-nineteenth century, however, all states have limited the right to vote to citizens of the United States.[5]

NJ: Chatham House, 1996), pp. 320–26. The role of activists in the presidential nomination process is analyzed in Jeane Kirkpatrick, *The New Presidential Elite* (New York: Russell Sage, 1976); and Alan I. Abramowitz and Walter J. Stone, *Nomination Politics: Party Activists and Presidential Choice* (New York: Praeger, 1984).

[5] Alexander Keyssar, *The Right to Vote: The Contested History of Democracy in the United States* (New York: Basic Books, 2000), pp. 32–33.

The surge in both legal and illegal immigration into the United States since 1970 has resulted in a dramatic increase in the number of voting-age residents who are barred from participation in the electoral process because they are not citizens.[6]

According to the U.S. Census Bureau, the number of noncitizens of voting age rose from approximately 2.7 million, or 2.2 percent of the voting-age population in 1970, to approximately 16.2 million, or 8 percent of the voting-age population in 2000. However, the proportion of noncitizens in the population varies considerably from state to state. According to the 2000 Census, noncitizens made up less than 1 percent of the voting-age population in Wyoming and West Virginia, but they comprised 13.5 percent of the voting-age population of New York and 19.8 percent of the voting-age population of California.

A good part of the decline in turnout among the voting-age population since 1970 can be explained by increased legal and illegal immigration and the growing number of noncitizens in the U.S. population. Many of these recent immigrants, like earlier generations of immigrants, will eventually become U.S. citizens and be eligible to vote but about half will probably never become citizens.[7] Thus, for the foreseeable future, the U.S. population will include a substantial number of residents, many of them permanent, who are unable to participate in the political process.

Felon Disenfranchisement

In 47 states and the District of Columbia, prisoners who have been convicted of felonies are barred from voting. In addition, 32 states extend this prohibition to convicted felons who are on parole or probation, 14 states prohibit ex-convicts from voting even after they have completed their sentences, and 10 states bar ex-felons from voting for life. While most Americans probably take **felon disenfranchisement** laws for granted, these policies are much harsher than those found in the vast majority of the world's democracies. Most

---

[6] For a analysis of the impact of rising immigration on voter turnout, see Michael P. McDonald and Samuel L. Popkin, "The Myth of the Vanishing Voter," *American Political Science Review* 95 (December 2001), pp. 963–74.

[7] According to INS data, by 1995, 46 percent of U.S. residents who had immigrated to the United States in 1977 had become U.S. citizens. For additional information on the citizenship status of recent immigrants, see the tables posted on the INS website: www.ins.usdoj.gov/graphics/aboutins/statistics/299.htm.

other countries allow ex-convicts to vote once they have completed their sentences and many, including Israel and South Africa, even permit those in prison to vote.[8]

Since the 1960s, the U.S. prison population has risen dramatically as a result of tougher sentencing laws and a dramatic increase in the number of drug convictions. The United States now has one of the highest proportions of incarcerated residents of any industrialized nation. As a result, the number of Americans legally barred from voting is quite substantial. Using Justice Department statistics, Michael McDonald and Samuel Popkin estimated that in 2000 there were more than 2.8 million disenfranchised felons in the United States. About three-fifths of these convicted criminals were not in prison, but on parole or probation. In addition, McDonald and Popkin estimated that there were at least 1.4 million permanently disenfranchised ex-convicts in the U.S. population.[9]

Laws barring convicts and former convicts from voting have a very uneven impact on different groups in American society. Black males make up a disproportionate share of those convicted of felonies in the United States. In addition, southern states with large black populations are more likely to extend the prohibition on voting to parolees, probationers, and former convicts than northern states with smaller black populations. According to a 1998 study co-sponsored by The Sentencing Project and Human Rights Watch, three southern states—Florida, Texas, and Virginia—accounted for a majority of disenfranchised ex-felons in the United States. In Florida alone more than 436,000 ex-felons, almost one-third of the national total, were prohibited from voting.[10]

The end result of these policies is that, intentionally or unintentionally, laws barring felons and ex-felons from voting have a disproportionate impact on African American citizens. Nationwide, according the 1998 Sentencing Project and Human Rights Watch study, 13.1 percent of black males were disenfranchised because they were either in prison or had been convicted of felonies. In some states the percentage was much higher: in Alabama and Florida, according to

---

[8] For a discussion of felon disenfranchisement in the United States, see Keyssar, *The Right to Vote*, pp. 302–8. For a critical analysis of the consequences of felon disenfranchisement laws in the United States and comparisons with other democracies, see the report of The Sentencing Project, "Losing the Vote: The Impact of Felon Disenfranchisement Laws in the United States," which can be found on their website: www.sentencingproject.org/pubs/hrwfvr.html.

[9] McDonald and Popkin, "The Myth of the Vanishing Voter," p. 971.

[10] See the report of The Sentencing Project, "Losing the Vote," Table 3.

the same study, nearly one-third of black males were barred from voting.[11]

The discriminatory effects of felon disenfranchisement laws may be compounded by the ways in which these laws are enforced. In the 2000 election, for example, the state of Florida paid a private consulting firm to produce a list of convicted felons who were barred from voting. Without checking the accuracy of this list, the Secretary of State's office distributed it to county election officials who used the list to purge their voting rolls. The overwhelming majority of those who were purged were African American. Subsequent investigations revealed that the list contained many errors and that its use had resulted in the disenfranchisement of thousands of persons who had never committed a crime and many others whose voting rights had been legally restored by other states.[12]

THE U.S. ELECTORAL AND PARTY SYSTEMS

The American electoral and party systems have important consequences for popular participation in the electoral process. From the national level down to the local level, a **single-member, simple plurality (SMSP) electoral system** is generally used in the United States. The large majority of elected officials are chosen in single-member districts and, in each district, only the candidate who finishes first is elected. It is therefore a winner-take-all system. Similarly, in presidential elections, the candidate who finishes first in a state generally receives all of that state's electoral votes.

Because minor party candidates rarely finish first, the use of SMSP elections strongly favors the existence of a two-party system.[13]

[11]See "Losing the Vote," Table 2.

[12]For an in-depth analysis of these events, see Scott Hiassen, Gary Kane, and Elliot Jaspin, "Felon Purge Sacrificed Innocent Voters," *The Palm Beach Post,* May 27, 2001, p. 1A. See also Melanie Eversly and Gary Kane, "Black Leaders Sense Sinister Motive in Purge," *The Palm Beach Post,* May 27, 2001, p. A17.

[13]The classic statement of the relationship between SMSP elections and a two-party system is Maurice Duverger, *Political Parties: Their Organization and Activity in the Modern State,* translated by Robert and Barbara North (New York: John Wiley and Sons, 1954). For a discussion of SMSP elections and other institutional barriers to third parties in the United States, see Diana Dwyre and Robin Kolodny, "Barriers to Minor Party Success and Prospects for Change," in Paul S. Herrnson and John C. Green, eds., *Multiparty Politics in America* (New York: Rowman and Littlefield, 1997).

Minor parties generally try to appeal to voters who are dissatisfied with both major parties but these protest parties rarely enjoy much success and they often disappear after a few elections because even voters who are dissatisfied with the two major parties are frequently reluctant to "waste" their votes on a party that has little or no chance of winning. Thus, the use of SMSP elections encourages discontented citizens to work for change within the established parties rather than supporting third-party movements.

The domination of elections by the two major parties in the United States in combination with an SMSP electoral system has two major consequences for popular participation in the electoral process. First, the existence of a two-party system discourages participation by citizens who are dissatisfied with the choices offered by the two major parties. In addition, the use of SMSP elections results in limited competition between the major parties in many areas and, therefore, limited mobilization of voters.

Limited Options

In the American two-party system, citizens who are dissatisfied with the Democratic and Republican candidates have three options: they can vote for whichever major party candidate they find least offensive, they can vote for a minor party candidate who has no chance of winning, or they can stay at home. Until fairly recently, voters who were dissatisfied with both major parties in the United States were most commonly found on the far left and far right ends of the ideological spectrum. These extremist voters generally saw little difference between the Democrats and Republicans. As a result, most third parties in the United States were also found on either the far left or the far right.[14] However, even during times of crisis, extreme liberals and conservatives made up only a small percentage of the American electorate. In 1932, for example, in the midst of the Great Depression, minor party candidates received only 3 percent of the presidential vote. While some extremist voters may have stayed home rather than

---

[14]See Paul S. Herrnson, "Two-Party Dominance and Minor Party Forays in American Politics," in Herrnson and Green, eds., *Multiparty Politics in America*, especially pp. 28–30. See also Steven J. Rosenstone, Roy L. Behr, and Edward H. Lazarus, *Third Parties in America: Citizen Response to Major Party Failure*, rev. ed. (Princeton, NJ: Princeton University Press, 1996).

vote for "the lesser of two evils," this probably did not have a major impact on the overall level of voter turnout in most elections.

Since the 1970s, however, increasing ideological polarization and partisan rancor in Washington have led to rising discontent with both major parties among political independents as well as many moderate Democrats and Republicans. In 1980, moderate Republican Congressman John Anderson of Illinois, running as an independent, won almost 7 percent of the national popular vote by appealing to independent and moderate voters dissatisfied with the choice between Jimmy Carter and Ronald Reagan.[15] Twelve years later, Texas businessman H. Ross Perot, running a much better financed independent campaign, won 19 percent of the national popular vote by appealing mainly to independents and moderates dissatisfied with the choice between George Bush and Bill Clinton.[16] This was the largest vote for a third-party or independent presidential candidate in 80 years. According to the exit polls, Perot won 30 percent of the vote among independents, 15 percent of the vote among moderate Democrats, and 23 percent of the vote among moderate Republicans.

In the 1992 presidential election, turnout surged to 55 percent of the voting-age population—its highest level in 20 years—primarily because of voters who were drawn to the polls by Perot's candidacy. Almost 13 million more voters turned out in 1992 than in 1988. Four years later, Ross Perot was still on the ballot as the candidate of the Reform Party, but his popular appeal had diminished considerably. Perot received only 8 percent of the national vote in 1996 and turnout fell to only 49 percent of the voting-age population, its lowest level since 1948. Eight million fewer voters turned out in 1996 than in 1992 and the decline was especially large among independents and moderates. Based on exit poll data, we can estimate that while the total number of voters declined by just under 8 percent between 1992 and 1996, the number of moderate voters declined by about 11 percent

[15]For a discussion of the impact of John Anderson's candidacy on the 1980 presidential election, see Gerald M. Pomper, "The Presidential Election," in Pomper, ed., *The Election of 1980: Reports and Interpretations* (Chatham, NJ: Chatham House, 1981), pp. 83–85.

[16]For an analysis of Perot's appeal and his impact on the 1992 and 1996 presidential elections, see John C. Green and William Binning, "Surviving Perot: The Origins and Future of the Reform Party," in Herrnson and Green, eds., *Multiparty Politics in America* (Lanham, MD: Rowman and Littlefield, 1997), pp. 87–102. See also Ted Jelen, ed., *Ross for Boss: The Perot Phenomenon and Beyond* (Albany, NY: State University of New York Press, 2001).

and the number of independent voters declined by more than 13 percent. It appears that many independents and moderates who were attracted to the polls by Ross Perot in 1992 decided to stay at home in 1996.

The declining appeal of Ross Perot along with the one-sidedness of the presidential race led to a steep drop in public interest in the presidential election between 1992 and 1996. According to National Election Study (NES) surveys, the proportion of Americans who were very interested in the presidential election fell from 39 percent in 1992, the highest level since 1968, to 27 percent in 1996, the lowest level in the history of the NES surveys. The decline was even greater among political independents: the proportion of independents claiming to be very interested fell from 34 percent in 1992 to 18 percent in 1996. Even in 2000, despite the closeness of the presidential race, only 29 percent of all respondents and 22 percent of independents in the NES survey claimed that they were very interested in the presidential election.

Limited Competition

Recent public opinion polls as well as the results of the 2000 and 2002 elections indicate that the strength of the two major parties in the United States is almost even. Surveys of the national electorate show that the Democratic advantage in party identification, which averaged between 15 and 20 percentage points during the 1960s and 1970s, has almost disappeared.[17] The 2000 presidential election was one of the closest in American history and, despite Republican gains in the 2002 midterm elections, the balance of power in Congress remains extremely close—a shift of only 2 seats in the Senate and

---

[17]Based on almost 45,000 interviews conducted during 2002, the Gallup Poll found that 33 percent of Americans identified themselves as Republicans, 32 percent as Democrats, and 34 percent as independents. With leaning independents assigned to their respective parties, the totals were 44.7 percent Democrats and 45.1 percent Republicans. Given the normal Republican advantage in turnout, these results suggest that the GOP now enjoys a modest advantage in party loyalty among actual voters. However, the Gallup party identification question is worded in a way that gives more weight to the current political situation than the NES question. As a result, the Gallup party identification measure shows more variation over time than the NES measure. For a state-by-state analysis of the Gallup results and a comparison with 1993 data, see Jeffrey M. Jones, "Special Report: State-by-State Analysis Reveals Republican Shift," which can be found online at www.gallup.com.

12 seats in the House of Representatives would return control to the Democrats. Similarly, control of the nation's governorships and state legislatures is almost evenly divided between the two major parties. Competition between the two major parties for control of Congress and the presidency has never been more intense; however, because of the winner-take-all electoral system that is used in almost all elections in the United States, competition in individual states and House districts is very limited. In the 2000 presidential election, for example, despite the closeness of the national popular vote, there was real competition in only 19 of the 50 states.[18] Thirty-one states, including California, Texas, and New York, the three most populous states, were generally considered safe for either Al Gore or George W. Bush. As a result, these states received little or no attention from either candidate during the campaign. Similarly, in both 2000 and 2002, only about half of gubernatorial elections, one-third of Senate elections, and one-tenth of House elections were truly competitive. In the remaining contests, there was little or no competition because there was only one major party candidate or only one major party candidate had enough money to wage a visible campaign.[19]

In the absence of meaningful competition, there is little incentive for the media to cover a campaign or for the parties and candidates to make much of an effort to mobilize their supporters. As a result, voters in House districts and states where there is little or no competition are less likely to be aware of the candidates, less likely to care about the outcome, and less likely to turn out on Election Day than voters in House districts and states where competition is present.[20]

Competition had a significant impact on voter turnout in the 2002 midterm elections. In the seven states with the most competitive

[18]For an analysis of the impact of the Electoral College on campaign strategies and competition in presidential elections, see William G. Mayer, Emmett H. Buell, Jr., James E. Campbell, and Mark Joslyn, "The Electoral College and Campaign Strategy," in Paul D. Schumaker and Burdett A. Loomis, eds., *Choosing a President: The Electoral College and Beyond* (New York: Chatham House, 2002), pp. 102–12.

[19]See Gary C. Jacobson, "Terror, Terrain, and Turnout: Explaining the 2002 Midterm Elections," *Political Science Quarterly*, forthcoming.

[20]See Gregory A. Caldeira, Samuel C. Patterson, and Gregory A. Markko, "The Mobilization of Voters in Congressional Elections," *Journal of Politics* 47 (1985), pp. 490–509; Franklin D. Gilliam, Jr., "Influences on Voter Turnout for U.S. House Elections in Non-Presidential Years," *Legislative Studies Quarterly* 10 (1985), pp. 339–52; and Robert A. Jackson, "A Reassessment of Voter Mobilization," *Political Research Quarterly* 49 (1996), pp. 331–49.

Senate races, turnout averaged 51 percent of the voting-age citizen population; in contrast, in the 17 states with the least competitive Senate races, turnout averaged only 43 percent of the voting-age citizen population. Similarly, in the 12 states with the most competitive gubernatorial elections, turnout averaged 46 percent of the voting-age citizen population while in the 10 states with the least competitive gubernatorial elections, turnout averaged only 43 percent of the voting-age citizen population.

In two states, South Dakota and Hawaii, voter turnout was actually higher in the 2002 midterm election than in the 2000 presidential election.[21] South Dakota was the scene of an extremely close and hard-fought Senate contest while Hawaii had a very competitive gubernatorial election. In contrast, the 2000 presidential contests in both states were one-sided affairs in which neither party made much of an effort.

A multivariate analysis confirms the influence of competition on voter turnout in the 2002 midterm elections. Table 4.1 presents the results of a multiple regression analysis of turnout in 45 states with Senate or gubernatorial elections in 2002. The dependent variable in this analysis is the proportion of the voting-age citizen population that turned out to vote in the 2002 midterm election. The independent variables are whether a state had a Senate election in 2002, whether a state had a gubernatorial election in 2002, the competitiveness of the Senate and gubernatorial elections, and the turnout of the voting-age citizen population in the 2000 presidential election in the state.

Each regression coefficient in Table 4.1 represents the estimated effect on voter turnout of an increase of one unit on that independent variable while controlling for all of the other independent variables. The results indicate that the competitiveness of the gubernatorial and especially the senatorial elections significantly influenced turnout in the 2002 midterm elections. Since the values of the competitiveness scale ranged from 0 (noncompetitive) to 3 (highly competitive), having a highly competitive gubernatorial election increased turnout by about four percentage points (3×1.32 percentage points) compared with having a noncompetitive gubernatorial election; similarly, having a highly competitive senatorial election increased

[21] In Hawaii, the number of votes increased from approximately 368,000 in 2000 to approximately 376,000 in 2002; in South Dakota, the number of votes increased from approximately 316,000 in 2000 to approximately 337,000 in 2002.

TABLE 4.1 Results of Regression Analysis of Turnout in 2002 Midterm Election

Independent Variable	B	(S.E.)	*t*-ratio	Significance
2000 Turnout	.745	(.097)	6.94	.001
Competitiveness of gubernatorial race	.013	(.009)	1.52	.10
Competitiveness of senatorial race	.016	(.007)	2.40	.01
Gubernatorial election present	.021	(.026)	0.80	N.S.
Senate election present	.010	(.019)	0.55	N.S.
Constant	−.046			
Adjusted R^2	.61			

Source: Data compiled by author.

Note: Based on 45 states with senatorial or gubernatorial elections in 2002. Turnout is based on number of votes in 2002 Senate or governor's race as a proportion of voting-age citizen population in 2000 Census. Competitiveness scales based on Congressional Quarterly ratings: 0 = Safe Dem or Safe Rep, 1 = Dem Favored or Rep Favored, 2 = Leans Dem or Leans Rep, 3 = No Clear Favorite.

N.S. = not statistically significant.

turnout by almost five percentage points (3 × 1.64 percentage points) compared with having a noncompetitive senatorial election. These effects are cumulative, so turnout in a state with highly competitive senatorial and gubernatorial elections would have been almost nine points higher than turnout in a state with noncompetitive senatorial and gubernatorial elections.

THE COSTS OF VOTING

In 1964, the Twenty-fourth Amendment to the U.S. Constitution officially abolished poll taxes. However, there are significant nonmonetary costs involved in voting and these costs are generally higher in the United States than in other countries with democratic political systems. That is because in the United States to a greater extent than in other democracies, these costs are borne by individual voters rather than by political parties or the government.

Registration

The U.S. **personal voter registration** system imposes an additional burden on citizens that is not present in any other advanced industrial democracy in the world—the necessity of registering to vote sometime before the actual date of an election. In 43 states and the District of Columbia, citizens must be registered to vote up to 30 days before an election to be eligible to vote. Despite the passage of the **National Voter Registration Act of 1993,** or **Motor Voter Law,** which allows citizens to register to vote when they apply for a driver's license or at other government offices, surveys conducted by the Census Bureau show that the percentage of Americans registered to vote has continued to decline.[22] According to the Census Bureau data, the percentage of voting-age Americans registered to vote fell from 68 percent in 1992 to 64 percent in 2000. The decline was especially large among the group targeted by the Motor Voter Law: young voters. Among Americans between the ages of 18 and 24, registration fell from 53 percent in 1992 to 45 percent in 2000.

While the Motor Voter Law has yielded disappointing results, one reform that has proven effective in increasing voter turnout is **Election Day registration.** Research by political scientists Steven Rosenstone and Raymond Wolfinger has shown that the later the cut-off date for registration in a state, the higher voter turnout tends to be.[23] Apparently, a substantial number of citizens do not pay attention to political campaigns until the last few days before the election and by that time it is too late to register in most states. However, six states—Idaho, Maine, Minnesota, New Hampshire, Wisconsin, and Wyoming—now allow their citizens to register to vote on Election

[22] U.S. Census Bureau, "Voting and Registration in the Election of November 2000," *Current Population Reports* (February 2002). According to an analysis conducted by Raymond Wolfinger and Jonathan Hoffman, more than 18 million Americans registered to vote under the provisions of the Motor Voter Law during its first full year of operation (1995–1996). However, the rate of turnout among those who registered at motor vehicle and other government offices was substantially lower than that of other registered voters. See Wolfinger and Hoffman, "Registering and Voting with Motor Voter," *PS: Political Science and Politics* 34 (2001), pp. 85–92. The failure of the Motor Voter Law to significantly increase registration and turnout in the United States has disappointed supporters such as Francis Fox Piven and Richard Cloward who argued that the personal voter registration system was largely responsible for the low rate of turnout in the United States compared with other industrial democracies. See Piven and Cloward, *Why Americans Don't Vote* (New York: Pantheon Books, 1988).

[23] Raymond E. Wolfinger and Steven J. Rosenstone, *Who Votes?* (New Haven, CT: Yale University Press, 1980), pp. 61–88.

Day and one state, North Dakota, does not require registration to vote. These states have substantially higher rates of voter turnout than the rest of the nation. In the 2000 presidential election, for example, voter turnout in the seven states that did not require advance registration averaged 63 percent of the voting-age population compared with the national turnout rate of 52 percent. Moreover, there has been no evidence of increased vote fraud in states that have adopted Election Day registration.[24] Several recent studies by political scientists have estimated that adoption of Election Day registration by all states would increase voter turnout in the United States by somewhere between six and nine percentage points.[25]

Getting to the Polls

Advance registration is not the only obstacle that Americans must overcome to vote. The United States, unlike many other democracies, does not hold its national elections on a holiday or a weekend. As a result, many citizens must take time off from work or school to travel to their polling place and wait in line, sometimes for several hours, to vote. Under federal law, employers are supposed to allow their employees to take time off from work to vote. Nevertheless, according to a U.S. Census Bureau survey, among citizens who were registered but did not vote in the 2000 presidential election, by far the most common explanation for not voting was that they were simply "too busy."[26]

The cost in time and effort required to get to the polls is compounded by the frequency with which elections are held in the United States. With primary elections, midterm elections, and the separation of many local elections from state and national elections, Americans are asked to vote far more often than citizens of other democracies. The result, not surprisingly, is **voter fatigue.** Public inter-

---

[24]See the testimony of Steven Carbo to the Governmental Administration and Elections Committee of the Connecticut General Assembly on March 11, 2002, "Election Day Registration: A Proven Innovation," available online at www.demos-usa.org.

[25]See Craig L. Brians and Bernard Grofman, "Election Day Registration's Effect on U.S. Voter Turnout," *Social Science Quarterly* 82 (2001), pp. 171–83; Committee for the Study of the American Electorate, "Creating the Opportunity: Voting and the Crisis of American Democracy," *Policy Studies Review* 9 (1990), p. 585; and Mark J. Fenster, "The Impact of Allowing Day of Registration Voting on Turnout in U.S. Elections from 1960 to 1992," *American Politics Quarterly* 22 (1994), p. 84.

[26]U.S. Census Bureau, "Voting and Registration in the Election of November 2000," *Current Population Reports* (February 2002), p. 10.

est in many of these elections is very low. Turnout in primary elections is generally much lower than turnout in general elections, turnout in midterm elections is generally much lower than turnout in presidential elections, and turnout in local elections is generally much lower than turnout in state and national elections.

To reduce the time and effort required to vote, some states have eased their **absentee voting** requirements. Other states have experimented with **early voting** and **mail-in voting**. In Tennessee and Texas, registered voters are allowed to cast their ballots at selected polling places up to 2 weeks before an election; in 2000, Oregon conducted its first election entirely by mail. So far, however, these reforms have not produced a noticeable increase in turnout. In Tennessee and Texas the percentage of registered voters casting ballots has remained fairly stable since the adoption of early voting. Both states continue to have turnout rates well below the national average. In Oregon, turnout increased by 3.5 percentage points between 1996 and 2000, about the same as the national average.

ELECTORAL PARTICIPATION: TRENDS AND PATTERNS

In the remainder of this chapter, we will describe recent trends in electoral participation in the United States and compare the characteristics and beliefs of nonvoters with those of voters and the active minority of citizens whose participation goes beyond voting. We will address four major questions about participation in the electoral process in the United States:

1. To what extent do Americans participate in the electoral process?
2. Who participates in electoral activities?
3. Why do Americans choose to participate or not participate?
4. What are the consequences of participation for representative democracy?

Trends in Voter Turnout

Voter turnout in the United States has declined since the 1960s. However, the extent of that decline depends on how turnout is measured.[27] Figure 4.1 displays trends in voter turnout in presidential elections between 1952 and 2000 for two different sets of potential

[27] See McDonald and Popkin, "The Myth of the Vanishing Voter," pp. 963–74.

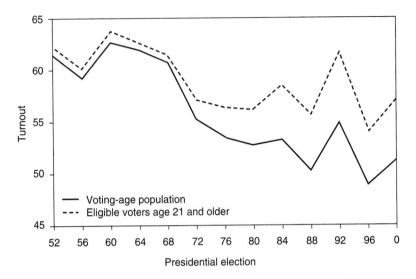

FIGURE 4.1 Voter Turnout in U.S. Presidential Elections, 1952–2000
Source: Michael P. McDonald and Samuel L. Popkin, "The Myth of the Vanishing Voter," *American Political Science Review* 95 (December 2001), Table 1.

voters—the entire voting-age population and the population of legally eligible voters over the age of 21. The latter group excludes 18 to 20 year olds, who were not eligible to vote before 1972, as well as ineligible convicted felons and noncitizens.

Between the first four elections in this series (1952–1964) and the last four elections (1988–2000), turnout among the entire voting-age population declined by 10 percentage points, from an average of 62 percent to an average of only 52 percent. However, among eligible voters over the age of 21, turnout fell by only four percentage points, from an average of 61 percent to an average of 57 percent. More than half of the decline in turnout among the voting-age population since the 1960s was caused by the addition of 18 to 20 year olds to the electorate along with the increasing proportions of noncitizens and disenfranchised felons in the U.S. population.

Who Votes?

No matter how it is measured, voter turnout in the United States is low compared with turnout in most other industrial democracies.[28] Moreover, the characteristics of nonvoters differ in important ways

[28] Dalton, *Citizen Politics*, pp. 43–47.

TABLE 4.2 Reported Turnout in 2000
Election by Selected Social Characteristics

	Citizens Reporting That They Voted
Total	59.5%
Age	
18–24	36.1
25–34	50.5
35–44	60.5
45–54	66.3
55–64	70.1
65–74	72.2
75 and over	66.5
Gender	
Male	58.1
Female	60.7
Race/Ethnicity	
White	60.5
Black	56.8
Asian and Pacific Islander	43.3
Hispanic	45.1
Education	
Grade school	39.3
Some high school	38.0
Graduated high school	52.5
Some college	63.1
College degree	75.4
Advanced degree	81.9
Annual family income	
Less than $5,000	34.2
$5,000–$9,999	40.6
$10,000–$14,999	44.3
$15,000–$24,999	51.3
$25,000–$34,999	57.8
$35,000–$49,999	61.9
$50,000–$74,999	68.7
$75,000 and over	74.9

Source: U.S. Census Bureau, Current Population Reports, February 2002.

from the characteristics of voters. Table 4.2 displays the percentages of various demographic groups voting in the 2000 election according to a survey conducted by the Census Bureau. Overall, almost 60 percent of the respondents in the survey reported voting in the presidential election. However, turnout varied dramatically depending on respondents' age, ethnicity, education, and income. According to the survey, younger Americans were less likely to vote than middle-aged and older Americans, blacks were less likely to vote than whites, and Americans of Hispanic or Asian ancestry were less likely to vote than Americans of European ancestry.

The most dramatic differences in Table 4.2 involve education and income, two of the major components of **socioeconomic status, or SES.** According to the Census Bureau survey, Americans of upper SES, those with a college education and family incomes above $50,000, were much more likely to vote in the 2000 election than Americans of lower SES, those with a grade school or high school education and family incomes below $25,000.

These results, which are very similar to those for other recent elections, indicate that the costs of registration and voting in the United States have a disproportionate impact on citizens of lower SES. The consequence is a strong class bias in voter turnout. In the United States, to a greater extent than in other industrial democracies, the wealthy and well educated are overrepresented in the electorate while the poor and less educated are underrepresented.[29] This can be politically significant because Americans of upper SES have different policy views and different candidate preferences from those of lower SES. For example, according to the Voter News Service national exit poll, support for George W. Bush in the 2000 presidential election ranged from 39 percent among voters with family incomes below $15,000 to 56 percent among voters with family incomes above $100,000.

Electoral Participation: Voting and Beyond

In addition to voting, there are many other ways in which citizens can participate in the electoral process They can try to influence friends and relatives, contribute money to a party or candidate, put

---

[29] For example, Dalton performed multiple regression analyses to estimate the relative effects of various social background characteristics and attitudes on voter turnout in the United States, France, Britain, and Germany during the early 1990s. He reports that the standardized regression coefficient measuring the effect of education was .36 in the United States, .12 in France, .04 in Britain, and .04 in Germany. See Dalton, *Citizen Politics,* pp. 56–58. For additional cross-national evidence, see Sidney Verba, Norman Nie, and J. O. Kim, *Participation and Political Equality* (New York: Cambridge University Press, 1978). For analyses of the effects of registration requirements and other voting costs on Americans of varying socioeconomic status, see Piven and Cloward, *Why Americans Don't Vote* (New York: Pantheon Books, 1988); and Ruy Teixeira, *The Disappearing American Voter* (Washington, DC: Brookings Institution, 1992).

TABLE 4.3 Participation in Electoral Activities
During Presidential Campaigns, 1956–2000

	1956–1964	1968–1976	1980–1988	1992–2000
Voting	76%	73%	72%	76%
Personal persuasion	31	34	32	34
Displaying button or sticker	18	12	8	11
Giving money	11	12	8	8
Attending meeting or rally	8	8	8	7
Working for party or candidate	5	5	4	3

Source: American National Election Studies.

up a yard sign, display a button or a bumper sticker, attend a campaign rally, make telephone calls, or distribute campaign literature in their neighborhood. By engaging in these activities, interested members of the public can influence the votes of their fellow citizens and possibly affect the behavior of candidates for office.

Table 4.3 displays the percentages of respondents in NES surveys between 1956 and 2000 who indicated that they had participated in a variety of election-related activities. These activities included voting, trying to influence the vote of a friend or relative, giving money to a party or candidate, displaying a button or sign, attending a meeting or rally, and actively campaigning for a party or candidate. A large majority of NES respondents claimed that they voted in each of these presidential elections.[30] However, only about one-third of respondents claimed that they tried to influence someone else's vote and only a small minority reported engaging in any of the more-intensive and time-consuming campaign activities: on average, about 10 percent of respondents reported giving money to a

[30] The NES surveys consistently report turnout rates at least 20 points higher than the Census Bureau's estimates of turnout among the voting-age population of the United States. Overreporting of voting only accounts for part of this discrepancy. In presidential election years, participation in the pre-election survey appears to increase interest in the campaign and turnout among NES respondents. In addition, several groups with very low rates of turnout are underrepresented in the NES sample including prisoners, hospital patients, and the homeless. For a discussion of these issues, see Michael W. Traugott and John P. Katosh, "Response Validity in Surveys of Voting Behavior," *Public Opinion Quarterly* 43 (1979), pp. 359–77.

party or candidate, less than 10 percent reported attending a campaign meeting or rally, and less than 5 percent reported working for a party or candidate.

The data in Table 4.3 show that the proportions of NES respondents reporting that they voted in the presidential election and that they tried to influence some else's vote have been fairly stable over time. However, there has been a modest decline in the proportions of respondents engaging in more-intensive electoral activities including displaying a campaign button or sign, giving money, and working for a party or candidate. Although only a small minority of American citizens has ever engaged in these activities, that active minority appears to be somewhat smaller today than it was 30 or 40 years ago.[31]

MEASURING ACTIVISM:
THE ELECTORAL ACTIVITY SCALE

Who are the members of the active minority of American citizens? To compare the characteristics and beliefs of the active minority with those of other citizens, we can combine respondents' answers to the electoral activity questions in the 1992, 1996, and 2000 NES surveys to create an electoral activity scale. This scale has values ranging from 0, for respondents who did nothing, to 6, for respondents who engaged in all of these activities. In the three combined surveys, 19 percent of respondents were completely inactive, 44 percent did nothing but vote, 25 percent voted and tried to influence the vote of a friend or neighbor, and 12 percent engaged in one or more additional activities such as displaying a button or sign, giving money to a party or candidate, attending a rally, or working on a campaign. Less than 1 percent of respondents achieved the maximum score of 6 by engaging in all of these activities.

THE CORRELATES OF ACTIVISM

Table 4.4 displays the correlations between the electoral activity scale and a variety of social background characteristics including age, gender, race, education, and income for the years 1992–2000. The data in this table show that there were statistically significant posi-

---

[31] For a more general discussion of the decline of civic involvement in the United States and its consequences, see Robert D. Putnam, *Bowling Alone: The Collapse and Revival of American Community* (New York: Touchstone, 2000).

TABLE 4.4 Correlations Between Social
Characteristics and Electoral Participation,
1992–2000

Social Characteristic	Correlation with Participation Scale
Age	.065
Gender (female)	−.103
Race (black)	−.083
Education	.273
Income	.253
Union household	.057
Marital status (married)	.145
Church attendance	.131
Region (non-South)	.065

Source: American National Election Studies.

Note: Coefficients shown are Pearson's *r*. All correlations are
statistically significant at the .01 level.

tive correlations between each of these social background characteristics and electoral activism. This means that higher levels of activism were found among older respondents, whites, males, married
persons, regular churchgoers, members of union households, and
northerners. However, by far the strongest correlations involved education and income. Wealthy, college-educated Americans were
much more active than lower-income, grade school– or high school–
educated Americans. These findings indicate that class bias in participation extends beyond the act of voting to other, more intensive
electoral activities.

The active minority differs from the less active majority of Americans in their political attitudes as well as their social background
characteristics. Table 4.5 displays the correlations between the electoral activity scale and a variety of political attitudes including **trust
in government** (belief in the honesty and trustworthiness of political
leaders), **internal efficacy** (confidence in one's own political skills
and capabilities), **external efficacy** (belief in the responsiveness of
leaders to the wishes of the public), **partisan intensity** (strength of
Republican or Democratic identification), and **ideological intensity**
(distance from the center of the liberal-conservative spectrum). With
the exception of trust in government, all of these correlations are positive and statistically significant.

Not surprisingly, active citizens were generally more self-
confident and more likely to perceive public officials as responsive
than less active citizens. This may be because positive attitudes lead

TABLE 4.5 Correlations Between Political
Attitudes and Electoral Participation,
1992–2000

Political Attitude	Correlation with Participation Scale
Trust in government	−.006*
Internal efficacy	.244
External efficacy	.127
Partisanship	.234
Ideological extremism	.260

Source: American National Election Studies.

Note: Coefficients shown are Pearson's *r*. Coefficient marked
with asterisk is not statistically significant. All other correlations are statistically significant at the .01 level.

to activism or because activism leads to positive appraisals of both
personal competence and governmental responsiveness. In all likelihood, both of these explanations are correct and there is a mutually
reinforcing relationship between political activism and positive attitudes about political participation.

The results in Table 4.5 also indicate that members of the active
minority were more partisan and more ideologically extreme than
their less active fellow citizens. Both partisanship and ideology appear to be important motivations for participation in the electoral
process in the United States. Strong Democrats and Republicans care
more about which party wins an election than weak partisans or independents and are therefore more motivated to support their preferred party. Similarly, liberals and conservatives perceive more at
stake in elections than moderates and are therefore more motivated
to work for the party that represents their policy preferences.[32]

EXPLAINING ACTIVISM

Thus far we have examined bivariate relationships between a variety
of individual characteristics and electoral activism. As shown in
Table 4.6, multiple regression analysis provides a technique for si-

---

[32] For evidence concerning the importance of ideology as a motivation for involvement
in presidential nominating campaigns, see James A. McCann, "Nomination Politics
and Ideological Polarization: Assessing the Attitudinal Effects of Campaign Involvement," *The Journal of Politics* 57 (1995), pp. 101–20. See also Abramowitz and Stone,
Nomination Politics, especially chapter 4.

TABLE 4.6 Results of Regression Analysis
of Electoral Participation Scale, 1992–2000

Independent Variable	Beta	t-ratio	Significance
Age	.065	3.89	.001
Gender (female)	−.046	−2.83	.005
Race (black)	−.011	−0.63	N.S.
Region (North)	.035	2.11	.05
Education	.123	6.78	.001
Income	.123	6.20	.001
Union household	.038	2.32	.05
Church attendance	.089	5.47	.001
Marital status	.016	0.87	N.S.
Political trust	−.047	−2.73	.01
Internal efficacy	.122	7.10	.001
External efficacy	.033	1.89	.05
Partisanship	.160	9.60	.001
Ideological extremism	.145	8.68	.001

Source: American National Election Studies.

Note: Entries shown are standardized regression coefficients. Significance levels based on one-tailed test.

N.S. = not statistically significant.

multaneously estimating the effects of all of these characteristics on electoral activism. The dependent variable that is being explained in this analysis is the six-item electoral activity scale. The independent variables include social background characteristics such as age, gender, race, education, and income, and political attitudes such as internal efficacy, external efficacy, partisanship, and ideological extremism. The entries in Table 4.6 are standardized regression coefficients, also known as beta weights. These coefficients show the relative influence of each independent variable on our dependent variable, the electoral activity scale.

The results in Table 4.6 indicate that income and education had by far the strongest effects on the electoral activity scale of any of the social background characteristics included in the regression analysis. This finding again confirms the existence of a strong class bias in electoral participation: after controlling for all of the other variables in the regression equation, citizens with higher incomes and more years of schooling were considerably more active than those with lower incomes and fewer years of schooling.

The findings in Table 4.6 also support our earlier conclusion that both partisanship and ideological extremism lead to higher levels of electoral activism. According to these results, partisanship and ideological extremism had the strongest effects on electoral participation of any of the attitudinal variables included in the regression analysis. After controlling for the effects of all other independent variables, strong Democrats and Republicans were much more active than weak party identifiers or independents. Similarly, extreme liberals and conservatives were much more active than ideological moderates.

COMPARING THE POLITICAL ATTITUDES
OF ACTIVE AND INACTIVE CITIZENS

The findings reported in Table 4.6 suggest that opinion leaders and activists may have attitudes on politically significant questions that differ from those of less active citizens. Table 4.7 presents evidence bearing on this issue. The data in this table compare the party loyalties, ideological orientations, and policy preferences of four types of citizens: the first type, inactive citizens, did nothing; the second type, voters, went to the polls but did nothing else; the third type, opinion leaders, voted and also tried to influence the vote of a friend or relative; the fourth type, activists, voted, tried to influence the vote of a friend or relative, and engaged in at least one additional activity such as contributing money, displaying a button or sign, attending a rally, or working on a campaign.

Compared with inactive citizens and voters, opinion leaders and activists were more likely to identify with the Republican Party and to describe themselves as conservatives. In addition, on the three economic issues included in Table 4.7—health insurance, government services and spending, and government responsibility for jobs and living standards—opinion leaders and activists were more conservative than voters and much more conservative than inactive citizens. However, on the one social issue included in Table 4.7, abortion policy, opinion leaders and activists held views that were very similar to those of voters and somewhat more liberal (pro-choice) than those of inactive citizens.

INTRAPARTY DIFFERENCES
IN POLITICAL ATTITUDES

The fact that opinion leaders and activists have different political attitudes than voters or inactive citizens is largely a reflection of their higher SES. Persons with higher incomes and more years of school-

TABLE 4.7 Political Attitudes by Electoral Participation, 1992–2000

	Inactive	Voter	Opinion Leader	Activist
Party identification				
Democrat	50%	53%	48%	48%
Independent	20	10	7	5
Republican	30	37	45	47
Ideological identification				
Liberal	25	25	27	31
Moderate	42	36	24	22
Conservative	34	39	49	47
Health insurance				
Government	53	46	42	41
Neutral	20	21	20	21
Private	27	33	38	38
Guaranteed jobs/ Living standards				
Favor	34	28	23	25
Neutral	23	21	22	20
Oppose	43	51	55	55
Government services/ Spending				
Increase	46	37	31	33
Maintain	29	34	30	27
Decrease	25	29	39	40
Abortion				
Pro-life	48	38	41	39
Neutral	14	17	14	13
Pro-choice	38	45	45	48

Source: American National Election Studies.

ing tend to be more politically active and are also more likely to identify with the Republican Party and to take conservative positions on economic issues than those with lower incomes and less schooling. However, we have seen that ideology itself is an important motivation for electoral activism. Individuals with very liberal or very conservative views tend to be more active than those with more moderate views. Therefore, when we examine the ideological positions and policy preferences of Democratic and Republican identifiers separately, we expect Democratic activists and opinion leaders to be more liberal than less active Democrats and Republican activists and opinion leaders to be more conservative than less active Republicans.

TABLE 4.8 Political Attitudes by Electoral Participation Among Democratic and Republican Identifiers, 1992–2000

| | Democratic Identifiers | | | |
	Inactive	Voter	Opinion Leader	Activist
Party identification				
Strong	22%	37%	43%	51%
Weak	45	35	31	23
Leaning	33	28	26	26
Ideological identification				
Liberal	30	40	50	58
Moderate	42	37	28	29
Conservative	28	22	22	13
Health insurance				
Government	56	56	58	66
Neutral	19	21	19	22
Private	25	23	23	12
Guaranteed jobs/ Living standards				
Favor	37	36	35	45
Neutral	25	25	26	22
Oppose	38	39	39	33
Government services/ Spending				
Increase	53	48	48	52
Maintain	28	34	36	32
Decrease	19	18	16	16
Abortion				
Pro-life	47	35	30	24
Neutral	15	16	13	11
Pro-choice	38	49	57	65

Table 4.8 presents data comparing the political attitudes of activists, opinion leaders, voters, and inactive citizens within each party. As expected, Democratic activists and opinion leaders were generally more liberal than less active Democrats and Republican activists and opinion leaders were generally more conservative than less active Republicans. On some of these questions, the differences between the opinions of the active minority and those of less active party supporters were quite striking. For example, only 30 percent of inactive Democrats and 40 percent of Democratic voters described

TABLE 4.8 (*continued*)

	Republican Identifiers			
	Inactive	Voter	Opinion Leader	Activist
Party identification				
Strong	13%	27%	40%	52%
Weak	44	42	31	23
Leaning	43	31	29	25
Ideological identification				
Liberal	16	8	7	5
Moderate	35	31	18	14
Conservative	49	61	75	81
Health insurance				
Government	43	30	25	17
Neutral	21	21	18	19
Private	36	49	57	64
Guaranteed jobs/ Living standards				
Favor	26	16	11	4
Neutral	20	16	17	17
Oppose	54	68	72	79
Government services/ Spending				
Increase	33	22	14	13
Maintain	28	31	24	23
Decrease	39	47	62	64
Abortion				
Pro-life	47	44	53	55
Neutral	11	18	16	16
Pro-choice	42	38	31	29

Source: American National Election Studies.

themselves as liberal compared with 50 percent of Democratic opinion leaders and 58 percent of Democratic activists. Similarly, only 49 percent of inactive Republicans and 61 percent of Republican voters described themselves as conservative compared with 75 percent of Republican opinion leaders and 81 percent of Republican activists.

In addition, on the issue of abortion, Democratic activists and opinion leaders were much more liberal than less active Democrats. Sixty-five percent of Democratic activists and 57 percent of Democratic opinion leaders took the most pro-choice position on the issue of abortion compared with only 49 percent of Democratic voters and 38 percent of inactive Democrats.

The gap between active and inactive Republicans was much smaller on the issue of abortion. However, on the issue of government services and spending, active Republicans were much more conservative than inactive Republicans. Sixty-four percent of Republican activists and 62 percent of Republican opinion leaders favored reductions in government services and spending compared with only 47 percent of Republican voters and 39 percent of inactive Republicans.

The end result of the activity patterns displayed in Table 4.8 is that there was a much greater degree of **ideological polarization** among the active minority than among less active party identifiers. For example, the difference between the proportions of self-identified conservatives ranged from 21 percentage points among inactive partisans to 39 percentage points among voters, 53 percentage points among opinion leaders, and 68 percentage points among activists. Similarly, on the issue of abortion, while there was almost no difference between the opinions of inactive Democrats and Republicans, Democratic voters were 9 percentage points more pro-choice than Republican voters, Democratic opinion leaders were 26 points more pro-choice than Republican opinion leaders, and Democratic activists were 36 points more pro-choice than Republican activists.

On all of the questions included in Table 4.8, the differences between active Democrats and Republicans were substantially larger than the differences between their less active fellow partisans. Therefore, to the extent that activists and opinion leaders exercise disproportionate influence in party affairs, the major effect of that influence should be to sharpen differences between the policy positions of the parties' candidates and officeholders.[33]

SUMMARY

Despite the easing of registration requirements and the elimination of such barriers to voting as poll taxes and literacy tests, today's generation of Americans is less likely to vote than the parents and grand-

[33] For evidence of increasing ideological polarization among Democratic and Republican elected officials in the United States since the 1970s, see David W. Rohde, *Parties and Leaders in the Postreform House* (Chicago: University of Chicago Press, 1991). See also Nolan McCarty, Keith T. Poole, and Howard Rosenthal, "Political Polarization and Income Inequality," unpublished paper available online at: http://voteview.uh .edu/default.htm.

parents were 40 or 50 years ago. And despite the pride that Americans take in their country's democratic institutions, they are less likely to vote in national elections than citizens in almost any other industrial democracy in the world.

Part of the explanation for the relatively low level of participation in the electoral process in the United States is the continued existence of certain legal barriers to voting. The surge in both legal and illegal immigration since the 1960s has resulted in a dramatic increase in the number of voting-age residents who are barred from participation in the electoral process because they are not U.S. citizens. More than two-fifths of the overall decline in turnout among the voting-age population since the 1960s can be explained by the increasing proportions of noncitizens and disenfranchised felons in the U.S. population.

The American electoral and party systems also have important effects on voter turnout. The domination of elections by the two major parties in combination with a single-member, simple plurality electoral system, discourages participation by citizens who are dissatisfied with the choices offered by the Democrats and Republicans. In addition, the use of SMSP elections results in limited competition between the two major parties in many areas and, therefore, limited mobilization of voters.

The costs of voting are generally higher in the United States than in other countries as well. The U.S. personal voter registration system, the cost in time and effort required to get to the polls, and the frequency with which elections are held in the United States result in low voter turnout.

The costs of registration and voting have a disproportionate impact on citizens of lower socioeconomic status. The consequence is a strong class bias in voter turnout. In the United States, to a greater extent than in other industrial democracies, the wealthy and well educated are overrepresented in the electorate while the poor and less educated are underrepresented.

While many citizens fail to exercise their franchise, voting is by far the most common form of political participation in the United States. A majority of eligible voters generally turns out to vote in presidential elections, but only a minority tries to influence the votes of friends or neighbors and only a small minority engages in more intensive campaign-related activities such as contributing money or working for a party or candidate. Moreover, this active minority appears to be somewhat smaller today than it was 30 or 40 years ago.

The active minority differs from the less active majority of Americans in terms of their social background characteristics and their political attitudes. Wealthy, college-educated citizens tend to be more active than lower-income, grade school– or high school–educated citizens. As a result, members of the active minority are more likely to identify with the Republican Party, to describe themselves as conservatives, and to take conservative positions on economic issues than less active citizens. However, because ideology is an important motivation for participation in the electoral process, Democratic activists and opinion leaders tend to be more liberal than less active Democrats while Republican activists and opinion leaders tend to be more conservative than less active Republicans. As a result, there is a much greater degree of ideological polarization among the active minority than among rank-and-file party supporters.

KEY TERMS AND CONCEPTS

absentee voting
active minority
early voting
Election Day registration
external efficacy
felon disenfranchisement
ideological intensity
ideological polarization
internal efficacy
mail-in voting

National Voter Registration Act
of 1993 (Motor Voter Law)
partisan intensity
personal voter registration
single-member, simple plurality
(SMSP) electoral system
socioeconomic status (SES)
trust in government
voter fatigue

DISCUSSION QUESTIONS

1. How do laws barring noncitizens and convicted felons from voting affect the electoral process in the United States? Are such laws justified?
2. How do the American electoral and party systems affect competition and popular participation in elections? How could the electoral system be changed to improve the prospects of third parties and increase competition?
3. What are the costs of voting and how do these costs affect turnout? What kinds of voters are most affected by these costs and what, if anything, should be done to reduce them?
4. Why have reforms aimed at increasing registration and turnout among young people been largely ineffective? What kinds of

reforms might be more effective at increasing electoral participation among Americans under the age of 25?

5. How does the eligible electorate differ from the voting-age population and how do these differences affect estimates of voter turnout in the United States?

6. What are the most important differences between the active minority and the less active majority of the electorate? How do these differences affect the political parties?

SUGGESTED READINGS

Dalton, Russell J. *Citizen Politics: Public Opinion and Political Parties in Advanced Industrial Democracies,* 3rd ed. New York: Chatham House Publishers, 2002. Dalton does an excellent job of placing the U.S. party system and electoral process in a comparative political perspective. He underscores major similarities and differences between the electoral process in the United States and other Western democracies.

Keyssar, Alexander. *The Right to Vote: The Contested History of Democracy in the United States.* New York: Basic Books, 2000. In this comprehensive history of the franchise in the United States, Keyssar demonstrates that the struggle for universal suffrage has been hard fought and marked by frequent setbacks.

McDonald, Michael P., and Samuel L. Popkin. "The Myth of the Vanishing Voter," *American Political Science Review* 95 (December 2001), pp. 963–74. McDonald and Popkin demonstrate that much of the decline in turnout among the voting-age population since the 1960s was due to the addition of 18 to 20 year olds to the electorate along with rising numbers of noncitizens and convicted felons in the U.S. population.

Putnam, Robert D. *Bowling Alone: The Collapse and Revival of American Community.* New York: Touchstone, 2000. Putnam argues that declining participation in a wide variety of civic activities in the United States since the 1960s has had negative consequences for American society and politics. While Putnam's work has attracted some critics, his central thesis of a decline in "social capital" remains highly influential.

Rosenstone, Steven J., and John M. Hansen. *Mobilization, Participation, and Democracy in America.* New York: Longman, 2003. Rosenstone and Hansen argue that the major reason for the low level of voter turnout in the United States compared with other Western democracies is the weakness of mobilization efforts by political parties and other organizations.

Teixeira, Ruy. *The Disappearing American Voter.* Washington, DC: Brookings Institution, 1992. Teixeira provides a comprehensive analysis of the causes and consequences of low turnout in modern U.S. presidential elections and evaluates proposals to raise turnout by lowering the costs or increasing the benefits of voting.

INFORMATION SOURCES ON THE INTERNET

Center for the Study of the American Electorate: www.gspm.org/csae. The Center, which is affiliated with the Graduate School of Political Management at George Washington University, provides in-depth analyses of voter turnout in the United States following every national election.

Federal Election Commission: www.fec.gov/elections.html. This section of the FEC website provides a wide range of useful data on trends in voter registration and turnout in recent presidential and midterm elections, patterns of registration and turnout among demographic groups, special reports on the impact of the National Voter Registration Act, and cross-national comparisons of voter turnout.

Center for Voting and Democracy: www.fairvote.org/turnout/index.html. This section of the CVD website includes information on turnout trends in U.S. presidential, midterm, and primary elections; data comparing voter turnout across states; cross-national turnout comparisons; special reports on voter turnout and proposed reforms; and links to other organizations interested in turnout issues.

International Institute for Democracy and Electoral Assistance (International IDEA): http://www.idea.int/voter_turnout/voter_turnout.html. This site provides information on turnout patterns and trends throughout the world including comparisons between new and established democracies, and between countries with parliamentary and presidential forms of government.

CHAPTER 5

The Battle for the White House, I

The Nomination

Since 1860, every victorious presidential candidate in the United States has been either a Republican or a Democrat. Numerous third-party and independent candidates have appeared on the ballot in recent presidential elections and a few, like Ross Perot in 1992 and 1996, have won a substantial number of popular votes. Even in 1992, however, when he won 19 percent of the popular vote, Ross Perot did not carry a single state and did not receive a single electoral vote. The last-third party or independent candidate to win any electoral votes was George Wallace who finished a distant third to Richard Nixon and Hubert Humphrey in 1968. Since 1860, only one third-party candidate, former President Theodore Roosevelt who ran as the candidate of the Progressive Party in 1912, has finished as high as second in either the popular or the electoral vote.[1] For all practical purposes, winning the nomination of one of the two major political parties is a prerequisite for winning the presidency. In the remainder of this chapter, we will examine the presidential nomination process in the United States, beginning with a brief overview of the 2000

---

[1] For an analysis of the role of third parties in American politics, see Steven J. Rosenstone, Roy L. Behr, and Edward H. Lazarus, *Third Parties in America: Citizen Response to Major Party Failure*, 2nd ed. (Princeton, NJ: Princeton University Press, 1996). See also Daniel A. Mazmanian, *Third Parties in Presidential Elections* (Washington, DC: Brookings Institution, 1976). Descriptions of third parties in U.S. history can be found in Immanuel Ness and James Ciment, eds., *The Encyclopedia of Third Parties in America* (Armonk, NY: Sharpe Reference, 2000). An excellent analysis of the Perot phenomenon can be found in Ted G. Jelen, ed., *Ross for Boss: The Perot Phenomenon and Beyond* (Albany, NY: State University of New York Press, 2001).

Democratic and Republican contests that resulted in the nominations
of Al Gore and George W. Bush.

THE 2000 PRESIDENTIAL NOMINATIONS

It took more than 4 weeks after Election Day 2000 for the American
people to find out who would be their next president. Eight months
before Election Day, however, Americans who were paying attention
to the presidential campaign knew that either George W. Bush or
Al Gore would almost certainly be taking the oath of office on January 20, 2001. By early March of 2000, even though the Republican and Democratic nominating conventions were several months
away, Bush and Gore had effectively secured their party's presidential nominations, thus ensuring that one of them would become the
43rd president of the United States.

The fact that Al Gore and George W. Bush managed to lock up
their party's presidential nominations in early March, long before
the Democratic and Republican nominating conventions, and before
many states had even held their presidential primaries, can be explained by certain features of the contemporary presidential nomination process as well as the special political circumstances of the
2000 election.[2]

The Democratic Nomination

On the Democratic side, Vice President Al Gore had been the clear
front-runner for his party's presidential nomination from the mo-
ment that he and Bill Clinton were reelected in 1996. During the nineteenth and early twentieth centuries, the vice presidency was generally considered a dead-end job. Between 1836 and 1960, not a single
incumbent vice president was nominated to run for the presidency
by a major party. In recent years, however, as the prestige and visibility of the office have increased, the vice presidency has emerged as
the most advantageous position from which to seek a party's presidential nomination. Since 1952, all four vice presidents serving

[2] In-depth analyses of the 2000 nomination campaign is provided in William G. Mayer,
"The Presidential Nominations," in Gerald M. Pomper, ed., *The Election of 2000* (New
York: Chatham House Publishers, 2001); as well as Harold W. Stanley, "The Nomina-
tions: The Return of the Party Leaders," in Michael Nelson, ed., *The Elections of 2000*
(Washington, DC: Congressional Quarterly Press, 2001).

under retiring presidents—Richard Nixon in 1960, Hubert Humphrey in 1968, George Bush in 1988, and Al Gore in 2000—have sought their party's presidential nomination and all four have been successful.

As the sitting vice president, Al Gore had several major advantages in seeking the Democratic presidential nomination in 2000. Gore enjoyed almost universal name recognition. He had the support of almost the entire Democratic Party establishment including the large majority of Democratic governors, members of Congress, mayors, and state and local party officials. He enjoyed close ties to key Democratic constituencies including organized labor, women's groups, African Americans, and Hispanics. Most important, he had the strong support of a Democratic president who was very popular among rank-and-file Democratic voters.

Not surprisingly, given the advantages enjoyed by the Vice President, almost all of Gore's potential Democratic challengers including, most notably, House minority leader Dick Gephardt, chose not to enter the race. The only Democrat who was not deterred by the seemingly long odds was one who did not have to risk losing any current office—former U.S. Senator Bill Bradley of New Jersey. Despite his long-shot status, however, Bill Bradley did have some advantages going into the contest. Bradley's celebrity status as a former NBA and college basketball star allowed him to compete with the Vice President in terms of media coverage and, just as important, fund-raising. In fact, Bill Bradley was able to almost match Al Gore dollar for dollar in campaign spending. In addition, as the Vice President's only challenger in the Democratic primaries, Bradley was the only option for voters who did not like Bill Clinton or Al Gore.

Like earlier **dark-horse candidates** such as George McGovern in 1972 and Jimmy Carter in 1976, Bill Bradley's strategy for winning the Democratic nomination in 2000 depended on winning New Hampshire's first-in-the-nation primary and using the momentum from that victory to generate support in subsequent contests in states with large blocs of delegates.[3] New Hampshire was an inviting target for a dark-horse candidate like Bradley because it has a small

---

[3] The role of the New Hampshire primary in the contemporary presidential nomination process is discussed in Niall A. Palmer, *The New Hampshire Primary and the American Electoral Process* (Westport, CT: Praeger, 1997). For an excellent earlier collection of essays on the New Hampshire primary and presidential nomination politics, see Gary R. Orren and Nelson W. Polsby, eds., *Media and Momentum: The New Hampshire Primary and Nomination Politics* (Chatham, NJ: Chatham House Publishers, 1987).

electorate, allowing an underdog to use personal appearances and door-to-door campaigning to neutralize the front-runner's normal advantages in money and visibility. Just as important, New Hampshire's election laws allow registered independents, who constitute the largest voting bloc in the state, to vote in either party's primary. These independent voters were a natural target for a candidate like Bradley who was challenging the Democratic Party establishment.

On primary day, Bill Bradley came very close to upsetting Al Gore in New Hampshire—Bradley won almost 46 percent of the vote compared to just under 50 percent for Gore and 5 percent divided among several minor candidates. According to the Voter News Service (VNS) exit poll, Bradley did very well among registered independents who made up 30 percent of the voters in the Democratic primary. Bradley defeated Gore by a 59 to 39 percent margin among this group. However, among registered Democrats, who made up 65 percent of Democratic primary voters, Gore defeated Bradley by 55 percent to 43 percent—enough to eek out a narrow victory.

Following his loss in New Hampshire, Bill Bradley faced a dilemma. Between February 1 and March 7, the only Democratic contests were nonbinding primaries in Delaware on February 5 and Washington State on February 29. To stem the growing perception that Al Gore's nomination was inevitable, Bradley decided to spend several days campaigning in Washington, even though no delegates were at stake in that state's "beauty contest" primary. In contrast, Al Gore spent almost no time in Washington, relying instead on the support of almost the entire Democratic Party establishment in the state. Despite his efforts, Bradley suffered a humiliating defeat, winning only 31 percent of the vote compared to 68 percent for Vice President Gore. One week later, on March 7, Al Gore ended Bill Bradley's slim remaining hopes by easily winning all 11 Democratic primaries, including those in New York, California, and Ohio. On March 9, Bradley officially withdrew from the race.

The Republican Nomination

The early emergence of Texas Governor George W. Bush as the clear front-runner for the 2000 Republican presidential nomination is somewhat harder to explain than the early front-runner status of Vice President Al Gore on the Democratic side. When a party does not have an incumbent president or vice president in the race, there is usually intense competition for its presidential nomination. Indeed, 11 other candidates, including four members of Congress, a former governor, a former cabinet secretary, and a former vice president, did announce their intention of seeking the 2000 Republican nomination. As early as the spring of 1999, however, both his rivals and the national media recognized Governor Bush as the clear front-runner.

A number of factors contributed to George W. Bush's early emergence from the GOP pack. As the son of the last Republican president, Bush enjoyed high name recognition. In fact, during the early months of the 2000 campaign, some voters apparently still confused him with his father. Bush's family ties and his work on his father's presidential campaigns had also enabled him to forge close connections with Republican party leaders, elected officials, and campaign contributors. Most important, many Republicans viewed George W. Bush as the candidate with the best chance of taking back the White House after 8 years of Democratic control. Bush had been overwhelmingly reelected governor of the nation's second most populous state in 1998. Despite a solidly conservative record, he had demonstrated an ability to appeal to some traditional Democratic constituencies, especially Hispanics. Finally, as a Republican governor, Bush had not been involved in the controversial and unsuccessful effort by congressional Republicans to impeach and remove President Clinton during 1998 and 1999.

In early July of 1999, the Bush campaign announced that it had already raised over $36 million, four times as much as its nearest competitor and almost twice as much as the other 11 Republican candidates combined. Over the next 3 months, five of Bush's GOP rivals dropped out of the race due largely to difficulty raising enough money to compete with the Texas governor. Of the six remaining Republican candidates, only two—Arizona Senator John McCain and publishing heir Steve Forbes—appeared to pose any real threat to Mr. Bush's nomination. McCain, a former Navy pilot and Vietnam POW, appealed to many independents and some Democrats because of his sponsorship of campaign finance reform legislation and his reputation as a party maverick. However, he had almost no support among Republican Party leaders or elected officials. Forbes, an unsuccessful candidate for the 1996 GOP nomination, had never held elected office, was a notoriously poor stump speaker, and appeared nervous and uncomfortable in public appearances. But he did have one thing going for him—by the end of 1999 he had contributed almost $29 million of his personal fortune to his campaign.

As in the Democratic contest, the New Hampshire primary loomed as a critical test for the dark-horse candidates in the Republican Party. Both John McCain and Steve Forbes needed a victory or at least a strong showing in New Hampshire to change the growing perception that George W. Bush's nomination was inevitable. In addition to making large media buys, both McCain and Forbes spent a great deal of time campaigning in the Granite State. In contrast, Governor Bush spent much less time campaigning in person, choosing instead to rely on a heavy media blitz in the week before the primary.

The Bush campaign's hopes of an smooth path to the Republican nomination were dashed on February 1 when John McCain scored a dramatic victory in the New Hampshire primary, winning 48 percent of the vote to only 30 percent for Mr. Bush. Steve Forbes, despite spending a considerable amount of time and money in the state, came in a distant third with only 13 percent of the vote. In the Republican primary, at least, New Hampshire voters had lived up to their reputation for ignoring the views of party leaders and rewarding dark-horse candidates.

John McCain's dramatic victory in New Hampshire produced a surge of favorable publicity and immediately established him as the main Republican rival to George W. Bush. Both his fund-raising and his standing in the national polls soared. Even as Senator McCain basked in the afterglow of his remarkable victory, however, there were good reasons to question his ability to duplicate his New Hampshire success in other states.

Senator McCain's victory in New Hampshire was based in large part on his ability to devote an enormous amount of time to personal campaigning, something that would be impossible in the later primaries where money and media would play a much larger role. In addition, a closer look at the New Hampshire results showed that Senator McCain benefited enormously from the peculiar makeup of the Republican primary electorate in that state. According to the VNS exit poll, only 53 percent of the voters in the New Hampshire Republican primary considered themselves Republicans while 41 percent considered themselves independents and 4 percent considered themselves Democrats. Further, only 51 percent of New Hampshire Republican primary voters described themselves as conservatives while 36 percent thought of themselves as moderates and 13 percent described themselves as liberals.

John McCain's decisive victory in New Hampshire was achieved by piling up huge margins among independent and moderate voters. According to the VNS exit poll, McCain won 62 percent of the vote among independents and 60 percent among moderates. In contrast, McCain won only 38 percent of the vote among Republican identifiers and only 37 percent among conservatives—groups that would make up a much larger proportion of the Republican primary electorate in most other states, especially those with closed primaries.

One important difference between the Republican and Democratic nomination contests in 2000 was that between February 1 and March 7, there were Republican primaries in several states including South Carolina on February 19, Michigan on February 22, and Virginia and Washington on February 29. Immediately following John McCain's dramatic victory over George Bush in New Hampshire, the attention of both campaigns and the national media shifted to these states and, especially, to the next state on the primary calendar: South Carolina.

The McCain forces saw the February 19 South Carolina primary as an opportunity to build on their victory in New Hampshire and demonstrate their candidate's vote-getting ability in another region of the country. Because South Carolina has no party registration, independents and Democrats as well as Republicans were eligible to vote in the Republican primary and there was no Democratic primary to draw away any of these voters—South Carolina Democrats chose their national convention delegates in caucuses at a later date. In addition, South Carolina has a large population of active and retired military personnel and the McCain campaign hoped that this group would strongly support the former POW and war hero.

John McCain soon discovered that South Carolina was not New Hampshire, however. The Republican primary electorate in South Carolina was considerably more conservative and included a much larger proportion of voters who identified with the religious right than did the Republican primary electorate in New Hampshire. The Bush campaign concentrated much of its effort in the Palmetto State on appealing to these voters, beginning with a controversial appearance by Mr. Bush at Bob Jones University, an institution noted for its hostility to both racial integration and the Catholic Church. While this strategy generated a great deal of criticism in the national media, it apparently succeeded in reaching its intended audience. According to the VNS exit poll, 61 percent of Republican primary voters in South Carolina described themselves as conservative, compared with 51 percent in New Hampshire, and Governor Bush outpolled Senator McCain by a 65 to 29 percent margin among this group; similarly, 34 percent of Republican primary voters in South Carolina identified with the religious right, compared with only 16 percent in New Hampshire, and Mr. Bush swamped Mr. McCain by a 68 to 24 percent margin among this group. Veterans, a group targeted by the McCain campaign, made up 27 percent of the Republican primary electorate, but they split their vote almost evenly between the two candidates.

In the end, John McCain won 42 percent of the vote in the South Carolina Republican primary compared with 53 percent for George W. Bush—a very respectable showing for a dark-horse candidate against a much better funded opponent who had the support of almost every Republican party and elected official in the state. However, in the aftermath of McCain's big win in New Hampshire and polls that showed him leading in South Carolina, the 11-point loss to Mr. Bush was a major disappointment. As in New Hampshire, Senator McCain outpolled Governor Bush by a wide margin among Democrats and independents in South Carolina but these groups were much too small to offset Mr. Bush's huge advantage among Republican identifiers who made up over 60 percent of the GOP primary electorate.

The outcome of the South Carolina primary underscored the fundamental problem with John McCain's strategy of appealing to independents and Democrats in the Republican primaries. In most states, especially those with closed primaries, there simply were not enough of these voters to overcome George W. Bush's advantage among hard-core Republicans. Senator McCain's campaign strategy could only work in states where the Republican electorate was unusually moderate or where large numbers of Democrats and independents could be convinced to vote in the Republican primary. In Michigan, for example, Mr. McCain scored a decisive victory over Mr. Bush on February 22. But that victory was based on overwhelming support from Democrats and independents, who made up over half of the voters in the Republican primary. One week later, on February 29, Mr. Bush decisively defeated Mr. McCain in both the Virginia and Washington State primaries.

After February 29, the battle for the Republican nomination entered a new phase with 11 states, including California, New York, and Ohio, holding primary elections on March 7. No longer could the candidates focus on one or two states at a time. Personal campaigning gave way to media campaigning and Mr. Bush's huge advantage in campaign funds allowed him to dominate the airwaves. On March 7 Governor Bush won 7 of the 11 Republican primaries, including those in California, New York, and Ohio. Mr. McCain's only victories came in four New England states: Connecticut, Massachusetts, Rhode Island, and Vermont. Moreover, because of the winner-take-all rule used by most state Republican parties in allocating convention delegates, Mr. Bush won almost 80 percent of the Republican delegates from the states holding primaries on March 7. With little money left, and no prospect of victory in any of the six southern primaries scheduled to take place on March 14, John McCain announced his withdrawal from the Republican race on Thursday, March 9, the same day that Bill Bradley announced his withdrawal from the Democratic race.

The Lessons of 2000

Despite some differences between the 2000 Democratic and Republican nomination contests—Al Gore had a somewhat easier time securing the Democratic nomination than George W. Bush had winning the Republican nomination—both contests reflected three basic features of the contemporary presidential nomination process:

1. A clear front-runner usually emerges long before the first caucus or primary takes place. This is not surprising when there is an incumbent president or vice president in the race. Even when a party does not have an incumbent president or vice president, however, as with the Republicans in 2000, one candidate usually emerges from the pack by raising substantially more money and gaining more support from party and elected officials than his or her rivals during the early period of competition that is sometimes referred to as the "**invisible primary.**"
2. The early delegate selection contests, especially the **New Hampshire primary,** provide the best opportunity for a dark-horse candidate to upset the front-runner. In New Hampshire, time and effort can overcome low name recognition and limited campaign funds and a dark-horse candidate can appeal to independent voters who make a large proportion of the primary electorate.

     The **Iowa precinct caucuses,** which usually take place a week or two before the New Hampshire primary, once provided a similar opportunity for upstart candidates. In 1976, a little-known former governor of Georgia named Jimmy Carter used a narrow victory in the Iowa caucuses to jump-start his presidential campaign. In recent presidential nomination contests, however, most voters who have taken the time and effort to participate in the Iowa precinct caucuses have tended to be strong partisans. The independent voters who are most likely to support an insurgent candidate make up a much smaller proportion of participants in Iowa than in New Hampshire. In 2000, for example, according to VNS exit polls, independents made up 41 percent of voters in the New Hampshire Democratic primary and 40 percent of voters in the New Hampshire Republican primary compared with only 17 percent of voters in the Iowa Democratic caucuses and only 15 percent of voters in the Iowa Republican caucuses. As a result, insurgent candidates like Bill Bradley and John McCain tend to skip the Iowa caucuses in order to concentrate their limited time and resources on the New Hampshire primary.

3. Even if the front-runner loses in New Hampshire, however, as George W. Bush did in 2000, he or she still has an excellent chance to recover, win most of the remaining primaries, and capture the nomination. The front-runner usually locks up the nomination very quickly once the campaign shifts from its initial phase of caucuses and primaries in small states like Iowa and New Hampshire to its second phase of multiple primaries in large states like California, New York, and Ohio. This is especially true in the Republican Party because its rules allow **winner-take-all primaries.** This allows the front-runner to very quickly achieve an overwhelming lead in the delegate race. In both parties, however, meaningful competition for the nomination almost always ends long before the national conventions and even before many states have held their primaries.

In the remainder of this chapter, we will try to explain these characteristics of the contemporary presidential nomination process. We will try to understand why a process in which the ultimate decisions are no longer made by party "bosses" but by ordinary voters nevertheless makes it very difficult for a dark-horse candidate like Bill Bradley or John McCain to win the nomination. First, however, we will briefly explore the history of the presidential nomination process in the United States in order to understand how the current system came about and what preceded it.

THE EVOLUTION OF THE
PRESIDENTIAL NOMINATION PROCESS

The Congressional Caucus

The origins of the first presidential nomination system can be traced to George Washington's decision not to seek a third term as president in 1796.[4] By this time, even though political parties in the mod-

---

[4] A concise description of the origins, operation, and eventual demise of the congressional caucus system is provided in John S. Jackson III and William Crotty, *The Politics of Presidential Selection* (New York: HarperCollins, 1996), pp. 21–27. Lengthier discus-

ern sense did not exist, the division between Federalists and Anti-Federalists in Congress was already well established. In response to Washington's decision, leaders of the two congressional factions met separately to select presidential and vice presidential candidates. The Federalists recommended that electors who supported their faction vote for John Adams and Thomas Pinckney while the Anti-Federalists, or Democratic-Republicans, recommended that their electors vote for Thomas Jefferson and Aaron Burr.

The presidential electors, who at that time were chosen by state legislatures rather than voters, followed the recommendations of their congressional leaders. The Federalist electors voted for John Adams while the Democratic-Republican electors voted for Thomas Jefferson. Adams won the election with 71 votes to 68 votes for Jefferson. However, before the adoption of the **Twelfth Amendment** in 1804, electors did not vote separately for president and vice president. Instead, each elector was supposed to vote for two candidates with the first-place finisher becoming president and the second-place finisher becoming vice president. To ensure that John Adams received more votes than the Federalist vice presidential candidate Thomas Pinckney, 12 Federalist electors withheld their votes from Pinckney. As a result, Jefferson finished second and became vice president.

After 1796, Federalists and Democratic-Republicans in the Congress continued the practice of meeting before each presidential election to recommend presidential and vice presidential candidates to their parties' electors. In 1812 and 1816, the Federalists, declining in membership and badly divided over the War of 1812, did not bother to hold a nominating caucus. Instead, a few leaders met in secret to choose the party's candidates. Shortly thereafter, the Federalists disappeared as a national party. Democratic-Republican members of Congress continued to meet to recommend presidential and vice presidential candidates until 1828. However, not all Democratic-Republican members attended these meetings and intraparty conflicts were common. In 1808, James Madison was chosen over James Monroe and George Clinton and in 1816 Monroe narrowly defeated William Crawford.

Growing criticism of the **congressional caucus system** as undemocratic contributed to declining participation by members of

---

sions of the caucus system can be found in William N. Chambers, *Political Parties in a New Nation* (New York: Oxford University Press 1963); and Joseph Charles, *The Origins of the American Party System* (New York: Harper and Row, 1961).

Congress. In 1824, the large majority of Democratic-Republican members boycotted the nominating caucus, which chose William Crawford as its candidate. Three other candidates—Henry Clay, Andrew Jackson, and John Quincy Adams—were nominated by state legislatures and conventions. Ultimately, no candidate received a majority of electoral votes and the election was thrown into the House of Representatives where Adams was elected with the votes of 13 of the 24 state delegations.

The Rise of National Party Conventions

William Crawford was the last candidate nominated by the Democratic-Republican caucus in Congress. The caucus system fell victim to two major political developments during the 1820s and 1830s: the spread of popular democracy and the reemergence of two-party competition.[5] By 1824, 18 of 24 states permitted popular voting for presidential electors, although the total number of votes cast was only about 366,000. Four years later, 22 states permitted popular voting and well over a million votes were cast in the presidential election.

The rise of popular democracy coincided with the reemergence of two-party competition after a hiatus of nearly 20 years. By the late 1820s, the Democratic-Republican Party, which had dominated American politics since the demise of the Federalists, was experiencing serious internal strains due to conflicts over the role of the federal government in promoting economic development and, especially, the power of the Bank of the United States.[6] President John Quincy Adams was a strong supporter of the Bank. However, most Democratic-Republicans viewed the Bank as an instrument of wealthy eastern elites and rallied behind the candidacy of Andrew Jackson, who had lost to Adams in 1824 despite winning more popular and electoral votes. Supporters of the Bank and President Adams then decided to form a new political party, the National Republican Party, which became known as the Whig Party after 1832. In the 1828 election, John Quincy Adams lost in a landslide to Andrew Jackson who captured 56 percent of the popular vote and 178 electoral votes to 83 for Adams.

[5]See John H. Aldrich, *Why Parties? The Origin and Transformation of Political Parties in America* (Chicago: University of Chicago Press, 1995), chapter 4.
[6]The classic account of this period is Arthur M. Schlesinger, Jr., *The Age of Jackson* (Boston: Little, Brown, 1947).

In 1831, leaders of the anti-Jackson National Republicans decided that they could attract attention to their cause by holding a **national nominating convention** to choose their presidential and vice presidential candidates, following the example of one of the minor parties of the time, the Anti-Masonic Party. Meeting in the same saloon in Baltimore that had been used earlier that year by the Anti-Masonic Party, the National Republicans nominated Henry Clay for president and John Sergeant for vice president. Not to be outdone, Jackson's Democratic-Republicans, or Democrats as they were known after 1828, decided to hold their own nominating convention in Baltimore the following year. That convention also served to ratify President Jackson's decision to replace his running mate John Calhoun with Martin Van Buren.

The shift from the congressional caucus to national conventions to nominate presidential candidates reflected the growing influence of state and local party elites in presidential politics. With the rise of popular voting and the reemergence of two-party competition after 1824, presidential candidates had to find a way of identifying and mobilizing their supporters in a rapidly expanding electorate. To do this, they had to depend on the state and local party organizations. National conventions provided a way to bring the leaders of these state and local organizations together and conduct the bargaining necessary to unite the party behind a national ticket.[7]

Except for 1836, when the Whigs ran three regional candidates against Martin Van Buren and did not hold a national convention, the two major political parties in the United States, first the Democrats and Whigs and later the Democrats and Republicans, have used national conventions to nominate their presidential and vice presidential candidates ever since 1832. By the mid-nineteenth century, the major parties had developed clear rules for determining each state's representation and conducting the business of the convention. These early conventions also began the practice of adopting policy statements, which evolved into the elaborate **party platforms** of the late nineteenth and twentieth centuries.

During the nineteenth century, the method of selecting delegates to the national convention was left up to each state party. Although

---

[7]See William Crotty and John S. Jackson III, *Presidential Primaries and Nominations* (Washington, DC: Congressional Quarterly Press, 1985), pp. 11–12. See also Richard P. McCormick, "Political Development and the Second Party System," in William N. Chambers and Walter D. Burnham, eds., *The American Party Systems: Stages of Political Development*, 2nd ed. (New York: Oxford University Press, 1975), pp. 102–14.

a variety of methods was used, including local and state conventions, caucuses, and special party committees, in almost all states the delegate selection process was closely controlled by top party and elected leaders. Delegates were chosen for their loyalty to the party organization and its leaders and there was very little opportunity for ordinary citizens to participate in the nomination process. At the national conventions, most important decisions were made behind closed doors through a process of bargaining among party and elected officials who controlled large blocs of delegates.[8] However, it was not unusual for these "**brokered conventions**" to take many ballots to agree on a presidential candidate. In 1924, the Democratic convention took a record 103 ballots to nominate John W. Davis, who went on to lose in a landslide to Republican Calvin Coolidge.

The First Presidential Primaries

During the late nineteenth century, progressive reformers in the United States made the adoption of the direct primary one of their principal goals. The reformers viewed the direct primary as a way to reduce the influence that party bosses exercised over many state and local governments by taking away their control of the nomination process. It wasn't long before the reformers also began to target the boss-dominated presidential nomination process for reform as well.[9] Florida Democrats held the first statewide primary to elect national convention delegates in 1904 and, by 1916, Democratic and Republican primaries took place in 20 states and over half of the delegates to both parties' conventions were chosen in primary elections.

Despite the rapid growth in the number of presidential primaries during the first two decades of the twentieth century, the results were disappointing to reformers. Turnout in presidential primaries was generally very low, many of the delegates chosen in primaries were not bound to specific candidates, and the results of the primaries seemed to have little bearing on the outcome of the nomination. Not surprisingly, most state and local party leaders disliked primaries because they threatened their own influence by allowing outsiders to participate in what the leaders regarded as internal party

[8]The major characteristics of the "brokered convention" system are described in Thomas R. Marshall, *Presidential Nominations in a Reform Age* (New York: Praeger, 1981).
[9]See Crotty and Jackson, *Presidential Primaries and Nominations*, pp. 12–20, for an account of the rise and fall of presidential primaries in the presidential nominating process from the early 1900s through the 1960s.

business. During the 1920s, as public interest in political reform diminished, party leaders in many states were able to convince their state legislatures to either repeal the presidential primary or to make its results merely advisory.

Between 1920 and 1968, fewer than half of the delegates to both parties' national conventions were chosen in presidential primaries, and many of the delegates chosen in primaries were not bound to a particular candidate. Most national convention delegates were chosen in caucuses or conventions—gatherings made up largely of party workers who could be counted on to follow the recommendations of their leaders. During these years, candidates sometimes ran in presidential primaries to demonstrate their popular appeal to party leaders. In 1960, for example, John F. Kennedy, a Roman Catholic, used his victory over Hubert Humphrey in the West Virginia primary to prove to Democratic Party leaders that he could win an election in an overwhelmingly Protestant state. Winning presidential primaries did not guarantee winning the presidential nomination, though. Consider Senator Estes Kefauver of Tennessee, who had achieved fame by chairing a series of televised hearings on organized crime. In 1952 the senator entered 13 of the 17 Democratic presidential primaries and won 12 of them but the Democratic Convention that year chose Senator Adlai Stevenson of Illinois as its presidential candidate. Stevenson was preferred by the party and elected leaders who controlled most of the delegates to the Democratic convention.

From Brokered Convention to Popular Choice

The 1964 Republican nomination contest revealed the existence of serious cracks in the brokered convention system. With Democratic President Lyndon Johnson running for reelection and enjoying high public approval ratings, Republican Party leaders were unable to unite behind a single candidate. Arizona Senator Barry Goldwater, an outspoken conservative, was able to capture the GOP nomination over a divided field of more moderate candidates by mobilizing amateur conservative activists in Republican caucuses and winning primary elections in southern and western states with conservative Republican electorates. Although Goldwater went on to lose the election in a landslide, his success in capturing the Republican nomination raised questions about the ability of both Republican and Democratic leaders to maintain control of the nomination process in the future.

In 1968, it was the Democrats' turn to experience a major challenge to the control of party and elected leaders over the presidential nomination process. Democrats opposed to the Vietnam War policies of President Lyndon Johnson rallied behind Senator Eugene Mc-Carthy of Minnesota and later Senator Robert Kennedy of New York. McCarthy and Kennedy won 11 of the 15 Democratic primaries that allowed voters to express a presidential preference that year. On June 4, 1968, Robert Kennedy was assassinated following his victory in the California primary. Despite not entering a single Democratic primary, Vice President Hubert Humphrey, the candidate preferred by outgoing President Johnson and most Democratic Party leaders, easily won the nomination at a bitterly divided Democratic convention in Chicago. In an effort to reunify the party, however, Democratic Party leaders agreed to create a commission after the election to recommend reforms of the nomination process.[10]

Following Hubert Humphrey's narrow loss to Richard Nixon in the 1968 election, the **McGovern-Fraser Commission,** named after its two chairmen, South Dakota Senator George McGovern and Minnesota Representative Donald Fraser, began its work during 1969. The commission recommended a number of reforms to open up the Democratic nomination process to greater rank-and-file participation. Most of these recommendations involved changes in the rules and procedures for conducting party caucuses such as publicizing the times and locations of caucus meetings. In response to the commission's recommendations, however, many state Democratic parties decided that the safest course of action was to switch from the traditional caucus system to a presidential primary.

Between 1968 and 1972, the number of states with Democratic presidential primaries increased from 17 to 23 while the proportion of Democratic convention delegates chosen in states with primaries increased from 38 percent to 61 percent. Moreover, since changes in primary election laws usually applied to both parties, Republicans as well as Democrats were affected by these reforms. Between 1968 and 1972, the number of states with Republican presidential primaries increased from 16 to 22 while the proportion of Republican convention delegates chosen in states with primaries increased from 34 percent to 53 percent.

After 1968, the presidential nomination process would never be the same. In 1972, George McGovern, the original chairman of the McGovern-Fraser Commission, took advantage of the new rules to

---

[10]For a detailed and thoughtful history of the reform movement and its consequences, see Byron E. Shafer, *Quiet Revolution: The Struggle for the Democratic Party and the Shaping of Post-Reform Politics* (New York: Russell Sage Foundation, 1983). See also Nelson W. Polsby, *Consequences of Party Reform* (New York: Oxford University Press, 1983).

challenge the candidate favored by most Democratic Party leaders, U.S. Senator and 1968 vice presidential candidate Edmund Muskie of Maine. Other candidates included former Alabama governor and 1968 independent presidential candidate George Wallace and former vice president and 1968 presidential candidate Hubert Humphrey who decided to enter the race after Muskie's disappointingly narrow victory in the New Hampshire primary.

Running on an anti–Vietnam War platform, Senator McGovern mobilized many of the liberal activists who had supported Eugene McCarthy and Robert Kennedy in 1968. In the Democratic primaries, Hubert Humphrey actually won slightly more total votes than Senator McGovern, with George Wallace finishing a close third. However, by taking full advantage of the delegate selection rules and by scoring a narrow victory in California's winner-take-all primary, McGovern was able to win the presidential nomination on the first ballot at the Democratic convention in San Francisco.[11]

Like Barry Goldwater in 1964, George McGovern overcame the opposition of his party's establishment to win the presidential nomination and, like Goldwater, McGovern went on to suffer a crushing defeat in the general election. Four years later, however, another outsider, Georgia Governor Jimmy Carter, took advantage of the new rules and a divided opposition to win the Democratic nomination and the presidency.

By 1976, there were 29 states with Democratic presidential primaries and 28 states with Republican presidential primaries; 73 percent of the delegates to the Democratic national convention and 68 percent of the delegates to the Republican national convention were chosen in states with presidential primaries. At the start of the nomination campaign, Jimmy Carter was virtually unknown outside of his home state of Georgia but he understood the logic of the reformed nomination process. By concentrating his time and resources in two states—Iowa and New Hampshire—Carter was able to compensate for his limited financial resources and low national visibility. Carter also benefited from the fact that there was no strong frontrunner in the Democratic field and all of the other candidates except George Wallace were northern liberals.

After scoring narrow victories in the Iowa caucuses and the New Hampshire primary and receiving an enormous amount of free publicity in the national media, Jimmy Carter quickly emerged as the

[11]Shafer, *Quiet Revolution,* pp. 525–39. See also Polsby, *Consequences of Party Reform,* and Jeane Kirkpatrick, *The New Presidential Elite* (New York: Russell Sage Foundation, 1976), pp. 35–60.

front-runner for the Democratic presidential nomination. Carter also benefited from another change in the nomination rules—the availability of public financing in the primaries. This reform, adopted by Congress in 1974 in the aftermath of the Watergate scandal, allowed candidates for the Democratic and Republican presidential nominations to receive federal matching funds by raising at least $100,000 in contributions of $250 or less in at least 20 states. The availability of these matching funds allowed a candidate like Jimmy Carter, who did not have a large war chest available at the beginning of the campaign, to capitalize more quickly on his success in the early primaries. To an even greater degree than the nomination of George McGovern in 1972, the nomination of Jimmy Carter in 1976 was a result of the post-1968 reforms of the presidential nomination process.[12]

Even incumbent presidents were not completely safe in the new primary-dominated nomination system. In 1976, Ronald Reagan, who had succeeded Barry Goldwater as the leader of the conservative wing of the Republican Party, challenged President Gerald Ford for the Republican nomination. Ford had never been elected president or vice president; he had been nominated to the vice presidency by Richard Nixon after the resignation of vice president Spiro Agnew and had become president after Nixon's resignation. As the incumbent, however, Ford did have the support of the large majority of Republican Party leaders and elected officials. Nevertheless, Reagan gave Ford a very difficult race, winning 10 of 26 Republican primaries and 46 percent of the total vote. After barely surviving Ronald Reagan's challenge, Gerald Ford went on to narrowly lose the presidential election to the Democratic nominee, Jimmy Carter.[13]

Four years later, it was President Carter who faced a tough challenge to his renomination from Massachusetts Senator Edward Kennedy. Carter, whose popularity had plummeted during 1980 as a result of a slowing economy, high inflation, and the Iran hostage crisis, survived Kennedy's challenge—winning 24 of 35 Democratic primaries and 51 percent of the total vote to 37 percent for Kennedy. However, Kennedy embarrassed the President by defeating him in four of the nation's most populous states: New York, Pennsylvania, New Jersey, and California. In November, Ronald Reagan, who had

---

[12]For an in-depth description of Jimmy Carter's rise to the presidency, see Jules Witcover, *Marathon: The Pursuit of the Presidency, 1972–1976* (New York: The Viking Press, 1977). See also Shafer, *Quiet Revolution*, pp. 525–39.

[13]Witcover, *Marathon*, pp. 371–625. See also Gerald M. Pomper, ed., *The Election of 1976: Reports and Interpretations* (New York: David McKay, 1977).

easily captured the Republican nomination, scored a decisive victory over Carter who carried only six states and the District of Columbia. For the second consecutive election, an incumbent president, wounded by a serious intraparty challenge, had been defeated for reelection.[14]

THE CONTEMPORARY PRESIDENTIAL NOMINATION SYSTEM

Democratic Party Rules Changes After 1980

The reforms enacted by the Democratic Party after the 1968 election and the subsequent proliferation of presidential primaries drastically altered the presidential nomination process. Presidential candidates were now chosen by voters in primaries rather than by party and elected leaders at the national conventions. The conventions themselves merely served to ratify the decisions made by primary voters. However, the results were not what Democratic reformers had hoped for. Between 1968 and 1992, Republicans won four out of five presidential elections.

After Jimmy Carter's defeat in 1980, many Democratic Party leaders concluded that the post-1968 reforms had gone too far in shifting power from party and elected officials to primary voters. A new reform commission chaired by North Carolina Governor James Hunt was created to recommend changes in the nomination rules to remedy some of the problems that had arisen as a result of earlier reforms. The most important change adopted as a result of the **Hunt Commission**'s deliberations was a requirement that several hundred Democratic Party and elected officials, including every Democratic governor and member of Congress, automatically be entitled to serve as delegates to the national convention. It was hoped that these **"superdelegates"** would use their prestige and influence to support candidates with broad electoral appeal and to unify the party after the convention. The Democratic National Committee also adopted another recommendation of the Hunt Commission—allowing state

---

[14]For analyses of various aspects of the 1980 campaign and election, see Gerald M. Pomper, ed., *The Election of 1980: Reports and Interpretations* (Chatham, NJ: Chatham House, 1981). See also Herbert A. Asher, *Presidential Elections and American Politics: Voters, Candidates and Campaigns Since 1952*, 4th ed. (Chicago: The Dorsey Press, 1988), chapter 6.

parties to require that candidates receive at least 20 percent of the vote in a caucus and at least 25 percent of the vote in a primary to win any national convention delegates. This change was intended to benefit the front-runner and reduce representation of fringe candidates at the convention.

The adoption of the Hunt Commission's recommendations resulted in a dramatic increase in the representation of party and elected officials at the 1984 Democratic convention. Several hundred Democratic members of Congress, governors, mayors, and party officials served as ex-officio delegates to the convention. However, the party's presidential nominee, former U.S. Senator and Vice President Walter Mondale, who was supported by the overwhelming majority of these superdelegates, lost in a landslide to President Ronald Reagan.[15] Once again, Democratic leaders found themselves searching for an explanation for their party's poor performance in presidential elections and, once again, the presidential nominating process emerged as a focus of concern.

The Rise of Front-Loading

In the aftermath of Walter Mondale's landslide defeat in the 1984 presidential election, a group of southern Democratic politicians led by Governor Charles Robb of Virginia came up with the idea of holding a southern regional primary early in the primary season to offset the influence of Iowa and New Hampshire. Robb and his allies hoped that a southern regional primary would improve the chances of a moderate and, in their view, more electable candidate winning the Democratic nomination. In addition, of course, the southern regional primary was intended to help candidates from the South.[16]

The first southern regional primary took place on March 8, 1988, which became known as **Super Tuesday** because of the number of

[15] For an account of the 1984 nomination and general election campaigns, see Paul R. Abramson, John H. Aldrich, and David W. Rohde, *Change and Continuity in the 1984 Elections* (Washington, DC: Congressional Quarterly Press, 1986), chapters 1–3. See also, Jack W. Germond and Jules Witcover, *Wake Us When It's Over: Presidential Politics of 1984* (New York: Macmillan, 1985).
[16] Charles D. Hadley and Harold W. Stanley, "The Southern Super Tuesday: Southern Democrats Seeking Relief from Rising Republicanism," in William G. Mayer, ed., *In Pursuit of the White House: How We Choose Our Presidential Nominees* (Chatham, NJ: Chatham House, 1996).

delegates at stake. On that date, 14 southern and border states along with two states outside the region—Massachusetts and Rhode Island —held presidential primaries. However, the results were disappointing to Super Tuesday's southern Democratic sponsors. Senator Albert Gore, Jr., the candidate preferred by most moderate southern Democrats, won primaries in Arkansas, Kentucky, North Carolina, Oklahoma, and his home state of Tennessee, but Massachusetts Governor Michael Dukakis won the Democratic primaries in Florida and Texas, the two most populous states in the South, along with those in his home state and neighboring Rhode Island. Even worse, from the standpoint of moderate southern Democrats, civil rights leader Jesse Jackson, the most liberal candidate in the field, used solid support from African American voters to capture Democratic primaries in Alabama, Georgia, Louisiana, Mississippi, and Virginia.

Super Tuesday did not give Al Gore, Jr., the boost he needed to win the Democratic nomination in 1988 but it did greatly benefit another southerner, Vice President George Bush of Texas. Bush swept all 14 Republican primaries held on March 8 and went on to easily win the Republican nomination.[17] In 1992, however, a scaled-down Super Tuesday did help a southern Democrat win his party's presidential nomination. Arkansas Governor Bill Clinton was able to overcome an early loss in New Hampshire by sweeping the six southern and border state primaries that were held 3 weeks later, on March 7. Clinton, went on to defeat President Bush and Ross Perot in the November election.[18]

The creation of Super Tuesday in 1988 marked the beginning of a trend that has drastically altered the presidential nomination campaign—the increasing **front-loading** of the delegate selection process. As party and elected officials came to realize that early primaries had a disproportionate influence on the outcome of the presidential nomination, more and more states moved the date of their presidential primary close to the beginning of the primary season.

[17]See Gerald M. Pomper, "The Presidential Nominations," in Gerald M. Pomper, ed., *The Election of 1988: Reports and Interpretations* (Chatham, NJ: Chatham House, 1989). See also Paul R. Abramson, John H. Aldrich, and David W. Rohde, *Change and Continuity in the 1988 Elections* (Washington, DC: Congressional Quarterly Press, 1989), chapter 1.
[18]See Ross K. Baker, "Sorting Out and Suiting Up: The Presidential Nominations," and Gerald M. Pomper, "The Presidential Election," in Gerald M. Pomper, ed., *The Election of 1992* (Chatham, NJ: Chatham House, 1993).

Between 1984 and 1996, the proportion of Democratic convention delegates chosen in the first 4 weeks of primaries increased from 24 percent to 51 percent and the proportion chosen in the first 8 weeks increased from 43 percent to 77 percent; during the same years, the proportion of Republican convention delegates chosen in the first 4 weeks of primaries increased from 27 percent to 44 percent and the proportion chosen in the first 8 weeks increased from 49 percent to 73 percent.[19]

The trend toward increasing front-loading of the primary calendar eased a bit in 2000 because New Hampshire officials decided to move the date of their traditional first-in-the-nation primary up to February 1. This left a gap of 5 weeks between the date of the New Hampshire primary and March 7, when the first large group of primaries would take place. These changes meant that a dark-horse candidate who scored an upset win in New Hampshire would have more time to capitalize on that victory by raising money and building a national organization before being forced to compete in multiple primaries in populous states. Nevertheless, the task facing such a dark-horse candidate remained formidable. After this 5 week hiatus, the primary calendar in 2000 was more compressed than ever: 64 percent of Democratic convention delegates and 55 percent of Republican convention delegates were chosen in consecutive weeks on March 7 and 14. On March 7 alone, 11 states including California, New York, and Ohio held presidential primaries. The cost of mounting an effective media campaign in so many states simultaneously would be staggering.

Financing the Nomination Campaign

The increased front-loading of the primary calendar places an enormous premium on early fund-raising. In 2000, for example, most political observers believed that a candidate needed to amass a campaign war chest of at least $25 million before the beginning of the primary season to seriously contend for the nomination. Eight of the 11 Republican candidates never came close to raising that much money and none of them was ever a factor in the race.

---

[19] For an examination of the development of front-loading and its impact on recent presidential nomination campaigns, see William G. Mayer, "The Presidential Nominations," in Pomper, ed., *The Election of 2000.*

In the past, the availability of **federal matching funds** has given a substantial boost to dark-horse candidates. After scoring victories in the early caucuses and primaries, candidates like Jimmy Carter in 1976 and Gary Hart in 1984 were able to augment increased private contributions with federal matching funds. Today, however, because of the front-loading of the primary calendar, a candidate cannot afford to wait until after the Iowa caucuses or the New Hampshire primary to begin amassing a substantial war chest. John McCain's fund-raising increased dramatically after his victory in the 2000 New Hampshire primary. He eventually raised $45 million including $14.5 million in federal matching funds but it was too little, too late. In the Super Tuesday primaries, McCain was badly outspent by George W. Bush.

Candidates who accept federal matching funds are required to abide by an overall spending limit as well as a spending limit in each state. In 2000, for example, the overall spending limit was about $45 million while the limits for individual states varied from a minimum of $676,000 in several small states to a maximum of over $13 million in California. The spending limit for each state is based on a formula that reflects the size of its voting-age population but not its political importance. For example, the spending limit for New Hampshire in 2000 was set at the minimum level of $676,000. Not surprisingly, candidates frequently try to evade spending limits in crucial states like New Hampshire through accounting gimmicks such as claiming that ads placed on Boston television stations to influence voters in southern New Hampshire were really aimed at voters in Massachusetts, which has a much higher spending limit.

Even with the use of creative accounting, candidates who accept federal matching funds in the primaries are at a severe disadvantage when they have to compete against candidates who do not depend on public financing. In the 2000 Republican nomination campaign, for example, both George W. Bush and Steve Forbes turned down federal matching funds. Bush raised so much money from individual contributors that he did not need federal matching funds while Forbes used his personal fortune to finance his campaign. As a result, Bush and Forbes, unlike John McCain, did not have to abide by either the overall spending limit or the spending limits for individual states. This allowed Governor Bush to outspend Senator McCain by a wide margin in the crucial round of primaries on March 7. As a result, Bush was able to dominate the airwaves in states like California, New York, and Ohio where television is the most efficient way of communicating with the electorate. Overall, even though John Mc-Cain was able to spend the legal limit of $45 million on his campaign, he was outspent by a 2-1 margin by George W. Bush.[20]

Open vs. Closed Primaries

Although money plays a vital role in the contemporary presidential nomination process, it is by no means the only factor that determines the winners and losers. The results also depend on who votes in presidential primaries. Here, the rules once again play a crucial role. The size and composition of the primary electorate in each state depends to a considerable extent on who is eligible to vote as well as the timing of the primary and the intensity of the campaign.

In 28 states, citizens are allowed to state a party preference when they register to vote. In some of these states, such as New York, only registered Democrats can vote in the Democratic primary and only registered Republicans can vote in the Republican primary. This is known as a **closed primary.** In states with closed primaries the proportion of voters who register as independents is usually fairly small. Other states, such as New Hampshire, have party registration but allow registered independents to vote in either the Republican or Democratic primary. In these states, not surprisingly, a much larger proportion of voters, sometimes well over half, typically register as independents. In addition, 22 states have no party registration. In these states any registered voter can vote in either party's primary. States with no party registration or where registered independents can vote in either party's primary have what is known as an **open primary.**

Of course, party registration is not always equivalent to party identification. In states with closed primaries, voters who consider themselves independents may choose to register as Republicans or Democrats to vote in primary elections. Moreover, when there is a dominant party in a state, it is not unusual for independents and supporters of the minority party to register with the dominant party to vote in its primary. Thus, during the era when the Democratic Party was so dominant in much of the South that victory in the Democratic primary was tantamount to election, many independents and Republicans registered as Democrats.

[20] Harold W. Stanley, "The Nominations: The Return of the Party Leaders," in Nelson, ed., *The Elections of 2000.* See also Mayer, "The Presidential Nominations," in Pomper, ed., *The Election of 2000.*

With the growth of two-party competition in many areas previously dominated by a single party, including the South, today there is much less reason for voters to register with a different party from the one with which they identify. As a result, party registration more closely reflects party identification and **crossover voting**—supporters of one party "crossing over" to vote in the opposing party's primary—is less common than in the past.[21]

In states with closed primaries, the large majority of voters in the Democratic primary are Democratic identifiers and the large majority of voters in the Republican primary are Republican identifiers. In the 2000 New York presidential primary, for example, 74 percent of the voters in the Republican primary were Republican identifiers and 80 percent of the voters in the Democratic primary were Democratic identifiers. Only 3 percent of the voters in the Republican primary were Democratic crossover voters and only 2 percent of the voters in the Democratic primary were Republican crossover voters.

In states with open primaries, independents and crossover voters are typically more prevalent than in states with closed primaries. However, the highest rates of independent and crossover voting generally occur when either only one party is holding a primary or only one party has competition in its primary. In 2000, for example, Michigan Democrats did not hold a presidential primary. They chose their national convention delegates through a caucus-convention process that began several weeks after the date of Michigan's presidential primary. As a result, independents and Democrats felt free to vote in the Republican presidential primary. According to the VNS exit poll, only 48 percent of voters in the Michigan Republican primary were Republican identifiers while 35 percent were independents and 17 percent were Democrats. This was by far the highest percentage of Democratic identifiers in any 2000 Republican primary for which exit poll data are available.

Even in states with open primaries, independent and crossover voting is generally limited when there is competition in both parties. In the 2000 Ohio presidential primary, for example, there were contests in both parties. John McCain was still battling George Bush for the Republican nomination while Bill Bradley had not yet dropped his challenge to Al Gore for the Democratic nomination. Even though Ohio has no party registration, so any registered voter

---

[21] See Earl Black and Merle Black, *Politics and Society in the South* (Cambridge, MA: Harvard University Press, 1987), chapter 11. See also Alexander P. Lamis, *The Two-Party South* (New York: Oxford University Press, 1988), chapter 3.

could have participated in either party's primary, 69 percent of the voters in the Republican primary were Republican identifiers and 77 percent of the voters in the Democratic primary were Democratic identifiers; only 7 percent of the voters in the Republican primary were Democratic crossover voters and only 3 percent of the voters in the Democratic primary were Republican crossover voters.

These statistics point to another major reason why insurgent candidates like John McCain and Bill Bradley generally do not fare well in the contemporary presidential nomination system. Anti-establishment candidates tend to appeal primarily to independents and crossover voters. In the 2000 Republican primaries, for example, John McCain did very well among independents and Democratic crossover voters. In eight Republican primaries for which exit poll data are available, McCain averaged 59 percent of the vote among independents and 75 percent among Democratic identifiers. However, independent and crossover voters combined make up less than a third of the electorate in most presidential primaries. Moreover, in appealing to independent and crossover voters, insurgent candidates risk alienating their own party's base. This appears to have been the case with John McCain. In the same eight primaries, McCain averaged only 32 percent of the vote among Republican identifiers.

Who Votes in Presidential Primaries?

In general, voter turnout in primaries is substantially lower than in general elections. In 2000, for example, the number of votes cast in the presidential primaries was about one-third the number of votes cast in the general election in the same states. However, turnout in presidential primaries varies considerably depending on the timing of the primary, the intensity of competition, and whether there are other major contests or issues on the ballot. The first two factors tend to go together—early primaries tend to be more competitive than later primaries because there are usually more serious candidates in the race in the early primaries. As a result these primaries generally have a higher than average turnout. In addition, states such as California that hold primaries for other offices or referenda at the same time as their presidential primary generally have a higher turnout than states that hold a separate presidential primary.

New Hampshire, in particular, generally has a very high turnout for its first-in-the-nation primary. In 2000, for example, the number of votes in the New Hampshire primary was about two-thirds the number of votes in the general election. This was by far the highest ratio of primary to general election turnout of any state. In contrast, turnout in many primaries held after March 7, when both parties' presidential nominations were effectively decided, was less than one-fourth of turnout in the general election.

Table 5.1 displays the social and political characteristics of Democratic and Republican primary voters in four states—California, New York, Ohio, and Georgia—that held presidential primaries on March 7, 2000, just before John McCain and Bill Bradley ended their campaigns. While no four states can adequately represent the entire nation, these four do represent every major region of the United States—the Northeast, the Midwest, the South, and the West. The California and New York primaries were closed: only registered Democrats and Republicans could vote in the Democratic and Republican primaries. The Ohio and Georgia primaries were open: neither state has party registration so any registered voter could choose either a Democratic or Republican primary ballot. In addition, the results of these four primaries were very similar to the results in the entire nation. On the Democratic side, Al Gore won an average of 76 percent of the vote in these four states to 23 percent for Bill Bradley. In all of the Democratic primaries, Gore won 76 percent of the vote to 20 percent for Bradley. On the Republican side, George W. Bush won an average of 59 percent of the vote in these four states to 36 percent for John McCain. In all of the Republican primaries, Bush won 63 percent of the vote to 30 percent for McCain.

Despite the fact that both Ohio and Georgia had open primaries and despite a major effort by John McCain to appeal to Democrats, crossover voters made up no more than 3 percent of Democratic primary voters and 8 percent of Republican primary voters in any of these states. Independent identifiers comprised about one-fifth of Democratic primary voters and about one-fourth of Republican primary voters. In all four states, the large majority of Democratic primary voters were Democratic identifiers and the large majority of Republican primary voters were Republican identifiers. Moreover, it is likely that many of the independents were "leaners" who voted in the primary of the party that they usually support.

Given their partisan orientations, it is not surprising that the social and political characteristics of Democratic and Republican primary voters in these four states generally reflected the characteristics of each party's identifiers in the electorate. Democratic primary voters were disproportionately female and nonwhite. The large majority reported family incomes below $75,000 and they included a substantial number of Jews and individuals with no religious preference. Republican primary voters were almost evenly divided between males and females. They were overwhelmingly white, and

TABLE 5.1 Social and Political Characteristics of Presidential Primary Voters in Four States, 2000

	Democrats				Republicans			
	NY	CA	OH	GA	NY	CA	OH	GA
Gender								
Female	58%	56%	60%	59%	45%	52%	47%	49%
Race/Ethnicity								
White	63	62	81	56	93	84	97	96
Black	21	11	17	41	2	1	2	2
Hispanic	14	17	1	1	4	8	0	1
Asian, Other	2	10	2	2	1	6	1	1
Religion								
Protestant	30	38	59	70	39	64	65	80
Catholic	35	27	27	11	50	21	25	13
Jewish	20	9	1	4	6	1	1	2
Other or none	15	26	14	15	5	13	9	5
Age								
18–29	9	12	8	12	9	9	13	9
30–44	24	30	28	28	23	27	25	30
45–59	31	28	34	31	29	28	37	33
60 or older	36	29	30	28	39	36	25	28
Education								
College graduate	53	47	27	43	44	47	41	46
Income								
Under $30,000	28	25	30	21	20	15	20	12
$30–75,000	41	46	54	57	46	42	49	48
More than $75,000	31	28	17	21	34	43	31	39
Party identification								
Democrat	80	85	77	81	3	2	7	8
Independent	18	13	21	17	23	16	24	29
Republican	2	2	3	2	74	82	69	62
Ideology								
Liberal	54	50	42	44	14	6	14	10
Moderate	35	42	49	44	35	33	39	29
Conservative	10	8	10	12	51	61	47	61

Source: VNS Exit Poll data compiled by CNN.

Note: Based on results from California, Georgia, New York, and Ohio. All entries shown are percentages.

overwhelmingly Christian. Although most had family incomes below $75,000, a larger minority of Republican than Democratic primary voters reported incomes of more than $75,000. Both sets of primary voters were older, wealthier, and better educated than the populations of their respective states.

Some regional differences in the political ideologies of Democratic and Republican primary voters are evident in this table. However, these differences were much smaller in 2000 than in the past. In all four states, the overwhelming majority of Democratic primary voters described themselves as liberal or moderate. In all four states a plurality or majority of Republican primary voters described themselves as conservative. Democratic primary voters in Georgia were only slightly less liberal than Democratic primary voters in New York and California and Republican primary voters in New York were only slightly less conservative than Republican primary voters in Georgia.

Candidate Choice in Presidential Primaries

In explaining candidate choice in general elections, political scientists have focused on three sets of factors: party identification, issue positions, and evaluations of candidates' personal characteristics. Party identification plays a particularly important role because it influences evaluations of candidates' issue positions and personal characteristics and because voters who know little or nothing about the candidates can still rely on party affiliation to make a choice.[22] In primary elections, however, the candidates all share the same party affiliation and their issue positions are frequently very similar. In 2000, for example, Bill Bradley's and Al Gore's positions on most issues were almost indistinguishable and all of the major Republican candidates were pro-life conservatives. As a result, perceptions of candidates' personal qualities and characteristics can have a stronger influence on voter decision-making in primaries than in general elections. However, disparities in the financial resources and visibility of candidates are often even greater in primaries than in general elections so many candidates are eliminated from consideration simply because voters know little or nothing about them.

---

[22] The classic account of the role of party identification in voter decision-making is found in Angus Campbell, Philip E. Converse, Warren E. Miller, and Donald E. Stokes, *The American Voter* (New York: John Wiley & Sons, 1960), chapter 6.

Despite the fact that all of the candidates share the same party affiliation, party loyalties can influence voter decision-making in primary elections. In recent presidential nomination contests, most prominent party and elected officials have lined up very early behind a particular candidate who seemed to have the best chance of uniting the party and winning the general election. In 1996, for example, many Republican officials were early supporters of Bob Dole, the party's leader in the Senate and a former GOP vice presidential candidate. In the 2000 presidential primaries, Al Gore, the incumbent vice president, and George W. Bush, the governor of Texas and son of the last Republican president, received the overwhelming majority of endorsements made by Democratic and Republican elected and party officials.

Endorsements by prominent party and elected officials send a signal to primary voters that a particular candidate has the best chance of uniting the party and leading it to victory in November. In 2000, for example, according to the exit polls, most primary voters viewed George W. Bush and Al Gore as the candidates with the best chance of winning the general election and the overwhelming majority of these primary voters cast their ballot for the candidate whom they perceived to have the best chance of winning.

Of course not all primary voters are equally receptive to endorsements made by party and elected officials. An endorsement, like any persuasive communication, tends to be most effective when it comes from a trusted source. Therefore, voters who identify with a party are much more likely to be influenced by the endorsements of party leaders than independents or crossover voters, and strong identifiers are more likely to be influenced than weak identifiers. In the 2000 presidential primaries, for example, exit polls consistently showed that Republican and Democratic identifiers were much more likely to support George W. Bush and Al Gore, the candidates endorsed by most party leaders, than were independents and crossover voters.

THE PARTY CONVENTIONS TODAY

Since the 1950s, the Democratic and Republican presidential nominations have almost always been settled long before the national party conventions in July and August. With the growing front-loading of the primary calendar since 1988, the outcome of the presidential nomination has been decided by the end of March, before many states have even held their primaries. The conventions themselves no longer choose the presidential candidates. The voters in the primaries, and especially the voters in first few rounds of primaries, choose the presidential candidates. Nevertheless, despite sagging television ratings and suggestions by some reformers that the conventions be abolished, the parties continue to hold national nominating conventions because presidential candidates and party leaders believe that they serve two major purposes: unifying the party and kicking off the general election campaign.

The relative importance of these goals depends on the divisiveness of the nomination campaign. The more divisive the campaign, the more attention the eventual nominee must devote to healing internal party rifts. This may involve accepting provisions in the platform favored by one's opponents, allowing defeated candidates or their supporters to speak to the convention during prime time, or even choosing a defeated rival as one's running mate, as John F. Kennedy did in choosing Lyndon Johnson in 1960 and Ronald Reagan did in choosing George Bush in 1980.

Locking up the nomination early, as both Al Gore and George W. Bush did in 2000, minimizes the need to make concessions to intraparty rivals and allows a nominee to focus mainly on appealing to the general electorate at the convention. Thus, Gore's and Bush's convention strategies were aimed at appealing to undecided or wavering voters by correcting flaws in their public images. This was particularly evident in their vice presidential choices.[23] Bush's selection of former Secretary of Defense Richard Cheney was aimed as assuaging voter concerns about his own lack of foreign policy experience and knowledge. In addition, the Bush campaign believed that Cheney's calm, reassuring style would be more important to swing voters than his conservative voting record in the House of Representatives during the 1970s. Gore's selection of Connecticut Senator Joseph Lieberman, the first Jew ever chosen for a national ticket by a major party, was intended to counteract the Vice President's reputation as a cautious, calculating politician by projecting an image of boldness and imagination. At the same time, the Gore campaign hoped that Lieberman's centrist voting record and long involvement with the Democratic Leadership Council would appeal to moderate and independent swing voters.

[23] Mayer, "The Presidential Nominations," pp. 38–40.

THE 2004 NOMINATION CAMPAIGNS

By January 2003, a year before the Iowa caucuses and the New Hampshire primary, the 2004 presidential nomination campaign was already well underway. It appears unlikely that President Bush will face any serious opposition for the Republican nomination. However, the President's high approval ratings in the polls during 2002 and early 2003 have not deterred a number of prominent and not-so-prominent Democrats from throwing their hats into the presidential ring. By late January 2003, the Democratic field consisted of six candidates: former Vermont governor Howard Dean, Missouri Representative and former House Minority Leader Richard Gephardt, North Carolina Senator James Edwards, Massachusetts Senator John Kerry, Connecticut Senator and 2000 Democratic vice presidential nominee Joseph Lieberman, and New York civil rights leader Al Sharpton. Waiting in the wings and reportedly considering a run was former Colorado Senator Gary Hart.

It is already clear that, in some ways, the 2004 Democratic nomination campaign will be very different from the 2000 Democratic and Republican nomination campaigns. The decision of former vice president and 2000 presidential nominee Al Gore to take his name out of consideration means that there is no obvious front-runner for the Democratic nomination. As a result, the early delegate selection contests, and especially the Iowa caucuses and the New Hampshire primary, may play a larger role in determining the ultimate nominee than they did in 2000. A number of the Democratic candidates have already devoted considerable time and effort to organizing their Iowa and New Hampshire campaigns.

Despite the absence of a clear front-runner, however, there are some important similarities between the 2004 Democratic nomination campaign and the 2000 Democratic and Republican campaigns. Because of the continued front-loading of the primary calendar, the outcome of the Democratic nomination contest will probably be settled very quickly and money will play a large role in determining which candidates are able to compete effectively in the critical round of large state primaries that will occur within a few weeks of the New Hampshire primary. One of the major reasons why the Democratic candidates are starting their campaigns so early is to begin raising the money that will be necessary to campaign simultaneously in these large state primaries. So while it is difficult in early 2003 to predict who will emerge from the Democratic pack, we can predict with a high degree of confidence that a front-runner will quickly emerge and lock up the nomination well before the date of the national convention.

SUMMARY

Obtaining the nomination of one of the two major political parties is a prerequisite for winning the presidency. Since the 1960s, the process by which Democrats and Republicans choose their presidential candidates has undergone dramatic changes. Superficially, the process has become more open and democratic than ever before. The vast majority of delegates to the parties' national nominating conventions are now chosen in primary elections: voters, rather than party bosses decide who will head the parties' tickets in November. In addition, candidates for the Democratic and Republican nominations can obtain public financing in the form of matching funds to cover a large portion of their campaign expenses.

Despite these reforms, however, most recent nomination contests have followed a fairly predictable path. Even when there is no incumbent in the race, one candidate usually emerges as the clear front-runner well before the first delegates are chosen in Iowa and New Hampshire by raising more money and collecting more endorsements from party leaders than his or her rivals. Moreover, the increasing front-loading of the primary calendar clearly works to the advantage of the front-runner. Since 1988, more and more states have moved up the dates of their presidential primaries to increase their influence on the outcome of the nomination. As a result, even if a dark-horse candidate manages to upset the front-runner in Iowa or New Hampshire, it is very difficult for that candidate to raise money quickly enough to compete in primaries in several populous states on the same date.

Front-loading is not the only problem that a dark-horse candidate faces in challenging the front-runner in the primaries. To defeat a front-runner supported by the party establishment, a dark-horse candidate must appeal to independents and crossover voters. Even in states with open primaries, however, independents and crossover voters usually comprise less than a third of the electorate and a candidate who openly campaigns for the support of crossover voters risks alienating many of his or her own party's loyalists.

Ideological realignment has also reduced the ability of dark-horse candidates to exploit intraparty ideological divisions in the primaries. Increasingly, voters have been choosing their party identification on the basis of their policy preferences rather than maintaining the allegiance that they inherited from their parents: conservatives have been moving toward the Republican Party while liberals have been moving toward the Democratic Party. The result has been a more conservative Republican primary electorate and a more liberal Democratic primary electorate than in the past. This increased ideological homogeneity makes it more difficult for a dark-horse candidate to challenge a front-runner who comes from the ideological mainstream of the party.

KEY TERMS AND CONCEPTS

brokered convention	McGovern-Fraser Commission
closed primary	national nominating convention
congressional caucus system	New Hampshire primary
crossover voting	open primary
dark-horse candidate	party platform
federal matching funds	superdelegates
front-loading	Super Tuesday
Hunt Commission	Twelfth Amendment
invisible primary	winner-take-all primaries
Iowa precinct caucuses	

DISCUSSION QUESTIONS

1. What major advantages did George W. Bush and Al Gore enjoy in seeking the Republican and Democratic presidential nominations in 2000? How did John McCain and Bill Bradley seek to counteract these advantages and why were their efforts unsuccessful?
2. How did the congressional caucus nomination system arise, what were its most important characteristics, and what led to its demise?
3. What was the McGovern-Fraser Commission, why was it created, and what impact did it have on the presidential nomination process?
4. What have been the most important changes in the presidential nomination process since 1980 and how have these changes affected nomination campaigns and their outcomes?
5. What are the most important factors influencing the size and composition of the electorate in presidential primaries?

6. What role do the national conventions play in the contemporary presidential nominating process? Why and how has that role changed since the 1960s?

SUGGESTED READINGS

Jackson, John S. III, and William Crotty. *The Politics of Presidential Selection.* New York: HarperCollins, 1996. Jackson and Crotty provide a comprehensive overview of contemporary presidential nominations and general election campaigns from a modified rational choice perspective.

Nelson, Michael, ed. *The Elections of 2000.* Washington, DC: Congressional Quarterly Press, 2001. Nelson has put together a strong set of essays on various aspects of the fascinating 2000 election. Harold Stanley's chapter provides an excellent analysis of the 2000 presidential nominations.

Palmer, Niall A. *The New Hampshire Primary and the American Electoral Process.* Westport, CT: Praeger, 1997. Palmer provides an up-to-date analysis and defense of the extraordinary role of the New Hampshire primary in the presidential nominating process.

Pomper, Gerald M., ed. *The Election of 2000.* New York: Chatham House, 2001. This is the most recent entry in a series of postelection reports that Pomper and various collaborators have produced every 4 years since 1976. The chapters by William Mayer on the presidential nominations and Anthony Corrado on campaign finance are especially worthwhile.

Shafer, Byron E. *Quiet Revolution: The Struggle for the Democratic Party and the Shaping of Post-Reform Politics.* New York: Russell Sage Foundation, 1983. Shafer provides a detailed history of the post-1968 reforms of the Democratic Party's presidential nomination process and an insightful analysis of their intended and unintended consequences for the presidency and the American political system.

INFORMATION SOURCES ON THE INTERNET

Federal Election Commission, Presidential Primary Results: www.fec.gov/pubrec/fe2000/2000presprim.htm. This section of the FEC website provides a comprehensive listing of results from the 2000 presidential primaries.

Federal Election Commission, Presidential Primary Voting Requirements: www.fec.gov./votregis/primaryvoting.htm. Here you'll find information about requirements and procedures for voting in state presidential primaries.

Iowa Precinct Caucuses: www.iowapoliticalhotline.com. When they're not campaigning in New Hampshire, chances are the Democratic presidential candidates are preparing for the 2004 Iowa precinct caucuses, which precede the New Hampshire primary. This website provides reports and data on the Iowa precinct caucuses and other political developments in the Hawkeye state.

New Hampshire Presidential Primary: www.primarymonitor.com. This website provides historical data and current information on New Hampshire's first-in-the-nation presidential primary. Many of the candidates for the 2004 Democratic nomination have already spent considerable time campaigning in New Hampshire.

Washington Post 2004 Election News: www.washingtonpost.com/wp-dyn/ politics/elections/2004. Visit this site to review recent articles and special reports on the 2004 elections, including the race for the 2004 Democratic presidential nomination.

CHAPTER 6

The Battle for the White House, II

The General Election

THE STRATEGIC ENVIRONMENT

As the battle for the White House shifts from the nomination to the general election phase, both the participants and the rules of the game change dramatically. Perhaps the most important changes involve the size and composition of the electorate. Instead of relatively small state primary electorates consisting mainly of ideologically distinctive party loyalists, the candidates must appeal to the much larger and more diverse general electorate and especially to the independents and weak partisans who hold the balance of power. In addition, the candidates' strategies in the general election are shaped by a campaign finance system that was created during the 1970s and by an institution that was created in 1787—the **Electoral College**. Before examining the characteristics of the presidential electorate, we will discuss the ways in which the Electoral College and campaign finance laws influence the conduct of modern presidential campaigns.

The Electoral College

In the aftermath of the 2000 election, many Americans learned for the first time that the winner of a presidential election is determined by the electoral vote rather than the popular vote: a candidate must receive a majority of electoral votes to become president. For this reason, the Electoral College has a powerful influence on the campaign strategies of modern presidential candidates.[1]

The Constitution gives each state as many electors as the total of its U.S. Representatives and Senators. Thus, each state is entitled to a minimum of three electoral votes. In addition, the **Twenty-third Amendment,** adopted in 1961, gives the District of Columbia three electoral votes. To be elected president, a candidate must receive a majority of the total number of electoral votes. Since there are now 538 electoral votes, (435 Representatives plus 100 Senators plus 3 votes for the District of Columbia), a candidate must receive at least 270 votes to be elected. If no candidate receives a majority of electoral votes, the Constitution provides that the election be decided by the outgoing House of Representatives with each state delegation casting one vote regardless of its size. However, this procedure has not been used since 1824 when the House chose John Quincy Adams over Andrew Jackson even though Jackson had received more popular and electoral votes.[2]

Because every state has two U.S. Senators, states with small populations are overrepresented in the Electoral College while states with large populations are underrepresented. In the 2000 election, for example, Wyoming had one electoral vote for every 165,000 residents while California had one electoral vote for every 627,000 residents. For this reason, proposals to abolish the Electoral College have been opposed by members of Congress who represent states with small populations. However, despite the overrepresentation of states with small populations in the Electoral College, presidential candidates typically pay very little attention to these states during the general election campaign. Instead, they spend most of their time, and most of their money, in states with large populations where the race is competitive. This is because of another feature of the Electoral

---

[1] For a recent summary of the research on the effects of the Electoral College on presidential campaign strategies, see William G. Mayer, Emmett H. Buell, Jr., James E. Campbell, and Mark Joslyn, "The Electoral College and Campaign Strategy," in Paul D. Schumaker and Burdett A. Loomis, eds., *Choosing a President: The Electoral College and Beyond* (New York: Chatham House, 2002).

[2] For a brief description of this election, see Congressional Quarterly, *Guide to U.S. Elections,* Volume 1 (Washington, DC: Congressional Quarterly Press, 2001), pp. 232–33. See also Arthur M. Schlesinger, Jr., *The Age of Jackson* (Boston: Little, Brown and Company, 1945); and George Dangerfield, *The Era of Good Feelings* (New York: Harcourt, Brace, 1952).

College—one that was not part of the framers' original plan—the **winner-take-all rule.**[3]

During the early nineteenth century, states began to award all of their electoral votes to the presidential candidate who won a plurality of the popular vote in the state. By awarding their state's electoral votes as a bloc rather than splitting them, political leaders hoped to increase their state's importance to the presidential candidates. Today, this practice continues. Every state except Maine and Nebraska awards all of its electoral votes to whichever presidential candidate receives a plurality of the popular vote in the state. Thus, in the 2000 presidential election, George W. Bush received all of Florida's 25 electoral votes even though his margin in the popular vote was less than 0.1 percent.

The use of the winner-take-all rule in awarding electoral votes provides a powerful incentive for presidential candidates to concentrate their campaign efforts in states with large blocs of electoral votes where the race is competitive. In these states, a relatively small swing in the popular vote can shift a large bloc of electoral votes.[4] In the 2000 election, for example, preelection polls showed the presidential race to be very close in Florida (25 electoral votes), Pennsylvania (23 electoral votes), and Michigan (18 electoral votes). Both Al Gore and George W. Bush made numerous visits and purchased large numbers of televisions ads in these three states during the final weeks of the 2000 campaign. In contrast, presidential candidates generally ignore states that are considered safe for one side or the other, regardless of how many electoral votes they award. Thus, neither Bush nor Gore invested much time or money in New York with its 33 electoral votes or Texas with its 32 electoral votes: New York was considered safe for Al Gore while Texas was considered safe for its native son, George W. Bush. Voters in these states saw little or nothing of the presidential candidates either in person or in television ads.

In a very close election, even states with only a few electoral votes may receive considerable attention from the presidential candidates if polls in those states show the presidential contest to be

---

[3] See Donald Lutz, Philip Abbott, Barbara Allen, and Russell Hanson, "The Electoral College in Historical and Philosophical Perspective," in Schumaker and Loomis, eds., *Choosing a President: The Electoral College and Beyond,* pp. 39–40.
[4] Mayer et al., "The Electoral College and Campaign Strategy," pp. 102–3.

highly competitive. In 2000, for example, the Bush and Gore campaigns invested considerable time and money in several small states including Arkansas (6 electoral votes), Iowa (7 electoral votes), Oregon (7 electoral votes), and New Hampshire (4 electoral votes). In all four of these states, preelection polls showed the presidential race to be very close and in all four of these states, the winning candidate's margin of victory was less than five percentage points. A shift of fewer than 4,000 votes in New Hampshire would have put Al Gore in the White House instead of George W. Bush.

Presidential candidates' decisions about where to allocate campaign resources are only as good as the information on which they are based, and this information is often imperfect. During the final week of the 2000 campaign, for example, the Bush campaign's internal polling indicated that the presidential race was tightening in California, a state that had been considered safe for Al Gore. With time running out, Mr. Bush flew to California to make several personal appearances and the Bush campaign invested thousands of dollars in television ads in Los Angeles and other major California media markets.[5] On Election Day, Al Gore, who spent no money on television advertising in California, carried the state by a wide margin.

In the election of 2000, George W. Bush became the first person since Benjamin Harrison in 1888 to win the presidency despite losing the popular vote. What made this possible was the closeness of the national popular vote along with the extraordinary events in Florida where voter confusion caused by Palm Beach County's "butterfly ballot" almost certainly cost Al Gore the state's 25 electoral votes.[6] Despite the controversial ending of the 2000 election, however, it is very unlikely that the Electoral College will be abolished or significantly reformed anytime soon.[7] As mentioned earlier, the Electoral College has strong support among politicians from small states that

---

[5] The Bush campaign was also under pressure from California Republicans to spend some time and money in the state to help GOP candidates for state and local office. See James Rainey and Jean O. Pasco, "Campaign 2000; Rivals Revisit California After Long Absences," *Los Angeles Times*, October 31, 2000, p. A1.

[6] The most thorough analysis of the effect of the butterfly ballot in Palm Beach County is found in Jonathan N. Wand, Kenneth W. Shotts, Jasjeet S. Sekhon, Walter R. Mebane, Jr., Michael C. Herron, and Henry E. Brady, "The Butterfly Did It: The Aberrant Vote for Buchanan in Palm Beach County, Florida," *American Political Science Review* 95 (December 2001), pp. 793–810.

[7] For an analysis of the political obstacles to reforming the Electoral College, see James W. Ceaser and Andrew E. Busch, *The Perfect Tie: The True Story of the 2000 Presidential Election* (New York: Rowman and Littlefield, 2001), chapter 8.

are overrepresented in relation to their populations. In addition, the fact that conflicts between the electoral vote and the popular vote are relatively rare makes it difficult for reformers to generate the public support that would be needed to convince two-thirds of the members of Congress and majorities in three-fourths of the state legislatures to amend the Constitution. For better or worse, the Electoral College is likely to remain an important part of the strategic environment of presidential elections for the foreseeable future.

Financing the General Election Campaign

Since the enactment of the 1974 amendments to the **Federal Election Campaign Act,** the Republican and Democratic presidential candidates have received direct federal funding to pay for their general election campaigns. The amount of this federal grant is adjusted every 4 years based on the rate of inflation.[8] In 2000, the Bush and Gore campaigns each received a total of $67.6 million—a rather small sum to run a national campaign. Minor party presidential candidates are also eligible for federal funding if their party's nominee received at least 5 percent of the popular vote in the previous presidential election. The amount depends on the share of the vote that the party's nominee received in the previous election. In 2000, for example, Reform Party nominee Patrick Buchanan received $12.6 million based on the 8 percent of the popular vote won by H. Ross Perot in 1996, but since Buchanan received less than 1 percent of the popular vote in 2000, the Reform Party's presidential candidate will not be eligible for federal funds before the 2004 campaign. However, under the provisions of the Federal Election Campaign Act, minor party or independent candidates can be reimbursed for campaign expenses after the election if they receive at least 5 percent of the popular vote.

Congress created the current system of **public financing** for presidential general election campaigns in the aftermath of the Watergate scandal and revelations concerning fund-raising abuses by the 1972 Nixon presidential campaign. The major goals of the post-

---

[8]For a history of campaign finance laws in presidential elections, see Herbert E. Alexander, *Financing Politics: Money, Elections, and Political Reform,* 4th ed. (Washington, DC: Congressional Quarterly Press, 1992). See also Frank J. Sorauf, *Money in American Elections* (Glenview, Illinois: Scott Foresman and Company, 1988). An excellent recent analysis of campaign finance law in the United States is found in Anthony Gierzynski, *Money Rules* (Boulder, Colorado: Westview Press, 2000).

Watergate reforms were to eliminate the dependence of presidential candidates on large private contributions and to equalize the financial resources of the candidates. For a while, the reforms seemed to be accomplishing these objectives. However, in recent elections these goals were seriously undermined by the rapid increase in campaign spending by political parties, and especially the explosive growth of **soft money** expenditures.[9]

Between 1992 and 2000, according to data compiled by the Federal Election Commission, the total amount of money raised by Democratic and Republican party committees increased from just over $500 million to more than $1.2 billion. During the same period, soft money contributions to party committees increased from $85 million, or 17 percent of all party funds, to $487 million, or 40 percent of all party funds.

It is impossible to determine what proportion of soft money expenditures in recent elections were specifically directed at the presidential race. However, presidential candidates, including Al Gore and George W. Bush, have played an active role in raising soft money for party committees and the presidential campaigns have had considerable influence in determining how these funds have been spent. The amount of soft money spent by party committees on behalf of the presidential candidates during the 2000 general election campaign was almost certainly much greater than the $67.6 million that the candidates were allowed to spend themselves. Thus, the rapid growth of soft money was seriously undermining one of the major goals of the campaign finance reforms of the 1970s: limiting the influence of large contributors. Wealthy individuals, corporations, and labor unions provided most of the funds that were spent on the 2000 presidential general election campaigns through soft money contributions to party committees.[10]

In response to rising public concern about the massive amounts of unregulated campaign cash flowing into the coffers of the two major parties, in April 2001 the U.S. Senate approved a bill co-sponsored by Senators John McCain (R-Arizona) and Russell Feingold (D-Wis-

---

[9]Gierzynski, *Money Rules*, chapter 4. See also Darrell M. West and Burdett A. Loomis, *The Sound of Money: How Political Interests Get What They Want* (New York: W. W. Norton and Company, 1999); and Thomas Gais, *Improper Influence: Campaign Finance Law, Political Interest Groups, and the Problem of Equality* (Ann Arbor: University of Michigan Press, 1998).

[10]Anthony Corrado, "Financing the 2000 Elections," in Gerald M. Pomper, ed., *The Election of 2000* (New York: Chatham House, 2001), pp. 92–124.

consin) to ban soft money contributions to national party committees. For almost a year, however, a nearly identical House bill co-
sponsored by Representatives Christopher Shays (R-Connecticut)
and Martin Meehan (D-Massachusetts) remained bottled up in committee due to opposition by Speaker Dennis Hastert and other Republican leaders. These GOP leaders were apparently worried that
banning soft money would reduce their party's overall financial advantage since Republican committees received over $100 million in
soft money contributions during 2001 compared with only $69 mil-
lion for their Democratic counterparts.[11]

In 2002, just as in 1974, a political scandal ultimately played a key
role in spurring the enactment of campaign finance reform legislation. Following revelations concerning large soft money contributions to the Bush presidential campaign by the failed Enron Corpo-
ration and its top executives, supporters of a soft money ban were
able to obtain the signatures of a majority of members of the House
of Representatives on a discharge petition, forcing a floor vote on
the bill. With 41 Republicans joining the overwhelming majority of
Democrats, the Shays-Meehan bill finally passed the House on February 13.[12] Five weeks later, the Senate voted 60-40 to accept the
House version of the bill. On March 27, 2002, President Bush, despite his earlier opposition to several of its key provisions, signed the
most significant campaign finance reform legislation since the 1970s
into law.[13]

Just how the **Bipartisan Campaign Reform Act of 2002** will
affect the conduct of presidential campaigns in 2004 and beyond
will depend on the outcomes of court challenges as well as the actions taken by party leaders and presidential candidates in response

---

[11] For a description of these events, see Karen Masterson, "Campaign Fund Reform
Advances; Measure Clears Senate 59–41," *Houston Chronicle*, April 3, 2001, p. A1. The
McCain-Feingold bill, like the Shays-Meehan bill in the House, included a number of
other provisions including one restricting "issue advertising" in federal campaigns.
Under the bill's provisions, interest groups sponsoring political advertisements
shortly before a primary or general election would not be permitted to mention the
names of the candidates. Opponents of McCain-Feingold and Shays-Meehan argued
that this provision violated the First Amendment's guarantee of freedom of speech.
[12] Peter Grier and Liz Marlantes, "A Campaign Finance Landmark," *Christian Science
Monitor*, February 15, 2002, p. 1.
[13] Elizabeth Bumiller and Philip Shenon, "Bush Signs Campaign Bill, Then Opens
Money Tour," *The New York Times*, March 28, 2002, p. A1. In a signal of his continued
reservations about several provisions of the new law, the President did not invite any
of the bill's major sponsors in the House or Senate to the signing ceremony.

to the legislation. Based on recent history, one should not underestimate the ability of party leaders and candidates to find creative ways to avoid restrictions on fund-raising. Some unregulated funds may still find their way into presidential campaigns through state party committees. It is also possible that the Bush reelection campaign will forego public financing and rely entirely on private donations to fund its 2004 general election campaign. Since the new law increases the limit on individual contributions to federal candidates from $1,000 to $2,000, it would be relatively easy for Mr. Bush to raise more in private contributions than he would receive in public funds. Such a move could allow the President to greatly outspend a publicly financed Democratic challenger.

VOTER TURNOUT

Far more Americans vote in presidential elections than in other types of elections in the United States. For example, more than 105 million citizens cast ballots in the 2000 presidential election compared with just over 73 million in the 1998 midterm elections. Nevertheless, turnout in U.S. presidential elections is far lower than turnout in national elections in most other Western democracies.[14] Moreover, students of American elections generally agree that turnout in the United States was higher during the 1950s and 1960s than it has been since 1972 although there is disagreement about whether voter turnout has continued to decline since 1972.[15]

Much of the disagreement about recent trends in voter turnout has to do with the way in which turnout is measured. Traditionally, most election analysts, along with the U.S. Census Bureau, have measured voter turnout as the percentage of the entire voting-age population that shows up at the polls. In the 2000 election, for example, the number of votes cast was about 51 percent of the estimated voting-age population of the United States, up slightly from 49 percent in 1996 but down from 54 percent in 1992. The problem with this definition is that the voting-age population includes millions of people who are not legally eligible to vote. Most of these ineligible voters are

---

[14]Russell J. Dalton, *Citizen Politics: Public Opinion and Political Parties in Advanced Industrial Democracies,* 3rd ed. (New York: Chatham House, 2002), p. 36.
[15]For an analysis of trends in voter turnout in U.S. elections, see Paul R. Abramson, John H. Aldrich, and David W. Rohde, *Change and Continuity in the 2000 Elections* (Washington, DC: Congressional Quarterly Press, 2002), chapter 4.

noncitizens, but some are citizens who are barred from voting because they have been convicted of felonies. Moreover, the proportion of ineligible voters in the population has grown substantially since the 1980s due mainly to increased legal and illegal immigration. According to political scientists Samuel Popkin and Michael McDonald, after removing noncitizens and ineligible convicted felons from the voting-age population, voter turnout in presidential elections has varied between 53 and 61 percent and has not declined significantly since 1972. They estimate that approximately 56 percent of the eligible population voted in the 2000 presidential election.[16]

The findings of Popkin and McDonald indicate that voter turnout in recent presidential elections was somewhat higher than generally acknowledged. Nevertheless, even after removing noncitizens and convicted felons from the population, almost half of Americans who were eligible to vote did not participate in the last two presidential elections. Moreover, as we showed in Chapter 3, these nonvoters were not a cross-section of the entire population—they consisted disproportionately of the young, the poor, and members of racial and ethnic minority groups.[17]

Findings such as these raise an important question. Does the low rate of voter turnout in the United States affect the outcomes of elections? Because turnout is lowest among groups that tend to vote Democratic, politicians and journalists as well as members of the public generally assume that low voter turnout helps Republican candidates and that any effort to reduce obstacles to voting or encourage higher turnout would benefit Democrats. Thus, many Republican politicians opposed passage of the **National Voter Registration Act,** or **Motor Voter Law,** in 1993, out of fear that the large majority of those who would register under the law's provisions would be Democrats.

Despite the fears of Republican politicians, however, the evidence regarding trends in voter registration since 1993 indicates that implementation of the Motor Voter Law has had little impact on either overall turnout in presidential elections or the characteristics of the electorate.[18] More generally, analyses done by political scientists

---

[16]Michael P. McDonald and Samuel L. Popkin, "The Myth of the Vanishing Voter," *American Political Science Review* 95 (December 2001), pp. 963–74.

[17]For a detailed comparison of turnout among social groups in the 2000 election, see Abramson, Aldrich, and Rohde, *Change and Continuity in the 2000 Elections,* pp. 77–84.

[18]Raymond E. Wolfinger and Jonathan Hoffman, "Registering and Voting with Motor Voter," *PS: Political Science and Politics* 34 (March 2001), pp. 85–92. See also Benjamin

indicate that reforms aimed at increasing voter turnout by easing registration requirements or extending voting hours would have little impact on either the partisan composition of the U.S. electorate or the outcomes of elections.[19]

There are two main reasons why reforms aimed at increasing turnout are unlikely to have a dramatic impact on either the social composition of the electorate or election outcomes. First, the additional voters would constitute a relatively small proportion of the entire electorate. Even if it were possible to increase turnout by 10 percentage points—a very optimistic projection—the additional voters would constitute less than one-sixth of the electorate. In addition, the individuals most likely to be affected by such reforms would not be hard-core nonvoters, those with little or no interest in government and politics, but marginal nonvoters, those with a moderate level of interest in government and politics. The social characteristics and partisan orientations of these marginal nonvoters tend to be similar to those of voters. Therefore, adding them to the electorate probably would not dramatically alter either the social composition of the electorate or the outcomes of elections.[20]

PARTISANSHIP AND VOTING

Since the publication of *The American Voter* in 1960, political scientists have generally divided the factors that influence voting decisions and election outcomes into two types: **short-term forces** and **long-term forces.** Short-term forces include the issues, candidates, and conditions peculiar to a given election while the most important long-term force is the distribution of **party identification** within the electorate. The authors of *The American Voter* found that party identification was far more stable than attitudes toward issues and candidates. As a result, party identification exerted a strong influence on individual voting decisions both directly and indirectly, through its influence on attitudes toward the candidates and issues.[21]

Highton and Raymond E. Wolfinger, "Estimating the Effects of the National Voter Registration Act of 1993," *Political Behavior* 20 (June 1998), pp. 79–104.

[19] Benjamin Highton and Raymond E. Wolfinger, "The Political Implications of Higher Turnout," *British Journal of Political Science* 31 (January 2001), pp. 179–223.

[20] Raymond E. Wolfinger and Steven J. Rosenstone, *Who Votes?* (New Haven, CT: Yale University Press, 1980).

[21] Angus Campbell, Philip E. Converse, Warren E. Miller, and Donald E. Stokes, *The American Voter* (New York: John Wiley and Sons, 1960).

More recent research has demonstrated that short-term forces such as attitudes toward issues and candidates can influence party identification.[22] However, this research has also confirmed the earlier finding that party identification is more stable than other political attitudes and exerts a much stronger influence on these attitudes than they exert on party identification during the course of a single election campaign. Therefore, the distribution of party identification remains a key influence on the outcomes of elections in the United States.[23]

Today, the American electorate is almost evenly divided between those who identify with the Democratic Party and those who identify with the Republican Party. According to the 2000 Voter News Service exit poll of over 13,000 voters across the United States, 39 percent of the voters in the presidential election identified themselves as Democrats, 35 percent as Republicans, and 27 percent as independents. This is similar to the partisan division of the electorate in other recent elections, but it represents a substantial change from the situation that existed during the 1960s and 1970s when Democratic identifiers greatly outnumbered Republicans. In the 1976 national exit poll, for example, Democrats outnumbered Republicans by a margin of 40 percent to 25 percent.

Just as striking as the nearly even division of the U.S. electorate between the parties was the high level of party line voting in the 2000 presidential election. According to the exit poll data, Democratic identifiers favored Al Gore over George W. Bush by an impressive margin of 86 percent to 11 percent. Despite the fears of Democratic Party leaders and strategists that many liberal Democrats would be attracted to the candidacy of consumer advocate and Green Party

---

[22] Benjamin I. Page and Calvin C. Jones, "Reciprocal Effects of Policy Preferences, Party Loyalties, and the Vote," *American Political Science Review* 73 (December 1979), pp. 1071–89; Charles H. Franklin and John E. Jackson, "The Dynamics of Party Identification," *American Political Science Review* 77 (December 1983), pp. 957–73; Michael B. MacKuen, Robert S. Erikson, and James A. Stimson, "Macropartisanship," *American Political Science Review* 83 (December 1989), pp. 1125–42.

[23] Philip E. Converse and Gregory B. Markus, "Plus Ca Change: The New CPS Election Study Panel," *American Political Science Review* 73 (March 1979), pp. 32–49; Gregory B. Markus and Philip E. Converse, "A Dynamic Simultaneous Equation Model of Electoral Choice," *American Political Science Review* 73 (March 1979), pp. 55–70; Morris P. Fiorina, *Retrospective Voting in American National Elections* (New Haven, CT: Yale University Press, 1981); M. Kent Jennings and Richard G. Niemi, *Generations and Politics* (Princeton, NJ: Princeton University Press, 1981); Paul R. Abramson and Charles Ostrom, "Macropartisanship: An Empirical Reassessment," *American Political Science Review* 85 (March 1991), pp. 181–92.

nominee Ralph Nader, only 2 percent of Democrats defected to Nader. Republican identifiers were even more loyal to their party's candidate, favoring Governor Bush over Vice President Gore by a 91 percent to 8 percent margin. Only 1 percent of Republicans cast their ballot for Nader and virtually none were drawn to the candidacy of Reform Party nominee and former right-wing talk-show host Pat Buchanan. Meanwhile, voters who identified themselves as independents split their ballots almost evenly, favoring Bush over Gore by a narrow 47 percent to 45 percent margin with only 6 percent opting for Nader and only 1 percent for Buchanan. With almost 90 percent of Democratic and Republican identifiers supporting their own party's nominee, the level of party line voting in the 2000 presidential election was the highest in any presidential election since at least 1976.

The results of the 2000 elections clearly contradict the conventional wisdom that party loyalty in the American electorate has been steadily declining and is now a thing of the past. In fact, there is convincing evidence that the widely heralded decline in partisanship in recent decades was exaggerated and that partisanship in the electorate has rebounded in recent decades.[24] Since the 1970s, the percentage of American voters who identify themselves as Republicans or Democrats and the percentage of these party identifiers who cast their presidential and congressional ballots along party lines have increased.

What explains this resurgence of partisanship in the U.S. electorate? As we saw in Chapter 3, at least part of the explanation appears to be that since the 1970s the U.S. electorate has undergone an **ideological realignment.** The increasing ideological polarization of Democratic and Republican leaders in the Reagan and post-Reagan eras has made it easier for voters to recognize the differences between the parties' policy stands. As a result, more voters have been choosing their party identification on the basis of their policy preferences rather than maintaining the party allegiance that they inherited from their parents. Many conservatives who were raised by Democratic or independent parents have shifted their allegiance to the Republican Party. At the same time, a smaller number of liberals who were raised by Republican or independent parents have shifted their allegiance to the Democratic Party. The major results of this realignment are that the advantage in party identification that the Democratic Party

---

[24]Larry M. Bartels, "Partisanship and Voting Behavior, 1952–1996," *American Journal of Political Science* 44 (January 2000), pp. 35–50.

enjoyed from the 1930s through the 1970s has been substantially reduced and there is now a closer correspondence between party identification and ideology in the overall electorate.[25]

Since 1980, the ideological center of the Democratic Party has
shifted left while the ideological center of the Republican Party has
shifted right. The increased correspondence between party identification and ideology in the American electorate means that these two
factors are more likely to reinforce each other than in the past and
fewer Democratic and Republican identifiers are likely to be attracted to the policies of the opposing party's candidates. The result
has been an increased level of party line voting, as seen in the 2000
presidential election.

SHORT-TERM FORCES IN
PRESIDENTIAL ELECTIONS

Party identification is the single best predictor of candidate choice in
presidential elections. However, the distribution of party loyalties in
the electorate is usually fairly stable from one election to the next
while election outcomes can vary considerably. For example, there
was very little change in the partisan composition of the electorate
between 1996 and 2000, but the results of the two elections were quite
different. With the electorate almost evenly divided between Democratic and Republican identifiers, the outcomes of recent presidential
elections have been determined by a relatively small group of **swing
voters:** independents and weak partisans whose decisions are based
on short-term factors such as the state of the economy, current policy issues, and perceptions of the candidates' personal qualities. The
closeness of the 2000 election reflected the facts that not only the
long-term forces but also the short-term forces were evenly balanced.

Personal Qualities

Evaluations of presidential candidates are strongly influenced by
party identification. However, the candidates' personalities do have
an independent impact on voter decision-making. Although few
Americans have an opportunity to meet presidential candidates in
person, most voters form opinions about the candidates' personal

---

[25] Alan I. Abramowitz and Kyle L. Saunders, "Ideological Realignment in the U.S. Electorate," *Journal of Politics* (August 1998), pp. 634–52.

qualities based on what they read or see in the media. Once formed, these **candidate images** can persist long after the information on which they were based has been forgotten.[26] Since the 1950s, television has played an increasingly important role in shaping the public's images of presidential candidates and voters who rely primarily on television for political information seem to be influenced more by evaluations of the candidates' personal qualities than voters who rely primarily on newspapers.[27]

Political scientists have found that two of the most important personal qualities that voters consider in evaluating a candidate for public office are competence and trustworthiness.[28] During the 2000 election campaign, Americans generally saw Al Gore and George W. Bush as having distinct and offsetting personal strengths and weaknesses. Voters generally gave Vice President Gore higher marks than Governor Bush on traits related to competence such as knowledge, intelligence, and experience; on the other hand, voters generally found Governor Bush to be more honest and trustworthy than the Vice President, perhaps due to Mr. Gore's close association with Bill Clinton and his spirited defense of the President during the Monica Lewinsky scandal. For example, a Newsweek Poll conducted 3 weeks before the 2000 election asked a national sample of registered voters to rate Gore and Bush on a variety of personal traits. Eighty-two percent of the respondents described Gore as "intelligent and well informed" compared with only 69 percent for Bush. On the other hand, 63 percent of the respondents described Bush as "honest and ethical" compared with only 52 percent for Gore.

Policy Voting

Political scientists generally divide issues into two types: **policy issues** and **performance issues.** Policy issues involve candidates' positions on controversial policy questions such as government regulation of abortion, affirmative action, and national health insurance. In contrast, performance issues involve the ability of the candidates to

[26]Milton Lodge, Marco R. Steenbergen, and Shawn Brau, "The Responsive Voter: Campaign Information and the Dynamics of Candidate Evaluation," *American Political Science Review* 89 (June 1995), pp. 309–26.

[27]Scott Keeter, "The Illusion of Intimacy: Television and the Role of Candidate Personal Qualities in Voter Choice," *Public Opinion Quarterly* 51 (Autumn 1987), pp. 344–58.

[28]See Arthur H. Miller, Martin P. Wattenberg, and Oksana Malanchuk, "Schematic Assessments of Presidential Candidates," *American Political Science Review* 80 (June 1986), pp. 521–40.

achieve consensual goals such as peace and prosperity. Policy voting requires that candidates take differing positions and that voters accurately perceive these positions.[29] In contrast, performance voting only requires that voters judge one candidate as more likely to achieve the desired goal. This judgment is, in turn, based largely on whether the voter considers the incumbent's recent performance to be satisfactory or unsatisfactory.[30] For this reason, performance voting requires less information and less attention to the current campaign than policy voting.

Some observers of American elections have argued that an important obstacle to policy voting is that, when it comes to their positions on controversial issues, the Republicans and Democrats are often as indistinguishable as Tweedledum and Tweedledee. In *An Economic Theory of Democracy,* Anthony Downs proposes a **spatial theory of voting** to explain this phenomenon. Downs argued that in a two-party system such as that found in the United States, where the ideological distribution of the electorate follows a normal, or bell-shaped curve, rational politicians have a strong incentive to position themselves as close as possible to the center of that ideological distribution to maximize their electoral support (see Figure 6.1). In addition, Downs argued that rational politicians will often try to be vague or ambiguous about their positions on controversial issues to avoid offending potential supporters on either side of the liberal-conservative divide.[31]

There are several reasons why the positions of the Democratic and Republican presidential candidates on controversial policy issues may not be as vague or indistinguishable as Downs's theory suggests, however. As we saw in Chapter 5, to be nominated, presidential candidates must appeal to their party's primary voters and activists. Democratic candidates must appeal to Democratic primary voters and activists, who tend to be quite liberal in their policy views, while Republican candidates must appeal to Republican primary voters and activists, who tend to be quite conservative.[32] After

---

[29] See Richard A. Brody and Benjamin I. Page, "Comment: The Assessment of Policy Voting," *American Political Science Review* 66 (June 1972), pp. 450–58.

[30] The impact of evaluations of past party performance on voter decision-making in different types of elections is examined in Morris P. Fiorina, *Retrospective Voting in American National Elections* (New Haven, CT: Yale University Press, 1981).

[31] Anthony Downs, *An Economic Theory of Democracy* (New York: HarperCollins, 1957), chapter 8.

[32] James McCann, "Nomination Politics and Ideological Polarization: Assessing the Attitudinal Effects of Campaign Involvement," *Journal of Politics* 57 (February 1995),

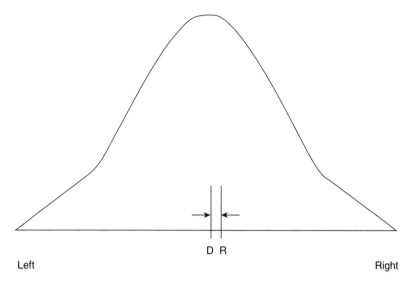

D R

Left   Right

FIGURE 6.1 A Spatial Model of Party Competition in the United States

winning their party's nominations, the Republican and Democratic presidential candidates cannot abandon the positions that they took during the primaries without appearing inconsistent or dishonest.

Beyond the need to appear consistent, the presidential candidates may take distinctive positions on policy issues during the general election campaign because of differences in voters' levels of interest and attentiveness. Generally speaking, citizens with extremely liberal or extremely conservative views care more deeply about policy issues, are better informed about candidates' positions on these issues, and are more likely to vote than citizens with more moderate views.[33] Therefore, the candidates may take distinctive positions to

pp. 101–20. See also Jeane Kirkpatrick, *The New Presidential Elite* (New York: Russell Sage Foundation, 1976), chapter 10. Several studies have found that the policy views of voters in primary elections are generally respresentative of the views of party identifiers in the electorate. On this point, see Barbara Norrander, "Ideological Representativeness of Presidential Primary Voters," *American Journal of Political Science* 33 (August 1989), pp. 570–87; John G. Geer, "Assessing the Representativeness of Electorates in Presidential Primaries," *American Journal of Political Science* 32 (November 1988), pp. 929–45; and Austin Ranney, "The Representativeness of Primary Electorates," *Midwest Journal of Political Science* 12 (May 1968), pp. 224–38.

[33] Thomas R. Palfrey and Keith T. Poole, "The Relationship Between Information, Ideology, and Voting Behavior," *American Journal of Political Science* 31 (August 1987), pp. 511–30.

TABLE 6.1 Mean Location of Voters and
Presidential Candidates on 7-Point Liberal-
Conservative Scale, 1972–2000

Year	Democratic Candidate	Average Voter	Republican Candidate
1972	2.36	4.15	4.91
1976	3.12	4.28	4.97
1980	3.63	4.33	5.36
1984	3.32	4.27	5.15
1988	3.04	4.45	5.27
1992	3.08	4.20	5.19
1996	3.02	4.42	5.22
2000	3.09	4.32	5.08

Source: American National Election Studies.

appeal to these liberal or conservative issue voters. In addition, some politicians may be concerned about more than just winning—they may have personal policy preferences that they want to advance. These preferences are usually liberal in the case of Democratic politicians and conservative in the case of Republican politicians.[34]

An examination of voters' perceptions of the ideological positions of the Democratic and Republican candidates in every presidential election between 1972 and 2000 does not support Downs's expectation that the candidates would converge at the center of the ideological distribution of the electorate (see Table 6.1). In every one of these elections, voters perceived a clear difference between the ideological positions of the major party candidates. In every election, the Democratic candidate was viewed as well to the left of the average voter while the Republican candidate was viewed as well to the right.

The impact of policy voting on the outcome of a presidential election depends on both the clarity of the differences between the candidates and the relative proximity of the candidates' positions to those of the voters.[35] In 1996 and 2000, voters perceived clear

[34]See John W. Kingdon, *Candidates for Office: Beliefs and Strategies* (New York: Random House, 1968).
[35]See Gerald M. Pomper, "From Confusion to Clarity: Issues and American Voters, 1956–1968," *American Political Science Review* 66 (June 1972), pp. 415–28; See also Brody and Page, "Comment: The Assessment of Policy Voting," *American Political Science Review* 66 (June 1972), pp. 450–58; John H. Kessel, "Comment: The Issues in Issue Voting," *American Political Science Review* 66 (June 1972), pp. 459–65; and Benjamin I.

differences between the positions of the Democratic and Republican presidential candidates on a variety of specific policy issues ranging from environmental regulation to abortion. On every one of these issues, the Democratic candidate was perceived as considerably more liberal than the Republican candidate. In both elections, however, the electorate was very closely divided in terms of perceived proximity to the major party candidates (see Table 6.2). On some issues, such as government spending and services, federal responsibility for jobs and living standards, and aid to blacks, a plurality or majority of voters preferred the position of the Republican candidate. On other issues, such as abortion, environmental regulation, and women's rights, a plurality or majority of voters preferred the position of the Democratic candidate. On average, in both elections, voters were almost evenly divided in terms of proximity to the presidential candidates. As a result, the impact of policy voting on the outcomes of both elections was probably slight. While Al Gore might have done better if he had been perceived as more moderate on certain issues, there is no evidence here that he lost the election because he was viewed as further to the left of the average voter than Bill Clinton was in 1996.

We can use data from the VNS national exit poll to assess the impact of policy preferences on individual voting decisions in the 2000 presidential election. In the exit poll, voters were asked about their general ideological orientation along with their views on a wide variety of specific policy issues. We can combine respondents' ideological self-identification as liberal, moderate, or conservative with their opinions on five specific policy issues—taxation, school vouchers, a federal prescription drug benefit, investment of social security funds in the stock market, and gun control—to create an overall liberal-conservative policy index with scores ranging from 1 (consistently liberal) to 8 (consistently conservative).

In Chapter 3 we showed that, since the 1980s, Americans have increasingly been choosing their party identification on the basis of their policy orientations.[36] It is not surprising, therefore, that the policy views of most voters in 2000 were consistent with their party identification: the mean score on the liberal-conservative policy index was 3.1 for Democrats compared with 3.9 for independents and 5.3 for Republicans. However, among the minority of voters whose

---

Page and Richard A. Brody, "Policy Voting and the Electoral Process: The Vietnam War Issue," *American Political Science Review* 66 (September 1972), pp. 979–95.

[36] Abramowitz and Saunders, "Ideological Realignment in the U.S. Electorate."

TABLE 6.2 Relative Issue Proximity to Candidates Among Voters in 1996 and 2000 Presidential Elections

Issue	1996	2000
Liberal-Conservative scale		
Closer to Democrat	40%	42%
Equal distance	14	14
Closer to Republican	46	44
Spending-Services scale		
Closer to Democrat	36	37
Equal distance	18	20
Closer to Republican	46	42
Jobs/Living Standards scale		
Closer to Democrat	31	29
Equal distance	22	24
Closer to Republican	47	47
Aid to blacks		
Closer to Democrat	28	27
Equal distance	22	24
Closer to Republican	50	49
Abortion		
Closer to Democrat	45	40
Equal distance	22	24
Closer to Republican	33	36
Environment/Job scale		
Closer to Democrat	40	38
Equal distance	29	29
Closer to Republican	31	33
Environmental Regulation scale		
Closer to Democrat	40	43
Equal distance	30	27
Closer to Republican	30	30
Women's Rights scale		
Closer to Democrat	42	32
Equal distance	37	51
Closer to Republican	21	17
Gun Control scale		
Closer to Democrat	NA	37
Equal distance	NA	30
Closer to Republican	NA	33
Average of eight issues		
Closer to Democrat	38	36
Equal distance	24	27
Closer to Republican	38	37

Source: American National Election Studies.

NA = data not available.

ideological orientation was inconsistent with their party identification—conservative Democrats and liberal Republicans—the rate
of partisan defection was much higher than among other partisans.

Forty-two percent of conservative Democrats (those with scores
of greater than 4 on the liberal-conservative policy index) voted for
George W. Bush compared with only 8 percent of all other Democrats. Similarly, 30 percent of liberal Republicans (those with scores
of less than 4 on the liberal-conservative policy index) voted for Al
Gore compared with only 5 percent of all other Republicans. In addition, policy orientation was strongly related to candidate choice
among independents—81 percent of liberal independents voted for
Al Gore compared with only 18 percent of conservative independents. Thus, even though policy issues may not have had a major impact on the outcome of the presidential election, they did influence
individual voting decisions.

Performance Voting

In addition to allowing voters to express their opinions about the
policies advocated by the candidates, a presidential election also provides voters with an opportunity to express their satisfaction or dissatisfaction with the performance of the incumbent president. Voting
based on one's evaluation of the performance of the incumbent president is known as **retrospective voting** and one of the most important
areas in which presidents are judged by the electorate is their management of the economy.[37] Although presidents share responsibility
for economic policy with Congress and the Federal Reserve Board,
it is much easier for the public to hold the president accountable for
the performance of the economy than these other actors. The president is an individual, not a collectivity, and his actions are much
more visible and understandable to the public than those of either
Congress or the Federal Reserve Board. Just as important, the president and vice president are the only public officials elected by the entire nation.

---

[37]Fiorina, *Retrospective Voting in American National Elections.* See also Gerald H.
Kramer, "Short-Term Fluctuations in U.S. Voting Behavior, 1896–1964," *American Po-
litical Science Review* 65 (March 1971), pp. 131–43; Michael S. Lewis-Beck, *Economics
and Elections: The Major Western Democracies* (Ann Arbor, MI: University of Michigan
Press, 1988); D. Roderick Kiewiet, *Macroeconomics and Micropolitics: The Electoral Effects
of Economic Issues* (Chicago: University of Chicago Press, 1983); and Robert S. Erikson,
"Economic Conditions and the Presidential Vote," *American Political Science Review* 83
(June 1989), pp. 567–73.

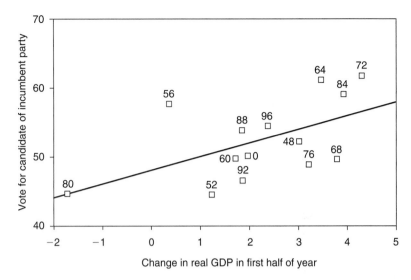

FIGURE 6.2 Vote by Real GDP Change in U.S. Presidential Elections, 1948–2000

Voters' evaluations of economic conditions are influenced by their party affiliation—those who identify with the president's party generally have a more positive view of economic conditions than those who identify with the opposition party. However, after controlling for party identification, there was a clear relationship between evaluations of economic conditions and voting decisions in the 2000 presidential election. This relationship was especially strong among independents, who comprise a large proportion of the swing vote in presidential elections. In the VNS exit poll, 72 percent of independents who rated economic conditions in the United States as "excellent" voted for Al Gore. In contrast, only 29 percent of independents who rated economic conditions as "not good" or "poor" voted for Gore.

If voters hold the president largely responsible for the economic condition of the nation, we should find a relationship between the performance of the U.S. economy and the outcomes of presidential elections. To test this hypothesis, Figure 6.2 displays the relationship between the percentage of the major party vote won by the candidate of the president's party and the change in real gross domestic product (GDP) during the first half of the election year, for all presidential elections since the end of World War II. The reason for using change in real GDP during the first half of the election year is that there may be a delay between changes in economic conditions and public awareness of these changes. Each point in this diagram represents a single presidential election. The straight line, called a regression line, shows the predicted vote for the candidate of the president's party based on the performance of the economy. If the outcomes of presidential elections could be predicted perfectly based on the performance of the economy, all of the points would fall exactly on this line.

As expected, the diagram shows that there is a positive relationship between the performance of the economy and the outcomes of presidential elections: the stronger the economy, the greater the vote for the candidate of the president's party. This is true whether that candidate is the president himself or someone else. However, the relationship between economic conditions and election results is far from perfect. The correlation between these two variables is .55, which means that only 30 percent of the variation in presidential election outcomes is explained by changes in real GDP. In some elections, such as 1956, the candidate from the president's party did far better than one would expect based on the performance of the economy. In other elections, such as 1968, the candidate from the president's party did considerably worse than one would expect based on the performance of the economy. In 2000, Vice President Gore did slightly worse than expected based on the growth rate of just under 2 percent during the first half of the year. He should have received about 51 percent of the major party vote instead of just over 50 percent.

The results in Figure 6.2 suggest that the outcomes of presidential elections are influenced by factors other than the performance of the economy. Managing the economy is only one part of the president's job description. The American people also expect the president to provide leadership in international affairs, recommend legislation to deal with domestic problems, and set a moral tone for the nation. The president's performance in all of these areas may affect the results of presidential elections.[38]

In the 2000 VNS exit poll, a national sample of voters were asked to express their opinion of President Clinton's overall job perfor-

---

[38] See Lee Sigelman, "Presidential Popularity and Presidential Elections," *Public Opinion Quarterly* 43 (Winter 1979), pp. 532–34. See also Richard Brody and Lee Sigelman, "Presidential Popularity and Presidential Elections: An Update and Extension," *Public Opinion Quarterly* 47 (Autumn 1983), pp. 325–28; and Michael S. Lewis-Beck and Tom W. Rice, "Presidential Popularity and Presidential Vote," *Public Opinion Quarterly* 46 (Winter 1982), pp. 534–37.

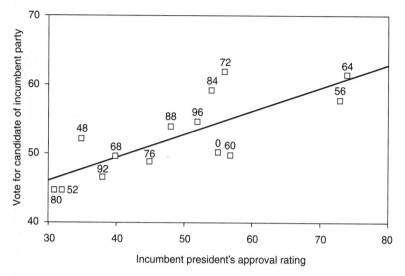

FIGURE 6.3 Vote by Incumbent President's Approval Rating at Midyear, 1948–2000

mance: 58 percent of the respondents approved of the President's performance while 42 percent disapproved. Although Bill Clinton was not on the ballot, there was a very strong relationship between voters' evaluations of the President's job performance and their candidate choice in the presidential election. Seventy-nine percent of voters who approved of President Clinton's job performance voted for the Democratic presidential candidate, Al Gore. In contrast, 91 percent of voters who disapproved of Mr. Clinton's job performance voted for the Republican presidential candidate, George W. Bush.

Since the 1940s, the Gallup Poll has regularly asked a representative sample of Americans to evaluate the president's overall job performance. Figure 6.3 displays the relationship between the incumbent president's approval rating at midyear in the Gallup Poll and the percentage of the major party vote received by the candidate of the president's party in all presidential elections since World War II. The reason for using the president's approval rating at midyear, before the national nominating conventions, is that it provides a measure of performance that is not influenced by either the conventions themselves or the subsequent general election campaign.

As expected, the data in Figure 6.3 show that there is a strong relationship between the incumbent president's approval rating and the outcomes of presidential elections: the higher the president's approval rating, the greater the vote for his party's candidate, whether that candidate is the president or someone else. This relationship is substantially stronger than the relationship between the performance of the economy and the outcomes of presidential elections. The correlation between these two variables is .78, which means that 61 percent of the variation in presidential election outcomes is explained by the incumbent president's approval rating. However, the relationship between presidential approval ratings and election outcomes is still far from perfect. In some elections, such as 1972, the candidate from the president's party did better than one would expect based on the incumbent president's approval rating. In other elections, such as 1960 and 2000, the candidate from the president's party did worse than one would expect based on the incumbent president's approval rating. Based on President Clinton's approval rating of 55 percent in June 2000, Al Gore should have received about 53 percent of the major party vote in November instead of just over 50 percent.

The Time for Change Factor

Why did Al Gore do worse than expected based on both the performance of the U.S. economy and President Clinton's approval rating prior to the 2000 election? Political observers have blamed Mr. Gore's defeat on a variety of factors including his failure to claim credit for the strong performance of the economy during the campaign, his weak showing in the presidential debates, and his reluctance to allow President Clinton to campaign for him in key states such as Arkansas and Tennessee. However, one major reason for Al Gore's defeat may have been the **time for change factor.** After a party has controlled the White House for 8 years or longer, regardless of the popularity of the president or the state of the economy, there is increased sentiment among the electorate that it's simply time for a change.[39]

Since 1900, there have been 10 elections in which the president's party had been in office for only 4 years. The candidate of the president's party won 9 of these 10 elections. During this same time period, there have been 16 elections in which the president's party had been in office for 8 years or longer. The candidate of the president's party won only seven of these elections while losing nine. Since World War II, the president's party has won five of six elections

[39] For a discussion of the time for change factor in presidential elections, see Alan I. Abramowitz, "An Improved Model for Predicting Presidential Election Outcomes," *PS: Political Science and Politics* 21 (December 1988), pp. 843–47.

and averaged 56.6 percent of the major party vote after one term in office while losing six of eight elections and averaging only 49.5 percent of the major party vote after two or more terms in office. Thus, in 2000, Vice President Gore may have been a victim of the time for change sentiment of the electorate after a party has controlled the White House for 8 years or longer.

PREDICTING RESULTS

If a presidential election is, to a large extent, a referendum on the performance of the incumbent president and his administration, we should be able to predict the outcomes of these contests with a high degree of accuracy based on factors that are known before the general election campaign begins. By using a statistical procedure called multiple regression analysis, we can test the accuracy of a model for predicting the outcomes of presidential elections based on three such factors: the growth rate of the economy during the first half of the election year, the incumbent president's approval rating in June, and the length of time that the president's party has held office. Regression analysis assigns a weight to each factor, or independent variable, to produce the most accurate possible prediction of our dependent variable: the percentage of the major party vote won by the candidate of the president's party.

A multiple regression analysis, based on data from all 14 presidential elections since the end of World War II, produces the following results:

$$PV = 42.0 + .193 \cdot APPROVE + 1.70 \cdot GDP - 4.93 \cdot CHANGE.$$

In this equation, PV represents the predicted share of the major party vote for the candidate of the president's party, APPROVE represents the incumbent president's approval rating in the June Gallup Poll, GDP represents the increase or decrease in real gross domestic product in the first two quarters of the election year, and CHANGE represents the time for change factor that takes on the value 0 if the president's party has held office for 4 years and 1 if the president's party has held office for 8 or more years. All of the estimated weights, or coefficients, are highly statistically significant ($p < .01$). This means that there is less than one chance in 100 that the results are due to chance factors. Taken together, our three predictors explain 89 percent of the variation in the outcomes of presidential elections since World War II.

TABLE 6.3 Accuracy of Referendum Model
of U.S. Presidential Elections

Presidential Election	Predicted Vote	Actual Vote	Difference (Actual − Predicted)
1948	49.0%	52.2%	+3.2%
1952	45.4	44.6	−0.8
1956	56.7	57.7	+1.0
1960	51.0	49.9	−1.1
1964	62.2	61.3	−0.9
1968	51.3	49.7	−1.6
1972	60.1	61.8	+1.7
1976	51.2	48.9	−2.3
1980	45.1	44.7	−0.4
1984	59.1	59.2	+0.1
1988	49.5	53.9	+4.4
1992	47.6	46.6	−1.0
1996	56.1	54.6	−1.5
2000	51.1	50.2	−0.9

Source: Data compiled by author.

The coefficient of the APPROVE variable (.193) means that an increase of one percentage point in the incumbent president's approval rating in June would be expected to increase the share of the major party vote for the candidate of the president's party in November by an average of almost 0.2 percentage points. Similarly, the coefficient of the GDP variable (1.70) means that an increase of one percentage point in real gross domestic product in the first 6 months of the election year would be expected to increase the share of the major party vote for the candidate of the president's party in November by an average of 1.7 percentage points. Finally, the coefficient of the CHANGE variable (−4.93) means that after controlling for both economic conditions and presidential popularity, the candidate of the president's party is penalized by almost five percentage points if his party has controlled the White House for 8 years or longer.

The results of this multiple regression analysis demonstrate that the outcomes of presidential elections are largely determined by factors that are known before the general election campaign begins. Taken together, the growth rate of the economy during the first half of the election year, the popularity of the incumbent president at midyear, and the length of time that the president's party has controlled the White House explain almost 90 percent of the variation in the outcomes of presidential elections.

Table 6.3 shows the relationship between the actual and predicted outcomes of all 14 presidential elections since the end of

World War II. The average margin of error of these predictions is only 1.5 percentage points. This is about half the average margin of error of the final preelection Gallup Poll. Nevertheless, the model predicts the wrong popular vote winner in 4 of these 14 elections: 1948, 1960, 1968, and 1988. However, the model does very well in predicting the outcome of the 2000 election. Based on President Clinton's 55 percent approval rating in June 2000, the 2.0 percent growth rate of the U.S. economy during the first half of the year, and the fact that the Democratic Party had controlled the White House for 8 years, Al Gore should have received 51.1 percent of the major party vote, only slightly more than his actual vote of 50.2 percent.

The results of the referendum model have important implications for the 2004 presidential election. We can make conditional predictions of George W. Bush's share of the major party vote in that election depending on his approval rating in June 2004 and the growth rate of the economy during the first half of that year. These predictions are presented in Table 6.4.

The predictions generated by the referendum model indicate that President Bush has an excellent chance of being reelected in 2004. Since 1900, only one U.S. president, Jimmy Carter in 1980, was defeated after his party had controlled the presidency for only 4 years. Carter was the victim of a devastating combination of high inflation, rising unemployment, and widespread dissatisfaction with his handling of the hostage crisis in Iran. However, since the end of World War II, first-term incumbents have averaged 56.5 percent of the major party vote and first-term Republican incumbents have averaged 59.6 percent of the major party vote. Based on these results,

TABLE 6.4 Conditional Predictions of George W. Bush's Share of Major Party Vote in 2004 Presidential Election

Change in Real GDP During First Two Quarters of 2004	Bush's Approval Rating in June				
	30%	40%	50%	60%	70%
−2.0%	44.4%	46.3%	48.3%	50.2%	52.1%
−1.0	46.1	48.0	50.0	51.9	53.8
+0.0	47.8	49.7	51.7	53.6	55.5
+1.0	49.5	51.4	53.4	55.3	57.2
+2.0	51.2	53.1	55.1	57.0	58.9
+3.0	52.9	54.8	56.8	58.7	60.6

Source: Data compiled by author.

if President Bush keeps his approval rating above 50 percent and avoids a recession during 2004, he should have a good chance of winning a second term in the White House.

DO PRESIDENTIAL CAMPAIGNS MATTER?

The results produced by the referendum model of presidential elections raise an important question about the effects of presidential campaigns. Since we can explain almost 90 percent of the variation in the results of presidential elections based on factors that are known before the campaign begins, do the campaigns themselves matter? The answer to this question is that presidential campaigns do matter, but they usually have approximately equal and offsetting effects on the electorate. That is because the Democratic and Republican presidential candidates usually have approximately equal resources and conduct equally aggressive and competent campaigns. For example, a recent study of state-level presidential campaigning found that both personal visits and television ad buys lead to increased support for a candidate. However, the same study found that the opposing candidate usually matches such efforts within 2 weeks, thereby neutralizing whatever short-term gains have been achieved.[40] As a result, the outcomes of most presidential elections reflect the attitudes held by the electorate before the campaign began. In fact, the candidate leading in the first Gallup Poll after Labor Day has gone on to win every presidential election since World War II except 1948 and 1960.

The assumption that the major party candidates have approximately equal resources and conduct equally aggressive and competent campaigns does not apply equally well in all presidential elections, however. Some of the discrepancies between the predicted and actual outcomes of presidential elections undoubtedly reflect differences in the resources, organizational capabilities, and political skills of the presidential candidates. For example, President Truman probably did better than predicted by our model in 1948 in part because he ran a much more aggressive campaign than his Republican challenger, New York Governor Thomas E. Dewey. While Truman was barnstorming across the country, attacking the record of the "do-nothing" Republican Congress, Dewey was making plans for his in-

[40] Daron R. Shaw, "The Effect of TV Ads and Candidate Appearances on Statewide Presidential Votes, 1988–96," *American Political Science Review* 93 (June 1999), pp. 345–62.

auguration and interviewing potential cabinet appointees.[41] Likewise, President Bush probably exceeded our model's prediction in 1988 because his Democratic challenger, Massachusetts Governor Michael Dukakis, ran an inept campaign: Dukakis took a weeklong vacation after the Democratic Convention and failed to respond to a barrage of television ads by the Bush campaign attacking his record as governor and his opposition to the death penalty.[42] Elections like 1948 and 1988 are unusual, however. Most of the discrepancies between the predictions of the referendum model and the actual results of presidential elections are fairly small. Despite the enormous amounts of time, money, and effort expended on general election campaigns, their effects on the outcomes of presidential elections are usually minor.

Since the 1960s, the largest share of presidential campaign funds have been spent on television advertising. However, despite the millions of dollars that are spent every 4 years producing and airing 30-second **spot advertisements,** they appear to change very few voters' minds. Instead they seem to produce a **reinforcement effect:** effective political advertisements reinforce positive or negative attitudes that voters already hold about the presidential candidates.[43] For example, the "Morning in America" spots produced by the Reagan campaign in 1984, which showed ordinary Americans enjoying life and expressing patriotic feelings, reinforced the widely shared view that President Reagan had restored American pride and prosperity in the aftermath of the hostage crisis in Iran and economic problems

---

[41] For a brief description of the 1948 campaign, see Congressional Quarterly, *Guide to U.S. Elections,* Volume 1 (Washington, DC: Congressional Quarterly Press, 2001), pp. 268–71.

[42] See Congressional Quarterly, *Guide to U.S. Elections,* Volume 1, pp. 286–89. See also Sidney Blumenthal, *Pledging Allegiance: The Last Campaign of the Cold War* (New York: HarperCollins, 1990).

[43] Thomas E. Patterson and Robert D. McClure, *The Unseeing Eye: The Myth of Television Power in National Elections* (New York: Putnam, 1976). Patterson and McClure found that while exposure to television ads had little impact on evaluations of the candidates or voting intentions in the 1972 presidential election, citizens did gain information from the ads about the candidates' issue positions. Further evidence that exposure to TV ads can increase awareness of candidates' issue positions is provided in Craig Leonard Brians and Martin P. Wattenberg, "Campaign Issue Knowledge and Salience: Comparing Reception from TV Commercials, TV News and Newspapers," *American Journal of Political Science* 40 (February 1996), pp. 172–93. For a more critical assessment of the effects of television advertising in presidential elections, see Kathleen Hall Jamieson, *Packaging the Presidency: A History and Criticism of Presidential Campaign Advertising* (New York: Oxford University Press, 1992).

that occurred under Mr. Reagan's predecessor, Jimmy Carter. However, the ads apparently had little impact on voters' preferences in the presidential election: Mr. Reagan maintained a comfortable lead over his Democratic challenger, Walter Mondale, throughout the campaign. Similarly, the famous "Daisy Girl" ad produced by President Johnson's reelection campaign in 1964, in which a scene of a young girl picking petals from a daisy is transformed into a nuclear explosion, reinforced voters' fears that Johnson's Republican challenger, Arizona Senator Barry Goldwater, would lead the United States into a nuclear confrontation with the Soviet Union. However, there is no evidence that this ad, or any of the other ads produced for the Johnson campaign, influenced voters' candidate preferences: Johnson held a huge lead over Goldwater from the very beginning of the campaign until the very end.

THIRD-PARTY AND INDEPENDENT CANDIDATES

The Democratic and Republican candidates are not the only alternatives available to the voters in presidential elections. Every 4 years, a number of independent and **third-party candidates** appear on the presidential ballot, with the exact number varying from state to state. In 2000, in addition to George W. Bush and Al Gore, three candidates received more than 0.1 percent of the national popular vote: Green Party nominee Ralph Nader won 2.7 percent of the vote, Reform Party nominee Patrick Buchanan won just over 0.4 percent, and Libertarian Party nominee Harry Browne won just under 0.4 percent. Twelve other candidates received a total of 0.1 percent of the vote.

The year 2000 was not good for third-party and independent candidates. Their overall share of the vote, just over 3.7 percent, was the lowest in any presidential election since 1988. By way of contrast, in 1992 H. Ross Perot, running as an independent, won 18.9 percent of the national popular vote. This was the largest total for any independent or third-party candidate since former President Theodore Roosevelt ran as the candidate of the Progressive, or Bull Moose, Party in 1912.

Two major factors seem to explain much of the variation in support for third-party and independent candidates in U.S. presidential elections: the extent of public dissatisfaction with the two major parties and their nominees, and the visibility and resources of the third-party or independent candidates.[44] The first factor appears to largely explain why independent and third-party candidates did not fare well in 2000. After 8 years of uninterrupted economic growth, with the country not facing any immediate crisis, relatively few Americans were dissatisfied with the choices offered by the two major parties. In addition, the closeness of the race between George W. Bush and Al Gore may have deterred some citizens from "wasting" their votes on a third-party or independent candidate. In contrast, in 1992, in the aftermath of a major recession, Texas businessman H. Ross Perot was able to capitalize on widespread discontent with both President Bush and his Democratic challenger, Bill Clinton. In addition, Perot spent over $60 million of his personal fortune on his campaign.[45]

The winner-take-all system used by 48 of the 50 states for awarding electoral votes makes it difficult for third-party or independent candidates to affect the outcomes of presidential elections. No third-party or independent candidate has won any electoral votes since George Wallace in 1968. Even Wallace, who carried five southern states, was unable to deny an electoral vote majority to the Republican candidate, Richard Nixon. However, even without winning any electoral votes, third-party and independent candidates can affect the outcome of a close presidential election by drawing popular support disproportionately from one of the major party candidates.

According to exit poll data, most independent and third-party candidates in recent presidential elections, including H. Ross Perot in 1992, have taken votes about equally from the Democratic and Republican nominees. In the 2000 presidential election, however, Ralph Nader apparently took far more votes from Al Gore than from George Bush. When Nader voters were asked in the VNS exit poll how they would have voted if their candidate had not been on the ballot, they chose Gore over Bush by a margin of 50 percent to 20 percent with the remaining 30 percent indicating that they would not have voted for either one. Projecting these results onto the national popular vote, it appears that if Ralph Nader had not been on the ballot, Al Gore would have defeated George W. Bush by a margin of

[44]Steven J. Rosenstone, Roy L. Behr, and Edward H. Lazarus, *Third Parties in America: Citizen Response to Major Party Failure* (Princeton, NJ: Princeton University Press, 1996).
[45]For analyses of the Perot movement and its impact on American politics, see Ted G. Jelen, ed., *Ross for Boss: The Perot Phenomenon and Beyond* (Albany, NY: State University of New York Press, 2001).

well over a million votes. More importantly, it seems very likely that Mr. Gore would have carried both Florida and New Hampshire and thereby had a clear majority in the Electoral College.

SUMMARY

In the general election, presidential candidates must appeal to a much larger and more diverse electorate than in the primaries, and especially to independents and weak partisans who hold the balance of power. The candidates' strategies are also shaped by the Electoral College and by a system of public financing that was intended to limit the influence of large donors.

A candidate must receive a majority of votes in the Electoral College to become president. Although states with small populations are overrepresented in the Electoral College, the use of a winner-take-all rule by every state except Maine and Nebraska provides a powerful incentive for candidates to spend the vast majority of their time and money in populous states where the contest is competitive. In these states a relatively small swing in the popular vote can shift a large bloc of electoral votes.

Under the provisions of the 1974 Federal Election Campaign Act, the major party candidates automatically receive a federal grant to pay for their general election campaigns. Since the 1980s, however, the Democratic and Republican parties have increasingly supplemented these public funds with unregulated soft money.

In response to growing concern about rapid growth of soft money, Congress in 2002 enacted the most significant changes in federal campaign finance law since the 1970s, cutting off the flow of unregulated cash into the presidential campaigns. If it survives an expected court challenge, this new law could force future presidential candidates to either opt out of the public finance system or rely on public funds to conduct their campaigns.

Voter turnout is much higher in presidential elections than in other types of elections in the United States. Nevertheless, almost half of American citizens have not bothered to vote in recent presidential elections. Moreover, these nonvoters were not a cross-section of the entire population—they consisted disproportionately of the young, the poor, and members of racial and ethnic minority groups.

Political scientists generally divide the factors that influence the outcomes of elections into two types: short-term forces and long-term forces. Short-term forces include the issues, candidates, and conditions peculiar to a given election while the most important long-term force is the distribution of party identification within the electorate.

The increased correspondence between party identification and ideology in the American electorate means that fewer Democratic and Republican identifiers are likely to be attracted to the policies of the opposing party's candidates. The result has been an increased level of party line voting.

Party identification is the single best predictor of candidate choice in presidential elections. However, with the electorate almost evenly divided between Democratic and Republican identifiers, the outcomes of recent presidential elections have been determined by short-term factors such as the state of the economy, current policy issues, and perceptions of the candidates' personal qualities. Of the latter, competence and trustworthiness are usually given the greatest weight in voters' calculations.

Political scientists have described two types of issue voting: policy voting and performance voting. Policy voting requires that candidates take differing positions and that voters accurately perceive these positions. Performance voting only requires that voters perceive one candidate as more likely than the other to achieve such consensual goals as peace and prosperity. In this regard, voters appear to judge the presidential candidates on the basis of the job that the current incumbent is doing. A presidential election is, largely, a referendum on the performance of the incumbent president even if the incumbent is not running for reelection: the stronger the performance of the economy and the higher the incumbent's approval rating, the more support his party's candidate can expect to receive. However, after a party has controlled the White House for two terms or longer, regardless of the popularity of the president or the performance of the economy, Americans begin to feel that it's time for a change.

The outcomes of presidential elections can be predicted with a high degree of accuracy based on factors that are known before the campaign begins: the state of the economy, the popularity of the incumbent president, and the length of time that the president's party has controlled the White House. However, this does not mean that presidential campaigns are irrelevant.

Support for independent and third-party candidates has varied considerably in recent presidential elections depending on the extent of public dissatisfaction with the major party candidates and the visibility and resources of the third-party and independent candidates.

However, since George Wallace in 1968, no independent or third-party candidate has carried a state. In most recent presidential elections, independent and third-party candidates appear to have taken votes about equally from the Democrats and Republicans. In the election of 2000, however, Green Party candidate Ralph Nader, despite winning less than 3 percent of the national popular vote, may have affected the outcome by taking far more votes from Al Gore than from George W. Bush.

KEY TERMS AND CONCEPTS

Bipartisan Campaign Reform
  Act of 2002
candidate images
Electoral College
Federal Election Campaign Act
ideological realignment
long-term forces
National Voter Registration Act
  (Motor Voter Law)
party identification
performance issues
policy issues

public financing
reinforcement effect
retrospective voting
short-term forces
soft money
spatial theory of voting
spot advertisements
swing voters
third-party candidates
time for change factor
Twenty-third Amendment
winner-take-all rule

DISCUSSION QUESTIONS

1. How does the Electoral College influence the campaign strategies of presidential candidates? How would proposed reforms, such as proportional allocation of electoral votes within states or direct popular election of the president, affect the conduct of presidential campaigns and the importance of various states in presidential elections?
2. How will the passage of the Campaign Finance Reform Act of 2002 affect the conduct of future presidential campaigns? Will this law favor either Democrats or Republicans?
3. Why have recent reforms such as the Motor Voter Law failed to significantly increase voter turnout in presidential elections? What, if anything, can be done to increase turnout in future presidential elections and how would these reforms affect election results?

4. What are the most important differences between policy voting and performance voting? What factors influence the importance of policy and performance voting and how did each type of voting affect the outcome of the 2000 presidential election?
5. What is the spatial theory of voting and how well does it explain the behavior of candidates and voters in U.S. presidential elections?
6. How much effect do political campaigns have on the outcomes of presidential elections? What effect did the Bush and Gore campaigns have on the outcome of the 2000 presidential election?
7. What factors influence the level of support for independent and third-party candidates in U.S. presidential elections? Why did third-party candidates Ralph Nader and Patrick Buchanan not do very well in the 2000 presidential election and how would you expect independent and third-party candidates to fare in 2004?

SUGGESTED READINGS

Abramson, Paul H.; John H. Aldrich; and David W. Rohde. *Change and Continuity in the 2000 Elections.* Washington, DC: Congressional Quarterly Press, 2002. This is a detailed examination of trends in public opinion, voter turnout, and candidate choice in the presidential and congressional elections using data from the National Election Studies and is the latest in a series by the authors analyzing every presidential election since 1984.

Dalton, Russell J. *Citizen Politics: Public Opinion and Political Parties in Advanced Industrial Democracies,* 3rd ed. New York: Chatham House: 2002. Dalton does an excellent job of placing the U.S. party system and electoral process in a comparative political perspective. He underscores major similarities and differences between the electoral process in the U.S. and other Western democracies.

Downs, Anthony. *An Economic Theory of Democracy.* New York: HarperCollins, 1957. Downs's pioneering effort to develop a theory of democratic politics based on the assumption of rationality has been the starting point for almost all subsequent scholars using a rational choice approach. The spatial theory of party competition developed in chapter 8 has been especially influential in the study of American party politics.

Nelson, Michael, ed. *The Elections of 2000.* Washington, DC: Congressional Quarterly Press, 2001. Nelson has put together a fine collection of essays on the fascinating 2000 election including a thoughtful, balanced discussion of the extended postelection controversy by the editor.

Pomper, Gerald M., ed. *The Election of 2000.* New York: Chatham House 2001. This collection of essays by well-known election scholars examines various aspects of the 2000 election including the presidential nomination and general election campaigns, public opinion, and the role of the media. The essays by William Mayer on the nomination process and Anthony Corrado on campaign finance are especially useful.

Rosenstone, Steven J.; Roy L. Behr; and Edward H. Lazarus. *Third Parties in America: Citizen Response to Major Party Failure.* Princeton, NJ: Princeton University Press, 1996. The authors present a brief history of third parties in American politics along with a theoretical explanation for third-party success and failure.

Schumaker, Paul D., and Burdett A. Loomis. *Choosing a President: The Electoral College and Beyond.* New York: Chatham House, 2002. The most comprehensive scholarly examination of the Electoral College in many years, this collection includes essays analyzing the impact of the Electoral College on the presidential campaign, its consequences for governance, and proposed reforms including direct popular election.

INFORMATION SOURCES ON THE INTERNET

American National Election Studies: www.umich.edu/~nes/nesguide/nesguide.htm. This is the website for the NES Guide to Public Opinion and Electoral Behavior. The guide provides a wide range of information about the social characteristics, political attitudes, and voting behavior of the American electorate since 1952.

Federal Election Commission: www.fec.gov. The FEC is the agency responsible for enforcing the nation's campaign finance laws. Although it is sometimes considered a toothless tiger by reformers, the agency's website provides valuable information about federal election laws and regulations, election results, and campaign spending.

Gallup Poll: www.gallup.com. This site of the Gallup Poll, the nation's oldest and one of its most respected public opinion polling organizations, provides links to recent poll results on a wide range of topics including attitudes toward foreign and domestic issues, evaluations of presidential performance, and support for presidential candidates.

U.S. Census Bureau: www.census.gov/population/www/socdemo/voting.html. This site provides current and historical data from government surveys on voter registration and turnout. The data is broken down by a wide variety of demographic variables including age, race, gender, education, and family income.

CHAPTER 7

The Battle for
Control of Congress

The battle for control of Congress in 2000, like the battle for the White House, was excruciatingly close.[1] Republicans entered the 2000 election holding 223 seats in the House of Representatives to 210 for the Democrats along with two independents—one aligned with the Republicans and one with the Democrats. In the upper chamber, Republicans held a 54-46 majority and were defending 19 of the 34 seats at stake in the election.

In the House elections, Republicans maintained their narrow majority as Democrats scored a net gain of two seats. Out of 400 incumbents seeking reelection, only six—four Republicans and two Democrats—were defeated. In the 35 open seat contests, each party picked up 6 seats from the other. The new House would have 221 Republicans and 212 Democrats along with the same two independents as the old House—the closest party division in almost 50 years.

Senate incumbents were not quite as successful as their House counterparts—six of the 29 who ran for reelection were defeated including 5 Republicans and 1 Democrat. In the five open seat races

---

[1] Several good accounts of the 2000 congressional elections are available. See Paul R. Abramson, John H. Aldrich, and David W. Rohde, *Change and Continuity in the 2000 Elections* (Washington, DC: Congressional Quarterly Press, 2002), chapters 9–10; Gary C. Jacobson, "Congress: Elections and Stalemate," in Michael Nelson, ed., *The Elections of 2000* (Washington, DC: Congressional Quarterly Press, 2001), pp. 185–210; Paul S. Herrnson, "The Congressional Elections," in Gerald M. Pomper, ed., *The Election of 2000* (New York: Chatham House Publishers, 2001), pp. 155–76; and Sunil Ahuja and Robert Dewhirst, "The Congressional Elections of 2000," in Ahuja and Dewhirst, eds., *The Roads to Congress 2000* (Belmont, CA: Wadsworth Publishing, 2002), pp. 1–12.

there was no net shift in party strength as Democrats picked up a previously Republican seat in Florida while Republicans picked up a
previously Democratic seat in Nevada. Overall, Democrats scored
a net gain of four seats, resulting in a 50-50 split—the first tie in over
a century. With Vice President Cheney casting the tie-breaking vote,
it appeared that Republicans would keep control of the upper chamber in the 107th Congress. In May 2001, however, James Jeffords
of Vermont, one of the most liberal Republicans in the Senate, announced that he was changing his party affiliation to independent
and joining the Democratic caucus, giving the Democrats a precari-
ous 51-49 majority.[2]

THE PARADOX OF
CONGRESSIONAL ELECTIONS

The results of the 2000 House and Senate elections clearly illustrate
the **paradox of congressional elections** in the twenty-first century.
Competition between Democrats and Republicans for control of the
House and Senate has never been more intense. In both chambers, a
switch of only a handful of seats from one party to the other would
result in a change in party control. Party organizations and interest groups are pouring record amounts of money into congressional
campaigns in an effort to sway the outcome in one direction or the
other. At the same time, however, the overwhelming majority of individual House contests and most Senate contests are low-key, one-
sided affairs. In 2000, for example, the average margin of victory was
37 percentage points in House elections and 24 percentage points in
Senate elections. The remainder of this chapter will attempt to explain this paradox.

Competition for Control of Congress

Political scientists have long recognized that the most important
long-term influence on voting behavior and election outcomes in the
United States is **party identification** and today the American electorate is almost evenly divided between those who identify with the

---

[2]Helen Dewar and Mike Allen, "Senator Jeffords May Quit GOP; Move by Vermont Moderate Would Give Democrats Control of Senate," *Washington Post*, May 23,
2001, p. A1.

Democratic Party and those who identify with the Republican Party.[3] According to the Voter News Service exit poll of over 13,000 voters across the United States, 39 percent of the voters in the 2000 election identified themselves as Democrats, 35 percent as Republicans, and 27 percent as independents. This is similar to the partisan division of the electorate in other recent elections, but it represents a dramatic change from the situation that existed during the 1960s and 1970s when Democratic identifiers greatly outnumbered Republicans. In the 1976 national exit poll, for example, Democrats outnumbered Republicans by a 40 to 25 percent margin. Republican gains in party identification since 1980 have been a major factor in the GOP's growing success in congressional as well as state and local elections.

Just as striking as the nearly even division of the U.S. electorate between the parties was the high level of party loyalty among voters in the 2000 Senate and House elections. Exit poll data from the 10 most hotly contested U.S. Senate races of 2000 — Delaware, Florida, Michigan, Minnesota, Missouri, Montana, New Jersey, New York, Virginia, and Washington — showed a consistently high level of party voting (see Table 7.1). In these 10 states, between 84 and 91 percent of Democrats voted for their party's Senate candidate while between 83 and 91 percent of Republicans voted for their party's Senate candidate. The average rate of loyalty was 86 percent for Democrats and 87 percent for Republicans.

In every one of these closely contested Senate races, the party with more identifiers in the electorate was victorious. As a result, Democrats picked up six previously Republican seats — Delaware, Michigan, Missouri, Florida, Washington, and Minnesota — while Republicans picked up one previously Democratic seat — Virginia. In the eight contests won by Democrats, Democratic identifiers made up an average of 40 percent of the electorate while Republican identifiers made up an average of only 32 percent of the electorate. In the two contests won by Republicans, Democratic identifiers, on average, made up only 32 percent of the electorate while Republican identifiers, on average, made up 37 percent of the electorate. Thus, Democratic gains in the 2000 Senate elections were mainly attributable to

[3] For a discussion of recent trends in party identification in the U.S. electorate, see Abramson, Aldrich, and Rohde, *Change and Continuity in the 2000 Elections,* chapter 8. The growth of Republican identification in the electorate since 1980 is analyzed in Alan I. Abramowitz and Kyle L. Saunders, "Ideological Realignment in the U.S. Electorate," *Journal of Politics* 60 (August 1998), pp. 634–52.

TABLE 7.1 Party Identification and Voting in 10 Closely Contested U.S. Senate Elections, 2000

State	Party Id	Percentage of Electorate	Percentage Voting for	
			Democrat	Republican
Delaware	Democrats	42%	85%	14%
	Independents	27	52	45
	Republicans	31	17	83
Florida	Democrats	40	87	12
	Independents	22	46	46
	Republicans	38	13	86
Michigan	Democrats	38	85	14
	Independents	30	46	50
	Republicans	32	12	87
Minnesota	Democrats	36	84	11
	Independents	33	49	39
	Republicans	31	8	88
Missouri	Democrats	39	88	12
	Independents	23	47	50
	Republicans	38	13	86
Montana	Democrats	29	87	13
	Independents	34	51	46
	Republicans	37	12	85
New Jersey	Democrats	41	85	13
	Independents	29	43	50
	Republicans	30	10	89
New York	Democrats	45	85	14
	Independents	27	46	49
	Republicans	28	14	85
Virginia	Democrats	35	91	9
	Independents	28	42	58
	Republicans	37	8	91
Washington	Democrats	37	86	13
	Independents	34	44	52
	Republicans	29	11	88

Source: Voter News Service Exit Polls.

a return to normal partisan voting patterns 6 years after the Republican landslide of 1994.

Although exit poll data are not available for individual House races, the national exit poll data show a very high level of party line voting in the 2000 House elections as well. Altogether, 87 percent of Democratic identifiers and 91 percent of Republican identifiers voted for their own party's House candidate. Just as in the presidential election, independents split their ballots almost evenly with 49 percent voting for a Republican candidate and 46 percent for a Democratic candidate.

From the presidential election on down, the 2000 election was extremely partisan, with the results closely reflecting the distribution of party loyalties in each constituency. The nearly even division between the parties in the presidential election, the House of Representatives, and the Senate all reflected the nearly even division between Democrats and Republicans in the national electorate.

Competition for Individual House and Senate Seats

Despite the intensity of the battle for control of Congress in 2000, the large majority of individual House races and most Senate races were not very competitive (see Figures 7.1 and 7.2). The main reason for this was the **advantage of incumbency.**[4] More than 98 percent of House incumbents who ran for reelection were successful—slightly more than the average of 95 percent for House elections since 1970. Sixty-one incumbents, 31 Democrats and 30 Republicans, had no major party challenger and the average incumbent with a major party challenger received 67.4 percent of the two-party vote—the highest average since 1988. Only 21 percent of House incumbents with major party opposition received less than 60 percent of the two-party vote and only 9 percent received less than 55 percent of the two-party vote. In contrast, open seat races were much more competitive: 69 percent of the winning candidates received less than 60 percent of the two-party vote and 49 percent received less than 55 percent of the two-party vote.

---

[4]For a discussion of the advantage of incumbency in congressional elections and its sources, see Gary C. Jacobson, *The Politics of Congressional Elections,* 5th ed. (New York: Longman Publishers, 2001), chapter 3.

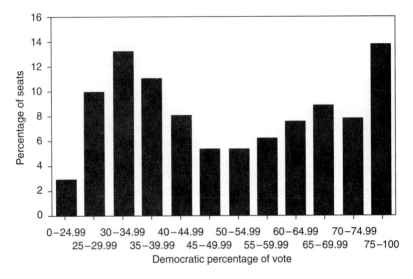

FIGURE 7.1 Democratic Percentage of Major Party Vote in Contested U.S. House Elections, 2000

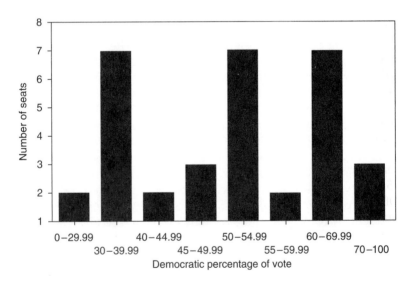

FIGURE 7.2 Democratic Percentage of Major Party Vote in Contested U.S. Senate Elections, 2000

As usual, a somewhat larger proportion of Senate than House races was competitive in 2000. Only one Senate incumbent, John Kyle of Arizona, did not have a major party challenger and only 79 percent of Senate incumbents who ran for reelection were successful—very close to the average of 83 percent for all Senate elections since 1970. Nevertheless, many Senate races were one-sided affairs. The average incumbent with a major party challenger received 62.2 percent of the two-party vote and only 32 percent of these incumbents received less than 60 percent of the two-party vote. In contrast, in the five open seat contests, all of the winning candidates received less than 60 percent of the two-party vote and three of the five received less than 55 percent of the two-party vote.

Competition in House and Senate Primaries

To have a realistic chance of becoming a member of Congress, a candidate must be nominated by one of the two major parties and almost all congressional candidates are nominated in primary elections. The timing of these primaries and the rules governing voter eligibility vary considerably from state to state.[5] Some states hold their primary elections early in the year while others hold them much closer to the general election. Some hold their congressional primaries at the same time as their presidential primary while others hold them at a separate time. Finally, some states allow any registered voter to participate in party primaries while other states allow only registered Democrats to vote in the Democratic primary and registered Republicans to vote in the Republican primary. Regardless of the timing and rules, however, meaningful competition in congressional primaries is relatively rare, especially in contests involving incumbents.

In the 2000 election, as usual, very few House incumbents faced serious competition for their party's nomination. In fact, more than 75 percent of incumbents were unopposed in their party's primary. Of the minority who did have opposition, most won by lopsided margins: out of 403 incumbents seeking another term in the House of Representatives, only 3 were defeated and only 7 won by a margin of less than 20 percentage points. This was fairly typical of recent

---

[5] See John F. Bibby, *Politics, Parties, and Elections in America* (Chicago: Nelson Hall Publishers, 1996), chapter 5, for a discussion of variations in state primary laws and their significance. For an analysis of competition in congressional primaries, see Paul S. Herrnson, *Congressional Elections: Campaigning at Home and in Washington* (Washington, DC: Congressional Quarterly Press, 1998), pp. 41–47.

elections, except for those that took place immediately after **redistricting.** Redistricting generally leads to increased competition in House primaries because it forces some incumbents to run in drastically redrawn districts and sometimes against another incumbent from the same party.[6] Since 1960, the number of House incumbents defeated in primary elections has averaged 13.8 in elections immediately after redistricting (1962, 1972, 1982, and 1992) compared with 4.3 in all other elections.

Although primaries in districts with open House seats are more likely to be competitive than those in districts with running incumbents, many of these contests are also rather one-sided affairs. Of the 60 major party candidates who won primary elections in open House seats in 2000, only 17, or fewer than one-third, survived highly competitive contests—ones decided by a margin of 10 percentage points or less. Sixteen nominees won their primary by a margin of more than 20 percentage points and another 19 were unopposed.

Since they don't have to worry about redistricting and they never have to run against another incumbent, senators are even less likely to encounter serious competition for their party's nomination than their colleagues in the House. In the 2000 election, 19 of the 27 incumbents running for reelection were unopposed in their party's primary and none of the remaining 8 faced a serious challenge. James Jeffords (R-Vermont) had the closest race and he trounced his challenger by a margin of 57 percentage points. In fact, since 1980, only two incumbent senators have been defeated in primary elections.

Open seat Senate primaries were even less competitive than those for open House seats. Of the 10 major party nominees in the five states with open Senate seats in 2000, 2 were unopposed, 5 won blowouts by margins ranging from 28 to 82 percentage points, and 1, Democrat John Corzine in New Jersey, defeated his closest rival by a margin of 16 percentage points. Only one open seat Senate nominee, Republican Bob Franks in New Jersey, survived a highly competitive primary, edging his closest rival by a margin of less than two percentage points.

These results indicate that there are often significant obstacles to competition in House and Senate primaries, even when there is no incumbent in the race. In many of these open seat contests, a high-profile front-runner with strong backing from party leaders emerged very early and deterred other serious candidates from running. In

---

[6]Jacobson, *The Politics of Congressional Elections,* chapter 2.

the Democratic Senate primary in Nebraska, for example, popular ex-Governor Ben Nelson, who announced his candidacy very early and was endorsed by almost every Democratic official in the state, faced only token opposition in his party's primary. In addition, the sheer cost of running a competitive campaign, which can run into millions of dollars in an open seat Senate primary, can dissuade potential candidates from challenging a well-financed front-runner. In the Democratic Senate primary in New York, for example, First Lady Hillary Clinton announced her candidacy very early and quickly accumulated a multi-million-dollar war chest. Despite considerable controversy over the fact that Clinton had never lived in New York State, no other serious candidate entered the Democratic primary.

CONGRESSIONAL DISTRICTS AND COMPETITION

One of the most important factors influencing the competitiveness of elections is the social and economic diversity of the electorate. Members of the U.S. Senate and House of Representatives are elected by voters within an individual state or district. Every state, regardless of population, elects two senators. As a result, the populations of senators' constituencies in 2002 ranged from less than 500,000 in the case of Wyoming to more than 30 million in the case of California. On average, each U.S. Senator represented approximately 5.6 million people. In contrast, the average House district in 2002 had a population of about 650,000. Because of their much larger populations, states generally have more diverse populations than House districts, which helps to explain why Senate elections tend to be more competitive than House elections.[7]

The number of House districts in each state is based on its share of the national population: seats are reallocated among the states every 10 years based on the results of the Census. This process is known as **reapportionment.** However, the seat shifts required by the

[7] Alan I. Abramowitz and Jeffrey A. Segal, *Senate Elections* (Ann Arbor: University of Michigan Press, 1992). See also Jonathan S. Krasno, *Challengers, Competition, and Re-election: Comparing Senate and House Elections* (New Haven, CT: Yale University Press, 1994); Alan I. Abramowitz, "A Comparison of Voting for U.S. Senator and Representative," *American Political Science Review* 74 (September 1980), pp. 633–40; and Thomas E. Mann and Raymond E. Wolfinger, "Candidates and Parties in Congressional Elections," *American Political Science Review* 74 (September 1980), pp. 617–32.

2000 Census were much smaller than those that occurred after the 1990 Census. Florida, Texas, Arizona, and Georgia each gained two seats in 2002 while New York and Pennsylvania both lost two seats. No other state gained or lost more than one seat in the House as a result of reapportionment. In contrast, after the 1990 Census, California gained seven seats, Florida gained four seats, Texas gained three seats, and New York lost three seats. Moreover, the gains and losses in 2002 were almost evenly balanced between states with predominantly Democratic delegations and states with predominantly Republican delegations.

Before 1964, states had a relatively free hand in drawing House district lines and the populations of these districts often varied considerably. In many states, rural areas were overrepresented in comparison with urban and suburban areas. In 1964, however, the Supreme Court ruled in *Wesberry v. Sanders* that the principle of "one person, one vote" applied to U.S. House elections. As a result, all states with more than one House district are now required to redraw their district lines after each Census to ensure that the populations of these districts are almost identical.[8]

To avoid partisan battles over redistricting, a few states have turned control of the redistricting process over to nonpartisan commissions. In the large majority of states, however, House district lines are drawn by the state legislature. In addition, in most states the governor has the power to veto a redistricting plan although a few states allow the legislature to override a gubernatorial veto by a simple majority vote. When one party effectively controls the redistricting process, its leaders will sometimes attempt to maximize their party's House seats by concentrating supporters of the opposing party in a few districts and/or by forcing opposing party incumbents into the same district so they have to run against each other in a primary. However, when party control of the redistricting process is divided, the outcome is more likely to be a plan designed to maintain the status quo by protecting as many incumbents from both parties as possible.

Following the 2000 election, Democrats had complete control of the redistricting process in nine states including California (53 districts) and Georgia (13 districts), while Republicans had complete

---

[8]The historical development of the one person, one vote doctrine is described in Alexander Keyssar, *The Right to Vote* (New York: Basic Books, 2000), pp. 284–87. For a discussion of the politics of redistricting and its consequences for congressional elections, see Jacobson, *The Politics of Congressional Elections,* chapter 2.

control in 14 states including Florida (24 districts), Pennsylvania (19 districts), and Ohio (18 districts). Excluding states with only one House district, Democrats controlled the redistricting process in states with 110 House districts while Republicans controlled the redistricting process in states with 104 House districts. Thus, neither party had a decisive advantage in redrawing House district lines before the 2002 election.[9] Moreover, the number of incumbents losing in primaries or choosing to retire or run for higher office was smaller in 2002 than in some previous elections following reapportionment and redistricting.

Whether the goal of those drawing the boundaries of House districts is to achieve partisan gains or to protect incumbents, the result is often the creation of districts that are relatively safe for one party or the other. This can be seen by examining the 2000 presidential vote in House districts. Because of the high level of partisan voting in the 2000 presidential election, the division of the vote between Al Gore and George W. Bush provided a very accurate indicator of the normal partisan voting patterns in House districts. In the 2000 election there were 196 House districts in which either Gore or Bush received at least 60 percent of the major party vote. Ninety-four percent of these districts chose a representative from the same party as the winning presidential candidate: 90 percent of the Bush districts elected a Republican representative while 98 percent of the Gore districts elected a Democratic representative. Only 6 of these 196 districts had a highly competitive House race—one in which the winning candidate received less than 55 percent of the two-party vote.

One major reason why Senate elections are generally more competitive than House elections is that state electorates tend to have a more even balance of Democratic and Republican identifiers than House district electorates.[10] This can be seen by comparing presidential voting in the states with presidential voting in House districts. In the 2000 election, Al Gore and George W. Bush received an average of 53 percent of the major party vote in states won by their party's Senate candidates. However, Gore and Bush received an average of 59 percent of the vote in districts won by their party's House candidates. Only 28 percent of states gave the winning presidential candidate at least 60 percent of the two-party vote compared with 45 percent of House districts.

[9] Charlie Cook, "Off to the Races: The Battle for the House Comes into Focus," *National Journal.com*, May 28, 2002.
[10] Abramowitz, "A Comparison of Voting for U.S. Senator and Representative."

Based on the partisan loyalties of Senate and House electorates, Senate races are much less likely than House races to be safe for one party or the other. This explains why elections for open Senate seats, those with no running incumbent, are more likely to produce a switch in party control than elections for open House seats. Since 1960, almost 40 percent of elections for open Senate seats have produced a switch in party control compared with only 25 percent of elections for open House seats.

CAMPAIGN FINANCE AND COMPETITION IN CONGRESSIONAL ELECTIONS

Along with the distribution of party loyalties in the electorate, campaign spending has a major influence on competition in House and Senate elections.[11] Spending by congressional candidates has increased dramatically in the past 20 years. According to data compiled by the Federal Election Commission, House and Senate candidates spent just over a billion dollars during the 1999–2000 election

[11]Gary C. Jacobson, *Money in Congressional Elections* (New Haven, CT: Yale University Press, 1980). Jacobson's conclusion that challenger spending had a much stronger influence than incumbent spending on the outcomes of congressional elections set off a debate among scholars on the relative efficacy of challenger and incumbent campaign spending. Several studies have produced evidence supporting the importance of incumbent spending. See, for example, Donald P. Green and Jonathan S. Krasno, "Salvation for the Spendthrift Incumbent: Reestimating the Effects of Campaign Spending in House Elections," *American Journal of Political Science* 32 (November 1988), pp. 884–907; Robert S. Erikson and Thomas R. Palfrey, "Campaign Spending and Incumbency: An Alternative Simultaneous Equations Approach," *Journal of Politics* 60 (May 1998), pp. 355–73; and Alan Gerber, "Estimating the Effect of Campaign Spending on Senate Election Outcomes Using Instrumental Variables," *American Political Science Review* 92 (June 1998), pp. 401–11; However, a number of other studies have produced evidence supporting Jacobson's original conclusion. See Gary C. Jacobson, "The Effects of Campaign Spending in House Elections: New Evidence for Old Arguments," *American Journal of Political Science* 34 (May 1990), pp. 334–62; Gary C. Jacobson, "Measuring Campaign Spending Effects," in Henry Brady and Richard Johnston, eds., *Capturing Campaign Effects* (Ann Arbor, MI: University of Michigan Press, in press); Christopher Kenny and Michael McBurnett, "A Dynamic Model of the Effect of Campaign Spending on Congressional Vote Choice," *American Journal of Political Science* 36 (November 1992), pp. 923–37; and Alan I. Abramowitz, "Incumbency, Campaign Spending, and the Decline of Competition in U.S. House Elections," *Journal of Politics* 53 (February 1991), pp. 34–56. Even among scholars who believe that incumbent spending is important, however, there is general agreement that inadequate spending by challengers is a major obstacle to competition in congressional elections.

cycle: a 36 percent increase over the amount spent during the 1997–1998 election cycle and almost three times the amount spent 20 years earlier. During the 1999–2000 election cycle, 2,083 House candidates spent a total of $572 million, an increase of 26 percent over the 1997–1998 election cycle, while 333 Senate candidates spent a total of $435 million, an increase of 51 percent over the 1997–1998 election cycle. Moreover, these figures reflect only hard money expenditures by House and Senate candidates—they do not include soft money expenditures by party committees or independent expenditures by outside individuals and groups, which have both increased dramatically in recent years.[12]

Although the total amount of money spent on congressional campaigns has grown considerably in recent years, not all candidates have benefited from the increased flow of campaign cash. The distribution of campaign money has always been highly unequal and it has become more unequal in recent years. One of the most important reasons for the lack of competition in House and Senate elections is the unequal distribution of campaign funds, and especially the inability of most challengers to raise enough money to get their message across to the electorate.[13]

Incumbency, Campaign Spending, and Election Outcomes

According to data compiled by the Federal Election Commission, the average House incumbent with a major party challenger spent $881,000 during the 1999–2000 election cycle while the average House challenger spent $287,000. The average Senate incumbent spent $4.5 million during the 1999–2000 election cycle while the average Senate challenger spent $2.6 million. However, these figures are very misleading because the average spending figures for House and Senate challengers are pulled up dramatically by a few big spenders. For this reason, a more revealing measure of campaign spending by incumbents and challengers is the median level of

[12] According to data compiled by the Federal Election Commission, soft money donations to national party committees increased from $86.1 million during the 1991–1992 election cycle to $495.1 million during the 1999–2000 cycle. Much of this money was used to support the campaigns of House and Senate candidates.

[13] The incumbency advantage in fund-raising is described in Anthony Gierzynski, *Money Rules: Financing Elections in America* (Boulder, CO: Westview Press, 2000), pp. 65–70. See also Paul S. Herrnson, *Congressional Elections: Campaigning at Home and in Washington*, chapter 6.

TABLE 7.2 Median Spending Levels of Incumbents and Challengers in House and Senate Elections by Competitiveness of Contest, 2000

Competitiveness of Contest	Median Challenger Spending (in $ thousands)	Median Incumbent Spending (in $ thousands)
House elections		
Noncompetitive (n = 266)	$ 23	$ 614
Competitive (n = 43)	431	1,120
Highly competitive (n = 29)	1,257	1,759
Senate elections		
Noncompetitive (n = 19)	400	3,131
Competitive (n = 2)	2,453	3,316
Highly competitive (n = 7)	8,801	6,610

Source: Federal Election Commission and data compiled by author.

spending—the amount surpassed by half of all incumbents and challengers.

During the 1999–2000 election cycle, median spending by House incumbents with major party challengers was $693,000 while median spending by House challengers was a paltry $41,000. This means that in a typical House race, the incumbent outspent the challenger by a greater than 15 to 1 ratio—the highest ratio of incumbent to challenger spending since accurate data on campaign spending in congressional elections became available in 1974. Half of all House challengers spent less than $41,000—not enough to make any impression at all on the electorate. Median spending by Senate incumbents was $3.7 million during the 1999–2000 election cycle while median spending by Senate challengers was just under $900,000. Thus, in a typical Senate race, the incumbent outspent the challenger by a greater than 4 to 1 ratio. Although not a record, this was one of the highest ratios of incumbent to challenger spending since 1974.

There is a very strong relationship between campaign spending and the outcomes of congressional elections.[14] Table 7.2 displays the median spending levels of incumbents and challengers in noncompetitive, moderately competitive, and highly competitive House and

[14] See Jacobson, *Money in Congressional Elections*, chapter 5. See also, Gierzynski, *Money Rules*, pp. 59–64; and James E. Campbell, "Is the House Incumbency Advantage Mostly a Campaign Finance Advantage?" paper delivered at the Annual Meeting of the New England Political Science Association, Portland, Maine, May 3–4, 2002.

Senate elections in 2000. In the House elections, the ratio of incumbent spending to challenger spending was almost 30 to 1 in noncompetitive races (those decided by more than 20 percentage points), less than 3 to 1 in moderately competitive races (those decided by between 10 and 20 percentage points), and less than 1.5 to 1 in highly competitive races (those decided by less than 10 percentage points). Three of the six House incumbents who lost were outspent by their challengers. Similarly, in the Senate elections, the ratio of incumbent to challenger spending was almost 8 to 1 in noncompetitive races, 1.3 to 1 in moderately competitive races, and only .75 to 1 in highly competitive races. Three of the six Senate incumbents who lost were outspent by their challengers.

The reason for the much lower ratio of incumbent to challenger spending in moderately and highly competitive races is that the challengers in these contests spent far more than challengers in noncompetitive races. Median spending by House challengers was a meager $23,000 in 267 noncompetitive races compared with $431,000 in 43 moderately competitive races and $1.26 million in 29 highly competitive races. Similarly, median spending by challengers was $400,000 in 19 noncompetitive Senate contests compared with $2.45 million in two moderately competitive contests and $8.8 million in seven highly competitive contests.

The overall amount spent by challengers in House and Senate elections has increased substantially since the 1980s. House challengers spent more than $97 million in the 2000 election compared with less than $37 million in the 1988 election. Similarly, Senate challengers spent more than $73 million in the 2000 election compared with $45 million in the 1988 election. Even after allowing for inflation, this represents a significant increase in total spending by both House and Senate challengers. However, while challengers are spending more money than in the past, the distribution of that money is highly concentrated, especially in House elections. A few challengers who are given a chance of winning by party leaders and political action committees are able to raise large sums of money while the rest get little or nothing. In the 2000 House elections, for example, the top 10 percent of challengers, those who spent more than $980,000, were responsible for 59 percent of total spending by challengers while the bottom half of challengers, those who spent less than $41,000, were responsible for only 2 percent of total spending. Challenger spending in the 2000 Senate elections was only slightly less concentrated: the top 10 percent of challengers, those who spent more than $10 million, were responsible for 46 percent of total spending by challengers while the bottom half of challengers, those who spent less than $1 million, were responsible for only 5 percent of total spending.

The data in Table 7.2 show that House and Senate incumbents responded to the threat posed by well-financed challengers by substantially increasing their own spending. However, this increased incumbent spending did not offset the effect of increased challenger spending. In both House and Senate elections, the more challengers spent, they better they did.

The most important limitation on competition in House and Senate elections is the inability of most challengers to raise enough money to conduct a serious campaign. This is even true in many districts and states where the partisan composition of the electorate appears to give the challenger a realistic chance of winning. For example, in the 2000 election there were 77 House districts that were carried by the presidential candidate from the challenger's party. However, half of the challengers in these districts spent less than $200,000 and 70 percent spent less than $500,000—the bare minimum that is needed to wage a competitive campaign. Similarly, there were 14 states that were carried by the Senate challenger's party in the 2000 presidential election, but half of the challengers in these states spent less than $1.7 million, not nearly enough to conduct a competitive campaign in most states.

Campaign Spending in Open Seat Elections

Relative spending by major party candidates is generally much more evenly balanced in **open seat contests** than in contests involving incumbents. Nevertheless, even in open seat House and Senate contests, one candidate often greatly outspends the other, and the candidate who wins the money race almost always wins the election.[15] In 2000, for example, one major party candidate outspent the other by a better than 2-1 margin in 16 of 34 open seat House races and two of five open seat Senate races. In 15 of the 16 House races and both Senate races, the higher-spending candidate won. In one of the Sen-

---

[15] For a discussion of the influence of campaign spending and other factors on the outcomes of open seat House elections, see Ronald K. Gaddie and Charles S. Bullock III, *Elections to Open Seats in the U.S. House: Where the Action Is* (New York: Rowman and Littlefield, 2000), especially chapter 2. For an analysis of the impact of campaign spending in open seat Senate elections, see Alan I. Abramowitz, "Explaining Senate Election Outcomes," *American Political Science Review* 82 (June 1988), pp. 385–403.

ate races, Democrat John Corzine, the former chairman of the Gold-
man Sachs investment firm, set an all-time record by spending
$63.2 million, almost all of it his own money. Despite outspending
his Republican opponent, former U.S. Representative Bob Franks, by
a better than 10 to 1 ratio, Corzine barely defeated Franks by a 51.5 to
48.5 percent margin, suggesting that campaign spending is subject to
diminishing returns. Overall, however, the higher-spending candidate won 30 out of 34 open seat House contests and four out of five
open seat Senate contests.

The Sources of Campaign Money

The overwhelming majority of money spent by congressional candidates comes from three sources—individual contributors, **political action committees (PACs),** and the candidates themselves.[16]
Table 7.3 shows the amount of money raised by congressional incumbents and challengers from these three sources in the 1992, 1994,
1996, 1998, and 2000 elections. The data in this table show that House
and Senate incumbents raised considerably more money from individual contributors than their challengers: House incumbents generally raised between two and three times as much from individual
contributors as their challengers and Senate incumbents generally
raised between one and a half and two times as much from individual contributors as their challengers. However, the largest disparity
in contributions to incumbents and challengers involved PACs. On
average, PACs gave about seven times more to House incumbents
than they gave to House challengers and about five times more to
Senate incumbents than they gave to Senate challengers.[17]

Because of difficulty in raising money from individual contributors and PACs, challengers are frequently forced to rely heavily on
their personal financial resources to fund their campaigns. The data
in Table 7.3 show that House challengers gave or loaned their own
campaigns about seven times more money than House incumbents.
About 20 percent of the funds raised by House challengers came
from contributions or loans to their own campaigns. The amount of
money that Senate challengers gave or loaned their own campaigns

---

[16]For a more detailed analysis of the sources of campaign money in U.S. elections, see
Gierzynski, *Money Rules,* chapter 5.

[17]For an in-depth examination of the role of PACs in the U.S. electoral process, see
Larry Sabato, *PAC Power: Inside the World of Political Action Committees* (New York:
W. W. Norton and Company, 1984).

TABLE 7.3 Sources of Funding for House and Senate Candidates, 1992–2000

Type of Candidate	Funding Source	1992	1994	1996	1998	2000
House incumbents	Individuals	$87.6	$108.2	$149.7	$150.8	$184.0
	PACs	90.6	100.4	113.1	123.9	149.8
	Candidate	2.4	2.5	2.3	2.6	3.1
House challengers	Individuals	33.2	43.8	56.7	44.8	64.1
	PACs	10.5	11.6	20.4	14.3	19.2
	Candidate	17.1	15.5	16.6	16.2	19.6
Senate incumbents	Individuals	57.5	68.1	55.5	90.9	80.6
	PACs	30.2	26.3	19.2	34.3	33.5
	Candidate	0.8	12.0	2.7	2.2	2.8
Senate challengers	Individuals	42.5	51.0	36.1	45.1	38.7
	PACs	7.3	5.0	6.0	6.1	6.4
	Candidate	4.6	42.0	13.2	25.6	23.5

Source: Federal Election Commission.

Note: Contributions in millions of current dollars.

varied tremendously from election to election because of a few wealthy individuals who financed all or most of their own campaigns. On average, however, Senate challengers gave or loaned their own campaigns about five times more money than Senate incumbents. Candidate contributions and loans made up almost a third of the total amount raised by Senate challengers in these five elections.

THE INCUMBENCY ADVANTAGE AND THE PERSONAL VOTE

Members of Congress do not ignore their constituencies between election campaigns. Most senators and representatives devote considerable time and effort to cultivating their constituencies. They use resources provided to all members of the Senate and House including the franking privilege, paid staff, and travel allowances to engage in activities such as advertising, credit claiming, and position taking.[18]

According to political scientist David Mayhew, advertising involves building a positive image through the use of mailings, per-

[18] David R. Mayhew, *Congress: The Electoral Connection* (New Haven, CT: Yale University Press, 1974).

TABLE 7.4 Results of Regression Analyses
of House and Senate Races, 2000

Independent Variable	House Elections		Senate Elections	
	B	(S.E.)	B	(S.E.)
District/State partisanship	**.447**	**(.021)**	.159	(.151)
Campaign spending	**14.5**	**(0.70)**	**14.8**	**(3.61)**
Incumbency status	**3.44**	**(.510)**	**4.52**	**(2.23)**
Constant	28.5		43.36	
Adjusted R^2	.95		.78	
(Total cases)	(370)		(33)	

Source: Data compiled by author.

Note: Based on contested races. Entries shown are unstandardized regression coefficients with accompanying standard errors. Coefficients shown in boldface are statistically significant ($p < .05$).

sonal appearances, and free media exposure; credit claiming involves building a reputation for obtaining government benefits for constituents; finally, position taking involves building a voting record that appeals to a majority of one's constituents. By engaging in these activities, members of Congress, especially those who represent districts or states where their party does not normally do well, seek to build a personal base of support above and beyond the normal level of support for their party. Their ultimate goal is to increase their chance of winning reelection regardless of who runs against them or what the national political climate may be.

The **personal vote** is the additional vote that an incumbent receives as a result of his or her personal popularity among constituents.[19] It is that portion of an incumbent's support that is not explained by either campaign spending or the normal party vote. We can therefore estimate the average size of the personal vote in House and Senate elections by estimating the impact of having a running incumbent in a district or state while controlling for the effect of campaign spending and the normal party vote.

Table 7.4 presents the results of regression analyses of contested House and Senate races in the 2000 election. The dependent variable in these analyses is the Democratic percentage of the major party vote in each state or district. The independent variables are the partisan composition of the electorate, the relative level of campaign

[19]The concept of a personal vote here is borrowed from the work of Cain, Ferejohn, and Fiorina on the U.S. House of Representatives and the British House of Commons. See Bruce Cain, John Ferejohn, and Morris Fiorina, *The Personal Vote: Constituency Service and Electoral Independence* (Cambridge, MA: Harvard University Press, 1987).

spending by the major party candidates, and the incumbency status of the candidates in the race. The partisan composition of the electorate is measured by the Democratic percentage of the major party presidential vote in 2000. Relative campaign spending is measured by the difference between the amount of money spent by the Democratic and Republican candidates divided by the total amount spent by both candidates.[20] Finally, incumbency status is coded as +1 for races with a Democratic incumbent, 0 for races with no incumbent, and −1 for races with a Republican incumbent.

The results in Table 7.4 indicate that our three independent variables explained over 90 percent of the variation in the outcomes of House elections and almost 80 percent of the variation in the outcomes of Senate elections. All three estimated regression coefficients were statistically significant in the House model and two of three were statistically significant in the Senate model despite the small number of cases.

Relative campaign spending had very similar and very powerful effects on the outcomes of both House and Senate elections. The estimated regression coefficients of 14.5 in the House model and 14.8 in the Senate model mean that when one candidate accounted for all of the spending in a race, that candidate gained an estimated advantage of 14.5 percentage points in a House election and 14.8 percentage points in a Senate election.

The results in Table 7.4 also indicate that the personal advantage of incumbency was very similar in House and Senate elections. The estimated coefficients for the incumbency status variable, 3.4 for House elections and 4.5 for Senate elections, mean that after controlling for the effects of campaign spending and district partisanship, the presence of an incumbent in a race was worth an average of 3.4 percentage points in House elections and 4.5 percentage points in Senate elections.

Based on the results in Table 7.4, we can also estimate the impact of both the partisan composition of the electorate and campaign spending on support for House and Senate incumbents. House incumbents gained an average advantage of 10.2 percentage points from campaign spending and 3.7 percentage points from the par-

[20] This measure of campaign spending was devised by James E. Campbell. It has the advantage of incorporating diminishing returns as well as reflecting the interactive character of campaign spending. For a more detailed explanation and justification of the measure, see Campbell, *The Presidential Pulse of Congressional Elections*, 2nd ed. (Lexington, KY: University of Kentucky Press, 1997).

tisan composition of the electorate. Senate incumbents gained an average advantage of 7.6 percentage points from campaign spending and 0.4 percentage points from the partisan composition of the electorate.

These results indicate that in both House and Senate elections, the largest factor in the electoral advantage of incumbency is the ability of incumbents to outspend their challengers.[21] Based on the results in Table 7.4, we can also estimate how these House and Senate races would have turned out if the challengers had been able to match the incumbents' campaign spending. This exercise indicates that, in the House of Representatives, far more incumbents were vulnerable than the six who actually lost their seats. If campaign spending had been equalized, a total of 37 House incumbents, instead of 6, would have lost their seats. However, because the losses would have been almost equally divided between the parties (17 Democrats and 20 Republicans), the party division of the House would have been almost unchanged—Democrats would have scored a net gain of three seats instead of two. In the Senate elections, six Republicans would have lost their seats instead of five Republicans and one Democrat. Thus, Democrats would have controlled the Senate even without James Jeffords's party switch.

Measuring the Personal Vote in House and Senate Elections

The estimates of the personal vote for House and Senate incumbents in Table 7.4 represent averages for all incumbents in contested races. However, we can estimate the size of the personal vote for individual incumbents by calculating the difference between their actual vote and the vote that would have been expected in their race based on campaign spending and district partisanship if no incumbent had been running. The results show that there was a great deal of variation in the personal vote for individual representatives and senators. In the House elections, the estimated personal vote ranged from −11.6 percent for freshman Democrat Tammy Baldwin in Wisconsin's Second District to +23.9 percent for fifth-term Democrat Gene Taylor in Mississippi's Fifth District. Baldwin won 51 percent of the

---

[21] These results are very similar to those obtained by James E. Campbell in a recent analysis of the incumbency advantage in U.S. House elections. See Campbell, "Is the House Incumbency Advantage Mostly a Campaign Finance Advantage."

vote in a district that Al Gore carried by 22 percentage points; Taylor won 79 percent of the vote in a district that Gore lost by 34 percentage points.

Twenty percent of House incumbents had negative personal vote scores. These 68 incumbents did worse than a candidate of their party should have done in an open seat race. On the other hand, 13 percent of House incumbents had positive personal vote scores of eight percentage points or higher. These 45 incumbents won by a much larger margin than expected based on the partisan makeup of their districts and the amount of money spent by their challengers. Based on these results it appears that some members of the House of Representatives have been doing a much better job of cultivating their constituencies than others.

Our estimates of the personal vote for Senate incumbents showed just as much variation as those for House incumbents. These estimates ranged from −7.4 percent for Republican Bill Roth of Delaware to +20.5 percent for Republican Jim Jeffords of Vermont. Roth, whose campaign was plagued by health-related problems, lost to Democratic Governor and former U.S. Representative Tom Carper by 12 percentage points despite outspending Carper—$4.4 million to $2.6 million. Jeffords crushed Democratic state auditor Ed Flanagan, 66 percent to 25 percent, running 25 points ahead of George W. Bush in the state. Of the 28 Senate incumbents in contested races, 7 had negative personal vote scores while 7 had positive scores of greater than 10 percentage points.

In the Senate, just as in the House of Representatives, it appears that some members have been much more successful than others at cultivating their constituencies. However, the Senate results also suggest that the personal vote can be influenced by perceptions of the challenger as well as perceptions of the incumbent. In the Delaware Senate contest, for example, incumbent Bill Roth's poor performance was undoubtedly due in part to the fact that his challenger, Tom Carper, was a popular two-term governor who had previously held the state's only seat in the House of Representatives. Similarly, the fact that Democrat Edward Kennedy of Massachusetts had the second highest personal vote score of any 2000 Senate incumbent, +17.6 percentage points, was undoubtedly due in part to the negative image of his Republican challenger, Jack E. Robinson, whose past run-ins with the law were widely publicized during the campaign. Because high-profile challengers are much more prevalent in Senate elections than in House elections, challengers probably have a much greater influence on the personal vote in Senate elections than in House elections.[22]

Ideological Position Taking and the Personal Vote

The personal vote allows many incumbents to survive in hostile political territory. In the 2000 election, for example, 37 out of 40 representatives and four out of five senators were reelected in districts or states where the opposing party's presidential candidate won at least 55 percent of the vote. Many of these incumbents faced well-financed challengers. Their success was based on having established a personal reputation for effectively representing their constituency.

A key factor in establishing a reputation for effective representation is the ability of members of Congress to "vote their constituencies."[23] Because party discipline is not strictly enforced in Congress, individual senators and representatives can cross party lines on issues when they perceive a clear conflict between the position of their party and the views of their constituents. Most members of Congress only occasionally perceive such a conflict: senators and representatives typically support their party's position on 80 to 90 percent of floor votes. However, Democrats who represent conservative, Republican-leaning constituencies and Republicans who represent liberal, Democratic-leaning constituencies tend to defect from their party's position much more frequently.

Political scientists Keith Poole and Howard Rosenthal have developed a widely used measure, the DW-NOMINATE scale, to measure senators' and representatives' ideological orientations based on

---

[22]See Abramowitz, "A Comparison of Voting for U.S. Senator and Representative." See also Krasno, *Challengers, Competition, and Reelection: Comparing Senate and House Elections,* chapter 4. The critical role of challengers in determining the amount of media coverage of Senate campaigns and the information available to voters in these contests is stressed in Kim F. Kahn and Patrick F. Kenney, *The Spectacle of U.S. Senate Campaigns* (Princeton, NJ: Princeton University Press, 1999).

[23]A recent study by Canes-Wrone, Brady, and Coogan on the impact of House incumbents' voting behavior provides strong support for this proposition. See Candice Canes-Wrone, David W. Brady, and John F. Coogan, "Out of Step, Out of Office: Electoral Accountability and House Members' Voting," *American Political Science Review* 96 (March 2002), pp. 127–40. For evidence that members of Congress in the early nineteenth century were held accountable for their votes, see William T. Bianco, David B. Spence, and John D. Wilkerson, "The Electoral Connection in the Early Congress: The Case of the Compensation Act of 1816," *American Journal of Political Science* 40 (February 1996), pp. 145–71.

their roll call votes.[24] Scores on this scale have a theoretical range from −1 to +1, with −1 representing the most liberal score and +1 representing the most conservative score. In the 106th Congress (1999–2001), members' actual scores ranged from a minimum of −.678 to a maximum of .896. The large majority of Democrats had negative (liberal) scores while the large majority of Republicans had positive (conservative) scores.

In the 106th Congress, there was a fairly strong correlation between members' DW-NOMINATE scores and the partisan orientations of their states or districts as indicated by the presidential vote. The correlation between conservatism scores and the percentage of the vote for George W. Bush in a state or district was .74 for House Democrats, .49 for House Republicans, .68 for Senate Democrats, and .62 for Senate Republicans. Thus, the voting records of members of Congress reflected the views of their constituents: Democrats who represented conservative, Republican-leaning states or districts had much more conservative voting records than Democrats who represented liberal, Democratic-leaning states or districts; Republicans who represented liberal, Democratic-leaning states or districts had much more liberal voting records than Republicans who represented conservative, Republican-leaning states or districts.

The ability of members of Congress to vote their constituencies has a significant positive impact on the reelection chances of those members who represent states or districts where their party is in the minority. By crossing party lines, moderate Democrats and Republicans can appeal to independents and opposing partisans whose support is crucial to victory in these states and districts.

Table 7.5 presents the results of regression analyses of all contested House and Senate races involving incumbents in the 2000 election. The dependent variable in these analyses is the incumbent's percentage of the major party vote. The independent variables are the partisan orientation of the electorate (measured by the percentage of the major party vote for the presidential candidate from the incumbent's party), campaign spending (measured by the difference between the amount spent by the incumbent and the amount spent by the challenger divided by the combined amount spent by the incumbent and the challenger), and the ideological extremism of the incumbent's voting record (measured by the liberalism of the incum-

TABLE 7.5 Results of Regression Analyses of House
and Senate Races Involving Incumbents, 2000

Independent Variable	House Elections		Senate Elections	
	B	(S.E.)	B	(S.E)
District/State partisanship	.557	(.025)	.387	(.202)
Campaign spending	13.7	(0.72)	18.0	(3.66)
Ideological extremism	−13.7	(1.91)	−26.7	(11.5)
Constant	30.3		40.3	
Adjusted R^2	.81		.60	
(Total cases)	(336)		(28)	

Source: Data compiled by anothor.

Note: Based on contested races. Entries shown are unstandardized regression coefficients with a
accompanying standard errors. Coefficients shown in boldface are statistically significant ($p < 0.5$).

bent's voting record for Democrats and the conservatism of the incumbent's voting record for Republicans).

The results in Table 7.5 show that ideological extremism had a
significant negative impact on support for incumbents in both House
and Senate elections. After controlling for district or state partisanship and campaign spending, representatives and senators with
moderate voting records did substantially better than their colleagues
with very liberal or very conservative voting records. According to
these results, a representative with a moderate voting record (DW-
NOMINATE score = 0) received an additional 6.5 percent of the
vote compared with an average representative while a senator with
a moderate voting record received an additional 7.7 percent of the
vote compared with an average senator. Thus, by building a moderate voting record, incumbents can sometimes overcome the disadvantage of representing a state or district where their party is relatively weak.

Why Incumbents Lose

Despite all of the advantages that they enjoy, some incumbents lose
their seats in every election. In the 15 elections between 1972 and
2000, an average of 23.9 representatives and 5.2 senators lost their
seats in either a primary or the general election. However, these
numbers represent a substantial decrease from earlier periods of
American history, especially for members of the House of Representatives. In the 13 elections between 1946 and 1970, an average of

39.8 representatives and 7.5 senators lost their seats in either a primary or the general election.

A variety of factors contribute to incumbent defeats in House and Senate elections. One such factor in House elections is redistricting. Between 1970 and 2000, an average of 35.3 incumbents were defeated in elections that followed redistricting compared with an average of 19.5 in all other elections.

The large majority of incumbents who lose in general elections represent districts or states where their party does not have a clear advantage in terms of voter loyalties. In the 2000 election, for example, five of the six representatives and five of the six senators who lost in the general election came from districts or states that were carried by the opposing party's presidential candidate. In some cases, this sort of mismatch between an incumbent and his or her constituency can result from changes in the partisan and ideological orientation of a constituency due to population shifts. During the 1990s, for example, ultraconservative Republican Representative Bob Dornan found the political orientation of his California district shifting to the left as a result of an influx of Hispanic voters. After cruising to a 20-point victory in 1994 over an Anglo Democratic challenger, Dornan lost a one-point decision in 1996 to a Hispanic Democrat, Loretta Sanchez. Two years later, Dornan made a comeback attempt. Despite spending $3.9 million, a record for a House challenger, Dornan lost to Sanchez by 17 percentage points.[25]

Scandals and controversies can also lead to the defeat of incumbents. In 2002, for example, Representative Gary Condit suffered a crushing defeat in the California Democratic primary in the aftermath of massive publicity over his relationship with missing congressional intern Chandra Levy. Condit, who had received 67 percent of the vote in the 2000 general election, lost the primary to state assemblyman Dennis Cardoza by a 55 to 37 percent margin.[26]

Usually, scandals involving members of Congress are isolated events, affecting no more than a handful of representatives or senators in a single election. In 1992, however, dozens of members of the House of Representatives from both parties found themselves caught up in a scandal as a result of revelations that they had been allowed to regularly overdraw their checking accounts with the House

[25]Dornan's 1996 defeat and his subsequent unsuccessful comeback attempt are described in Michael Barone and Grant Ujifusa, *The Almanac of American Politics 2000* (Washington, DC: National Journal, 1999), pp. 296–98.

[26]Jean Merl and Matea Gold, "Condit Loses Reelection Bid to Former Protégé," *Los Angeles Times*, March 6, 2002, p. A1.

bank without penalty. Although no public funds were involved and these representatives had broken no laws, the scandal led to a substantial number of early retirements, primary losses, and general election defeats.[27]

In politics "you can't beat somebody with nobody." Voters generally will not turn out an incumbent unless there is a viable challenger in the race. In addition to simply providing voters with an alternative to the incumbent, a competent and adequately financed challenger can raise questions in voters' minds about the performance of the incumbent. In the 1992 House banking scandal, for example, the likelihood of an incumbent losing depended not just on how many checks he or she had bounced, but how much money his or her challenger was able to spend. In the 2000 House and Senate elections, as well, all of the losing incumbents faced well-financed challengers. All six successful House challengers spent at least $800,000 and five spent more than a million dollars. Likewise, all six successful Senate challengers spent at least $2.5 million and five spent more than $7.5 million. Regardless of whatever other problems incumbents face, one common element in almost all incumbent defeats is the presence of a capable, well-financed challenger.

NATIONAL FORCES AND CONGRESSIONAL ELECTIONS

The numbers of House and Senate incumbents who lose vary considerably from election to election. Since the end of World War II, the number of representatives losing their seats in general elections has ranged from a low of 4 in 2002 to a high of 68 in 1948; the number of senators losing their seats in general elections has ranged from a low of 1 in 1960, 1966, 1990, and 1996 to a high of 10 in 1958. There have been five general elections—1946, 1948, 1964, 1966, and 1974—in which at least 40 House incumbents were defeated and five general elections—1948, 1952, 1958, 1976, and 1980—in which at least eight Senate incumbents were defeated.

Almost all of the elections in which a large number of House and Senate incumbents were defeated have involved strong **national forces** that produced substantial seat gains for one party or the other.

[27] For an analysis of the political consequences of the House banking scandal, see Gary C. Jacobson and Michael A. Dimock, "Checking Out: The Effects of Overdrafts on the 1992 House Elections," *American Journal of Political Science* 38 (August 1994), pp. 601–24.

In 1974, for example, in the aftermath of the Watergate scandal, 40 House incumbents were defeated and Democrats gained 49 seats in the House of Representatives.[28] Similarly, in 1980, in the midst of a recession and the hostage crisis in Iran, nine Senate incumbents were defeated and Republicans gained 12 seats in the Senate.[29]

In general, there is a strong relationship between the number of seats gained by one party at the expense of the other in an election (the **seat swing**) and the number of incumbents who lose their seats. This is because when a strong national tide is running in an election, the overwhelming majority of incumbents who lose their seats come from the party that is disadvantaged by that tide. Thus, in six House elections between 1954 and 2000 in which at least 30 incumbents were defeated, 94 percent of the defeated incumbents came from one party. Similarly, in six Senate elections between 1954 and 2000 in which at least six incumbents were defeated, 84 percent of the defeated incumbents came from one party.

National electoral forces clearly play a major role in producing incumbent defeats as well as seat swings in congressional elections. The weakness of these forces in recent elections helps to explain why so few incumbents have been defeated and why the seat swings in these elections have been relatively small. In this section, we will consider where these national forces come from, why they vary in strength from election to election, and why their effects have been weakening in recent years.

Surge and Decline I: Presidential Coattails

Political scientist James E. Campbell has observed that there is a "presidential pulse" to congressional elections. That is, to a considerable extent, the influence of national issues on congressional elections is mediated by presidential elections.[30] When a party wins a presidential election, it usually gains seats in the House and Senate as a result of **presidential coattails.** In the next midterm election,

[28] Eric M. Uslaner and M. Margaret Conway, "The Responsible Congressional Electorate: Watergate, the Economy, and Vote Choice in 1974," *American Political Science Review* 79 (September 1985), pp. 788–803. See also Jack M. McLeod, Jane D. Brown, and Lee D. Becker, "Watergate and the 1974 Congressional Elections," *Public Opinion Quarterly* 41 (Summer 1977), pp. 181–95.

[29] See Charles E. Jacob, "The Congressional Elections," in Gerald M. Pomper, ed., *The Election of 1980: Reports and Interpretations* (Chatham, NJ: Chatham House, 1981), pp. 119–41.

[30] Campbell, *The Presidential Pulse of Congressional Elections.*

2 years later or 6 years later, without the benefit of presidential coat-tails, the party that won the presidential election almost always loses seats in the House and usually loses seats in the Senate. This alternating pattern of **surge and decline** has been one of the most regular features of congressional elections in the United States.[31] In recent elections, however, the surge and decline pattern has been less regular than in the past.

Presidential elections are high-stimulus elections. There is extensive media coverage of the campaign and interest and turnout are relatively high. Independents and voters with weak party loyalties who turn out to vote for a particular presidential candidate tend to vote for House and Senate candidates from the same party. As a result, the party that wins the presidential election generally makes gains in the House and Senate elections and the larger the margin of victory in the presidential election, the larger the gains tend to be in the House and Senate.[32]

The number of seats that the party winning the presidency gains as a result of presidential coattails also depends on the number of **marginal seats** that the losing party is defending in the House and Senate. Marginal seats are especially vulnerable because the party holding them does not have a clear advantage in terms of party identification. Therefore, the more marginal seats the losing party has exposed, the more seats the party winning the presidential election tends to gain. This is known as the **exposure effect.** In 1948, for example, Democrat Harry Truman defeated Republican Thomas Dewey by only four percentage points in the presidential election but Democrats gained 75 seats in the House of Representatives. The Democrats were able to pick up so many seats in 1948 because Republicans were defending many marginal seats that they had won in the 1946 midterm election when they gained 55 seats.

The coattail effect, while still evident, has not been as important in recent elections as it was in the past.[33] Between 1900 and 1944, the

[31] See Angus Campbell, "Surge and Decline: A Study of Electoral Change," in Angus Campbell, Philip E. Converse, Warren E. Miller, and Donald E. Stokes, *Elections and the Political Order* (New York: John Wiley and Sons, 1966), pp. 40–62; and James E. Campbell, "The Presidential Surge and Its Midterm Decline in Congressional Elections, 1868–1988," *Journal of Politics* 53 (May 1991), pp. 477–87.

[32] See James E. Campbell, "Predicting Seat Gains from Presidential Coattails," *American Journal of Political Science* 30 (February 1986), pp. 165–83.

[33] Campbell, *The Presidential Pulse of Congressional Elections.* See also Randall L. Calvert and John A. Ferejohn, "Coattail Voting in Recent Presidential Elections," *American Political Science Review* 77 (June 1983), pp. 407–19.

party winning the presidency gained seats in the House of Representatives in 10 of 12 elections, with an average gain of 21 seats. Moreover, when a presidential candidate won the popular vote by a margin of more than 10 percentage points, the coattail effect was much more dramatic. The party winning the presidency gained seats in all seven of these elections, with an average gain of 47 seats. However, since the end of World War II, the party winning the presidency has gained seats in the House of Representatives in only 9 of 14 elections, with an average gain of only 12 seats. In four of the five postwar elections in which a candidate won a decisive victory in the presidential election, that candidate's party gained seats in the House, but the average gain was only 17 seats. Moreover, in the four most recent presidential elections—1988, 1992, 1996, and 2000—the party winning the presidency gained seats in the House only once, and the winning candidate's party lost an average of three seats in these elections. Even when Bill Clinton defeated Bob Dole by a margin of almost nine percentage points in 1996, Democrats gained back only 9 of the 53 seats that they had lost in the House of Representatives in the 1994 midterm election.

Between 1900 and 1944, the party winning the presidency gained Senate seats in 7 of 12 elections, with an average gain of four seats. Just as in House elections, however, the coattail effect was more evident when a presidential candidate won the popular vote by more than 10 percentage points. The party winning the presidency gained Senate seats in six of these seven elections, with an average gain of seven seats. Since the end of World War II, however, the coattail effect has been almost entirely absent in Senate elections. The party winning the presidency gained Senate seats in only 5 of these 14 elections, with an average gain of only one seat. Even in the five elections in which a presidential candidate won the popular vote by more than 10 percentage points, the party winning the presidency picked up Senate seats only twice and, on average, there was no change in the party makeup of the Senate.

Surge and Decline, II: Midterm Elections

The tendency of the president's party to lose congressional seats in **midterm elections** has been even more regular than the tendency of the party winning the presidency to gain seats in presidential election years.[34] Since 1900, the president's party has lost House seats in

---

[34] For a summary of this evidence, see Campbell, *The Presidential Pulse of Congressional Elections.*

23 of 26 midterm elections and Senate seats in 17 of 26 midterm elections. On average, the president's party has lost 31 House seats and 3.3 Senate seats in these elections.

According to the surge and decline theory, the losses suffered by the president's party in midterm elections are caused by the withdrawal of presidential coattails. Without a presidential race on the ballot, there is much less media coverage of the campaign, and voter interest and turnout decline. Because turnout is low and short-term forces are relatively weak, the outcomes of midterm elections generally reflect the distribution of party loyalties among hard-core voters. Therefore, the president's party tends to lose many of the marginal seats that it won 2 years earlier with the benefit of presidential coattails.

The more marginal seats the president's party wins with the benefit of presidential coattails, the more seats it risks losing 2 years later, or 6 years later in the case of Senate seats, when those coattails are withdrawn. This is another example of the exposure effect: the more marginal seats the president's party has exposed in a midterm election, the more seats it is likely to lose. For example, in 1966 Democrats had to defend an unusually large number of marginal House seats that the party had won during Lyndon Johnson's landslide victory over Barry Goldwater in the 1964 presidential election. This contributed to a Republican gain of 47 seats in the midterm election. Similarly, in 1986, 6 years after riding Ronald Reagan's coattails to a 12-seat gain and their first Senate majority since the 1950s, Republicans had to defend 22 of the 33 Senate seats at stake in the midterm election. Several of these Republican seats were in what were then Democratic strongholds such as Alabama and Georgia. Without the benefit of Reagan's coattails, Republicans lost eight seats and their majority.

Just as the gains produced by presidential coattails have declined in recent elections, the losses suffered by the president's party in midterm elections have also diminished, especially in House elections. In 12 midterm elections between 1902 and 1946, the president's party lost an average of 40 House seats and four Senate seats; in 14 midterm elections between 1950 and 2002, the president's party lost an average of 22 House seats and three Senate seats. In 1998, for the first time since 1934, the president's party gained seats in the House of Representatives in a midterm election. Four years later, with Republican George W. Bush in the White House, Republicans gained six seats in the House of Representatives and two seats in the Senate.

There are two closely related reasons why presidential coattails and midterm seat losses have been less significant in recent elections than they were during the first half of the twentieth century: declining party loyalty and the growing advantage of incumbency. Because party loyalties are weaker than they were during the first half of the twentieth century, contemporary voters are more likely to engage in **split-ticket voting**—casting a ballot for a presidential candidate from one party and a House or Senate candidate from the opposing party. They are also more likely to choose a candidate based on personal qualities and characteristics than party affiliation.

The principal beneficiaries of ticket splitting and candidate-based voting in congressional elections are incumbents. The overwhelming majority of voters who split their ticket vote for the incumbent. According to data from the 2000 National Election Study, in races involving incumbents, 81 percent of House ticket splitters and 75 percent of Senate ticket splitters voted for the incumbent. Likewise, those whose votes are based primarily on candidate qualities and characteristics, independents and party defectors, overwhelmingly support incumbents. According to the 2000 NES data, in House races involving incumbents, 88 percent of party defectors and 71 percent of independents voted for the incumbent; in Senate races involving incumbents, 80 percent of party defectors and 61 percent of independents voted for the incumbent.

Because of the increased advantage of incumbency, there are fewer marginal seats available in House and Senate elections than there were 40 or 50 years ago and more seats are insulated from the influence of national tides. As a result, the effects of surge and decline are smaller now than in the past. Presidential coattails are shorter and midterm losses are smaller. As James E. Campbell has argued, there is still a presidential pulse to congressional elections but because of the increased advantage of incumbency, that pulse is considerably weaker than it was in the first half of the twentieth century.[35]

The Midterm Election as a Referendum

According to the surge and decline theory, the outcomes of midterm elections are largely a reflection of what happened during the preceding presidential election: the mores seats the president's party won 2 years earlier, or 6 years earlier in the case of Senate elections, as a result of presidential coattails, the mores seats it can expect to

---

[35] Campbell, *The Presidential Pulse of Congressional Elections.*

lose in the midterm election when those coattails are withdrawn. However, surge and decline cannot account for all of the variation in the outcomes of midterm congressional elections. In some midterm elections, like 1974 and 1994, the losses suffered by the president's party are much larger than what would have been expected based solely on the number of seats won 2 years earlier. These elections demonstrate that while short-term forces are usually weaker than in presidential elections, national issues can influence the results of midterm elections.

The most salient national issue in most midterm elections is the performance of the incumbent president. Fairly or unfairly, Americans hold the president responsible for the well-being of the nation, including the condition of the economy. Since the president is not on the ballot, however, the only place where voters can express their opinion about the president's performance is in the congressional elections. Voters who approve of the president's performance are more likely to vote for House and Senate candidates from the president's party while voters who disapprove of the president's performance are more likely to vote for House and Senate candidates from the opposition party.[36]

The effects of positive and negative opinions about the president's performance are not equal, however. In midterm elections, discontented voters appear to be more motivated to turn out and to express their opinion about the president's performance than contented voters.[37] In seven midterm elections between 1974 and 1998, according to NES data, turnout among voters who disapproved of the president's performance was six points higher on average than turnout among voters who approved of the president's performance. Among those who disapproved of the president's performance, 76 percent voted for House candidates from the opposition party and 77 percent voted for Senate candidates from the opposition party; among those who approved of the president's performance, however, only 59 percent voted for House candidates from the president's

[36] See Alan I. Abramowitz, "Economic Conditions, Presidential Popularity, and Voting Behavior in Midterm Congressional Elections," *Journal of Politics* 47 (February 1985), pp. 31–43.

[37] Samuel Kernell, "Presidential Popularity and Negative Voting: An Alternative Explanation for the Midterm Congressional Decline of the President's Party," *American Political Science Review* 71 (March 1977), pp. 44–66. See also Richard Born, "Surge and Decline, Negative Voting, and the Midterm Loss Phenomenon: A Simultaneous Choice Model," *American Journal of Political Science* 34 (August 1990), pp. 615–45.

party and only 63 percent voted for Senate candidates from the president's party. The predominance of **negative voting** reinforces the tendency of the president's party to lose seats in midterm elections.

The impact of national issues on congressional elections, including midterm elections, can also be affected by the behavior of "**strategic politicians.**" Gary Jacobson and Samuel Kernell have demonstrated that both candidates and contributors behave strategically: their decisions are influenced by their expectations about the chances of winning. Therefore, when national conditions favor a party, that party will tend to attract stronger challengers and open seat candidates and raise more money than the opposing party. In a presidential election year, having a popular incumbent president at the top of the ticket can help a party to recruit experienced candidates and raise money. Similarly, in a midterm election year, having an unpopular opposition party president can help a party to recruit experienced candidates and raise money. In both types of elections, the behavior of strategic politicians serves to reinforce the influence of presidential popularity on House and Senate elections.[38]

In 13 midterm elections between 1950 and 1998, the correlation (Pearson's r) between the president's approval rating in the Gallup Poll at the time of the election and the number of seats lost by the president's party was −.71 for House elections and −.30 for Senate elections. Because of the small number of seats involved in each election, the relationship between presidential approval and midterm seat losses was not as consistent in Senate elections as it was in House elections. Nevertheless, in both Senate and House elections, the greater the president's popularity, the fewer seats his party tended to lose in midterm elections. In the six midterm elections in which the president's approval rating was below 50 percent, the president's party lost an average of 36.2 House seats and 5.5 Senate seats. On the other hand, in the four midterm elections in which the president's approval rating was above 60 percent, the president's party lost an average of only 5.5 House seats and 1.5 Senate seats. President Bush's

---

[38] Gary C. Jacobson and Samuel Kernell, *Strategy and Choice in Congressional Elections*, 2nd ed. (New Haven, CT: Yale University Press, 1983). See also Thomas A. Kazee, ed., *Who Runs for Congress? Ambition, Context, and Candidate Emergence* (Washington, DC: Congressional Quarterly Press, 1994); Richard Born, "Strategic Politicians and Unresponsive Voters," *American Political Science Review* 80 (September 1986), pp. 599–612; and William T. Bianco, Strategic Decisions on Candidacy in U.S. Congressional Districts, *Legislative Studies Quarterly* 9 (1984), pp. 351–64.

high approval rating at the time of the 2002 midterm election, and his active campaigning for GOP candidates, helps to explain why Republicans were able to gain seats in both the House and Senate.

LOOKING AHEAD TO 2004

In the aftermath of the 2002 midterm elections, the balance of power in both chambers of Congress remains extremely close. A shift of only two seats in the Senate and a dozen seats in the House in 2004 would return control to the Democrats. However, while a Democratic comeback is possible, Republicans now enjoy important structural advantages in competing for control of both the House and Senate.

In 2004, Democrats will have to defend many more vulnerable House districts than Republicans. In the current House, only seven Republicans represent districts in which Al Gore received at least 55 percent of the major party vote and not one Republican represents a district in which Gore received at least 60 percent of the major party vote. In contrast, 21 Democrats represent districts in which George Bush received at least 55 percent of the major party vote and nine represent districts in which Bush received at least 60 percent of the major party vote.

Although Democrats did briefly regain control of the Senate as a result of the 2000 election and the subsequent defection of James Jeffords, the Senate is not friendly territory for Democrats. That is because the constitutional formula for apportioning seats in the upper chamber—two seats for each state regardless of population—gives a substantial advantage to the Republican Party. The Democratic Party's strength is concentrated disproportionately in the most populous states—those with large urban centers and large minority populations. In the 2000 presidential election, Al Gore carried six of the nine most populous states. These states account for 51 percent of the U.S. population but only 18 percent of seats in the Senate. George W. Bush carried 15 of the 20 least populous states. These states account for only 10 percent of the population but 40 percent of seats in the Senate.

George W. Bush carried 22 of the 34 states with Senate contests in 2004 including 10 of the 19 states with Democratic incumbents. Bush carried five states now represented by Democrats—Indiana, South Dakota, North Dakota, South Carolina, and Georgia—by a margin of

10 points or more. Al Gore carried only one state now represented by a Republican—Illinois—by a margin of 10 points or more. Based on these voting patterns, Democrats will be hard pressed just to hold their own in the 2004 Senate elections.

SUMMARY

The 2000 and 2002 House and Senate elections illustrate the paradox of congressional elections in the twenty-first century. Competition for control of Congress has never been more intense. The American electorate is almost evenly divided between Democratic and Republican identifiers and the large majority of these identifiers cast their congressional ballots along party lines. As a result, in the past several elections both the national popular vote and the party division of seats in the House and Senate have been extremely close. The national parties and their interest group allies have been pouring record amounts of money into congressional elections in an attempt to tip the balance one way or the other. At the same time, however, the overwhelming majority of individual House contests and most Senate contests are low-key, one-sided affairs. In recent elections only about one in ten House races and 1 in 3 Senate races have been truly competitive, with both major party candidates having a realistic chance of winning.

The main reason for the absence of meaningful competition for individual House and Senate seats is the advantage of incumbency. In recent elections, few House or Senate incumbents have chosen to retire and almost none have been defeated in primaries. As a result, more than 90 percent of House races and close to 90 percent of Senate races have involved incumbents and the success rate of these incumbents has been extremely high.

There are several reasons why House and Senate incumbents have enjoyed such success in recent elections. Although two-party competition is now the norm in the large majority of states, many House districts are very safe for one party or the other. In addition, through skillful public relations, diligent casework, and aggressive pursuit of federal dollars, most senators and representatives are able to add a personal vote to their party's normal base of support. If they represent a district or state where their party is in the minority, members of Congress can appeal to independents and supporters of the opposing party by crossing party lines on key votes with little fear of reprisal from party leaders. However, the single largest factor in the electoral success of congressional incumbents is the inability of most challengers to raise enough money to mount effective campaigns. The overwhelming majority of House challengers and most Senate challengers spend too little money to make any impression on the electorate. Without a viable challenger, the incumbents in these races triumph by default.

In every election, a few incumbents lose their seats because of scandals, shifting demographics, or sheer incompetence. However, almost all elections in which a large number of House and Senate incumbents are defeated involve strong national forces that produce substantial seat gains for one party or the other.

To a considerable extent, the influence of national forces on congressional elections is mediated by presidential elections. There is a presidential pulse to congressional elections. When a party wins a presidential election, it usually gains seats in the House and Senate as a result of presidential coattails. In the next midterm election, 2 years later or 6 years later, the party that won the presidential election almost always loses seats in the House and usually loses seats in the Senate. This alternating pattern of surge and decline has been one of the most regular features of congressional elections in the United States. Since the end of World War II, however, both the gains produced by presidential coattails and the losses suffered by the president's party in midterm elections have diminished, especially in House elections. Because of the increased advantage of incumbency, there are fewer marginal seats available in House and Senate elections, and more seats are insulated from the influence of national tides. As a result, the effects of surge and decline are smaller than in the past: presidential coattails are shorter and midterm losses are smaller.

Midterm elections are also, to some extent, referenda on the performance of the incumbent president. Voters express their opinion about the president by voting for or against his party's candidates for the House and Senate. Usually, discontented voters are more motivated to turn out and express their opinion about the president's performance than contented voters. The predominance of negative voting in midterm elections reinforces the tendency of the president's party to lose seats in the House and Senate. In 2002, however, President Bush's intense campaigning apparently motivated Republican voters to turn out at a higher rate than Democratic voters, contributing to GOP gains in the House and Senate.

KEY TERMS AND CONCEPTS

advantage of incumbency
exposure effect
marginal seats
midterm elections
national forces
negative voting
open seat contests
paradox of congressional
   elections
party identification
personal vote

political action committees
   (PACs)
presidential coattails
reapportionment
redistricting
seat swing
split-ticket voting
strategic politicians
surge and decline
Wesberry v. *Sanders*

DISCUSSION QUESTIONS

1. What are the most important factors affecting competition in U.S. House and Senate elections? Why are Senate elections generally more competitive than House elections?

2. How does the current system of campaign finance affect competition in House and Senate elections? Will new restrictions on soft money lead to greater competition for congressional seats? What other reforms could lead to increased competition?

3. According to David R. Mayhew, "The organization of Congress meets remarkably well the electoral needs of its members." What did he mean? How do the organization and decision-making processes of Congress help members to cultivate their constituencies? Why are some members more successful at cultivating their constituencies than others?

4. Why is there a "presidential pulse" to congressional elections and why has it become weaker in recent years? What consequences does this trend have for the relationship between Congress and the President?

5. What will be the most important factors affecting the outcome of the 2004 congressional elections?

SUGGESTED READINGS

Abramowitz, Alan I., and Jeffrey A. Segal. *Senate Elections*. Ann Arbor, MI: University of Michigan Press, 1992. The authors provide an in-depth analysis of the factors that influence the national outcomes of Senate elections as well as the results of individual races along with case studies of several Senate campaigns.

Ahuja, Sunil, and Robert Dewhirst, eds. *The Roads to Congress 2000*. Belmont, CA: Wadsworth, 2002. These case studies of six House and six Senate campaigns in the 2000 election include competitive and noncompetitive races.

Barone, Michael; Richard E. Cohen; and Charles E. Cook, Jr. *The Almanac of American Politics 2002*. Washington, DC: National Journal Press, 2001. This is the latest edition of the definitive guide to the members of Congress and their constituencies. Along with demographic data and election statistics, Barone and his colleagues provide an in-depth analysis of each state and district and a description of recent campaigns.

Campbell, James E. *The Presidential Pulse of Congressional Elections*, 2nd ed. Lexington, KY: University of Kentucky Press, 1997. Campbell provides a clear explanation of presidential coattails and midterm losses in congressional elections and shows that the presidential pulse is somewhat weaker than in the past, but still an important factor in congressional elections.

Jacobson, Gary C. *The Politics of Congressional Elections*, 5th ed. New York: Longman Publishers, 2001. Jacobson gives provides a thorough overview of the factors influencing the behavior of candidates and voters in congressional elections as well as a comprehensive bibliography.

Kahn, Kim F., and Patrick J. Kenney, *The Spectacle of U.S. Senate Campaigns*. Princeton, NJ: Princeton University Press, 1999. Kahn and Kenny analyze candidate strategies, media coverage, and electoral consequences of U.S. Senate campaigns and emphasize the differences between competitive and noncompetitive campaigns.

INFORMATION SOURCES ON THE INTERNET

American National Election Studies: www.umich.edu/~nes/nesguide/nesguide.htm. This is the website for the NES Guide to Public Opinion and Electoral Behavior. The guide provides a wide range of information about the social characteristics, political attitudes, and voting behavior of the American electorate since 1952.

Center for Responsive Politics: www.opensecrets.org. The Center for Responsive Politics provides a critical perspective on current campaign finance laws and practices in the United States along with an extensive body of data on campaign spending in congressional and presidential elections.

Federal Election Commission: www.fec.gov. The FEC is the agency responsible for enforcing the nation's campaign finance laws and the agency's website provides valuable information about federal election laws and regulations, election results, and campaign spending.

Gallup Poll: www.gallup.com. This is the website of the Gallup Poll, the nation's oldest and one of its most respected public opinion polling organizations. The site provides links to recent poll results on a wide range of topics including attitudes toward foreign and domestic issues, evaluations of presidential performance, and support for the Democratic and Republican parties.

U.S. Census Bureau: www.censupopulation/www/socdemo/voting/vote-htabtcon.html. This site provides current and historical data from government surveys on voter registration and turnout in congressional elections. The data is broken down by a wide variety of demographic variables including age, race, gender, education, and family income.

United States Congress: http://thomas.loc.gov. This website is a service of the Library of Congress. It provides information on legislation, committee meetings, and roll call votes in the House and Senate.

CHAPTER 8

Electoral Reform and American Democracy

THE OUTLOOK FOR REFORM

Major electoral reforms in the United States generally occur in response to scandals or crises. By focusing attention on contradictions between democratic values and current political practices, scandals and crises can break down the normal resistance of the public and political leaders to federal intervention in the electoral process. Thus, public outrage over the murders of civil rights workers in Mississippi during the summer of 1964 expedited passage of the 1965 Voting Rights Act that authorized the use of federal registrars to register black voters in the southern states. Similarly, the **Watergate scandal** with its revelations of fund-raising abuses by the 1972 Nixon reelection campaign led Congress to pass the most important campaign finance reforms in American history, the 1974 Amendments to the Federal Election Campaign Act. More recently, the 2000 Florida election controversy, although it may not deserve to be classified as a major scandal or crisis, spurred enactment of the **Help America Vote Act** of 2002 authorizing federal assistance to states in modernizing their election equipment and training poll workers.

The National Outlook

In the absence of a new scandal or crisis, the outlook for significant electoral reform at the national level in the near future appears to be fairly dim. The main obstacles to any major changes in the nation's campaign finance or election laws are conservative opposition to additional federal regulation of the electoral process and the fact that such reforms would have to be enacted by officials who have benefited from the current system.

Republicans currently control both chambers of Congress and the White House. While a few Republicans such as Arizona Senator John McCain and Connecticut Representative Christopher Shays have been in the forefront of efforts to reform the nation's campaign finance laws, neither the Bush Administration nor Republican leaders in Congress seem eager to change a campaign finance system that benefits the GOP. In fact, the elimination of soft money may actually increase the Republican advantage in fund-raising. According to **Federal Election Commission (FEC)** data, during the first 18 months of the 2001–2002 election cycle, Republican Party committees raised $181.8 million in unregulated soft money compared with $126.4 million for their Democratic counterparts, giving the GOP a less than 3-2 soft money advantage. However, during the same period, Republican committees raised $283.4 million in regulated hard money compared with only $128.7 million for their Democratic counterparts, giving Republicans a better than 2-1 hard money advantage.

In the aftermath of the party's defeat in the 2002 midterm election, Democratic Party leaders, including current Democratic National Committee chairman Terry McAuliffe, seem more interested in finding ways to keep soft money flowing into party coffers than in proposing new federal regulations of campaign fund-raising.[1] In addition, unless the Supreme Court changes its mind and reverses the *Buckley* decision, any new regulation of campaign spending, to be effective, would have to be tied to public financing. Given current projections of massive federal budget deficits for the foreseeable future, it is unlikely that any Congress, and especially a Republican Congress, would be willing to find the money necessary to make a system of public financing work.

Major reform of the nation's registration and voting procedures also appears unlikely in the near future. Along with ideological opposition to new federal regulation and the normal inclination of elected officials to resist change in the status quo, another important obstacle to such reform is the highly decentralized structure of the

[1] See Don Van Natta, Jr., and Richard A. Oppel, Jr., "The 2002 Campaign: The Money; Parties Set Up Groups to Elude Soft Money Ban," *The New York Times*, November 2, 2002, p. A1. See also Lorraine Woellert, "Soft Money: Is It the End, or the End Run?" *Business Week*, July 8, 2002, p. 47.

American electoral system. Traditionally, individual states have had considerable discretion in establishing rules and procedures governing registration and voting. As a result, rules such as registration deadlines and voting hours vary widely from state to state. Moreover, as Americans learned in the aftermath of the 2000 Florida election controversy, important aspects of the electoral process, including the design of the ballot and the type of equipment used to record votes, can vary considerably from county to county within a single state. The Help America Vote Act of 2002 will provide states with financial assistance in replacing antiquated voting equipment and training poll workers. However, any effort to impose more uniform registration and voting procedures across the entire country would undoubtedly meet with strong resistance from state and local elected officials who might be adversely affected by such reforms.

The Outlook for Reform at the State and Local Level

While the decentralized structure of the American electoral system makes it difficult to impose uniform rules and procedures across the entire country, it also provides opportunities for reformers. In recent years, for example, several states have reformed their registration and voting laws to permit Election Day registration, early voting, and mail-in voting. Although the results of these reforms have been uneven, states that have adopted Election Day registration have had turnout levels far above the national average. In the 2000 presidential election, for example, voter turnout in the six states with Election Day registration averaged 63 percent of the voting-age population compared with a national turnout of 51 percent of the voting-age population. One recent study estimated that adoption of Election Day Registration would increase voter turnout by an average of seven percentage points.[2]

In recent years, state and local governments have been in the forefront of efforts to reform campaign finance practices in the United States. Seven states—Arizona, Hawaii, Maine, Massachusetts, Minnesota, Nebraska, and Wisconsin—now have voluntary public financing systems for all statewide and legislative candidates. Several other states provide public funds for statewide candidates or

---

[2]Craig L. Brians and Bernard Grofman, "Election Day Registration's Effect on U.S. Voter Turnout," *Social Science Quarterly* 82 (March 2001), pp. 171–83.

gubernatorial candidates.[3] Many of these **"clean election laws"** were
adopted by means of citizen-sponsored initiatives, thereby bypassing reluctant state legislatures. In addition, a number of major cities including New York, Los Angeles, Oakland, Cincinnati, and
Albuquerque have instituted public financing of their municipal
elections.

State and local public financing systems generally provide
matching funds or grants to candidates who raise at least a minimum amount of money in small contributions and who agree to
limit their total spending and/or the maximum size contribution that
they accept. Some plans provide extra funding for candidates whose
opponents do not accept public funds and who exceed a maximum
spending level. In this way, sponsors of these plans hope to encourage more citizens to contribute to campaigns, limit the influence of
large contributors, and stimulate competition by reducing disparities in financial resources among candidates.[4] Because acceptance of
public funds is voluntary, the plans are permissible under the guide-
lines laid down by the Supreme Court in the *Buckley* decision.

If they are successful, these state and local public financing laws
could serve as models for campaign finance reform in other states
and localities and, eventually, at the federal level. Although much
more research is needed to evaluate the effectiveness of these plans,
thus far the results appear to be encouraging.[5] In Maine's first election after implementing public financing, there was a 40 percent increase in the number of contested primaries and 53 percent of the
challengers who accepted public funds defeated their incumbent opponents. By 2002, a majority of both Democratic and Republican legislative candidates chose to accept public financing. In Arizona, too,
a growing number of candidates from both parties have chosen to ac-

[3] For an overview of campaign finance practices in the states, see Anthony Gierzynski, "Financing Gubernatorial and State Legislative Elections," in David B. Magleby,
ed., *Financing the 2000 Election* (Washington, DC: Brookings Institution Press, 2002),
pp. 188–212.
[4] A good summary of state public financing laws can be found on the website of Common Cause, a nonpartisan political reform advocacy group. See www.commoncause
.org/cf_financing.htm. Another good source of information on campaign finance laws
in the states is the website of the National Institute on Money in State Politics: www
. followthemoney.org.
[5] For an analysis of the impact of public financing on the 2000 elections in Arizona and
Maine, see Samantha Sanchez, "First Returns on a Campaign Finance Reform Experiment: Maine, Arizona and Full Public Funding." This report is available on the website of the National Institute on Money in State Politics at www.followthemoney.org/
press/MaineArizona/FullReport.phtml.

cept public financing and publicly financed candidates have generally done well. In the 2002 gubernatorial election, Democrat Janet Napolitano who accepted public financing defeated Republican Matt Salmon who refused public financing.[6] The total cost of public financing has been fairly small in both states: less than $1 per state resident in Arizona and 69 cents per state resident in Maine for the 2000 election.[7]

Although it has not attracted as much attention recently as campaign finance, the legislative redistricting process has been a target of reform groups such as the League of Women Voters in a number of states.[8] The main goal of reformers with regard to redistricting has been to end partisan and pro-incumbent gerrymandering by taking responsibility for drawing district lines away from the legislature and giving it to a nonpartisan organization or a special redistricting commission. As with campaign finance, pro-reform groups have utilized the initiative process to bypass reluctant state legislatures. Most recently, voters in Arizona approved an initiative in the 2000 election that shifted responsibility for redistricting from the state legislature to a special bipartisan commission.[9]

During the 2001–2002 round of redistricting, six states—Arizona, Hawaii, Idaho, Montana, New Jersey, and Washington—assigned responsibility for redrawing congressional and state legislative districts to special independent redistricting commissions. In addition, Iowa's nonpartisan Legislative Services Bureau has had the job of drawing new state legislative and congressional districts since 1980.

Not all of the plans produced by independent redistricting commissions have pleased reformers.[10] In general, however, states in

[6]See Marc Cooper, "Running Clean in Arizona," *The Nation,* October 14, 2002.

[7]For an early assessment of the results of voluntary public financing schemes in the states, see Robert Tanner, "States Try Public Financing of Races," *Associated Press Online,* September 6, 2002. Data on the results of the first publicly financed elections in Arizona and Maine can be found at www.publiccampaign.org.

[8]For a summary of the League of Women Voters' position on redistricting reform, see Todd A. Cox, "Redistricting: How to Keep It Honest," *National Voter* (September/October 2001). This article can also be found on the league's website at www.lwv.org/elibrary/nv/2001/voter_0901_1.html.

[9]Information on Arizona's reformed redistricting process can be found at www.azredistricting.org.

[10]In New Jersey, for example, a bipartisan commission drew districts designed to protect incumbents from both parties. For more information on the redistricting process in New Jersey and the other 49 states, see the website of the Center for Voting and Democracy: www.fairvote.org/redistricting/index.html.

which outside organizations control redistricting tend to have more competitive elections than states in which the legislature controls redistricting. During the 1990s, for example, both Iowa and Washington experienced much greater competition for their congressional seats than the nation as a whole. Based on presidential voting patterns, four of Iowa's five current House districts and five of Washington's nine current districts appear to be potentially competitive. In addition, Iowa's and Washington's congressional districts, in contrast with those in many other states, are relatively compact and generally follow city and county boundaries.[11]

In the past two decades, a small number of local governments in the United States have adopted a much more drastic type of electoral reform—replacing SMSP elections with **cumulative voting (CV).** CV is a semiproportional electoral system based on multimember districts. Under CV, voters are given as many votes as the number of seats in a district and they can distribute these votes among the candidates in any manner that they see fit, including giving all of their votes to one candidate. Approximately 80 cities, counties, and school districts in the United States, mostly in the southern states, now utilize CV. By allowing voters to cast multiple votes for one candidate, CV makes it easier for candidates from minority groups to be elected and encourages more of them to run.[12] In addition, voter turnout in local elections using CV appears to be somewhat higher than voter turnout in similar plurality elections.[13]

State and local politics often lacks the glamour and visibility of the national political stage. However, in an era in which the federal government is constrained by massive budget deficits and preoccupied with fighting terrorism, the state and local arena may be where reformers have their greatest chance of finding ways to in-

[11] For a favorable assessment of Iowa's redistricting process by a noted conservative columnist, see Fred Barnes, "Where Incumbents Tremble: In Iowa a `Good Government' Reform Actually Works," *The Weekly Standard,* September 8, 2002.

[12] See Richard L. Cole, Delbert A. Taebel, Richard L. Engstrom, "Cumulative Voting in a Municipal Election: A Note on Voter Reactions and Electoral Consequences," *Western Political Quarterly* 43 (March 1990), pp. 191–99. See also Elisabeth R. Gerber, Rebecca B. Morton, Thomas A. Rietz, "Minority Representation in Multimember Districts," *American Political Science Review* 92 (March 1998), pp. 127–44.

[13] See Shaun Bowler, David Brockington, and Todd Donavan, "Election Systems and Voter Turnout: Experiments in the United States," unpublished paper presented at the 1997 Annual Meeting of the American Political Science Association. A revised version of this paper is available on the website of the Center for Voting and Democracy: www.fairvote.org.

crease citizen participation, control the influence of money, and promote competition.

SUMMARY

In the absence of a major scandal or crisis, the prospects for significant electoral reform at the national level in the near future appear to be very limited. Such reform would have to overcome conservative opposition to new federal regulation of the electoral process and resistance to change by elected officials who have benefited from the current system.

The decentralized structure of the American electoral system makes it difficult to impose uniform rules and procedures across the country, but it also provides opportunities for reformers. In recent years, for example, several states have liberalized their registration and voting laws to permit Election Day registration, early voting, and mail-in voting. In addition, state and local governments have been in the forefront of efforts to reform campaign finance practices in the United States. Several states have adopted voluntary public financing systems in statewide and legislative elections and a growing number of cities have implemented similar systems for their municipal elections. Reformers have also succeeded in ending partisan and pro-incumbent gerrymandering in several states by shifting responsibility for drawing district lines from state legislatures to special redistricting commissions. In a number of states, citizens groups were able to bring about major reforms of campaign finance laws or redistricting by using the initiative process to bypass reluctant state legislatures. In an era in which the federal government is constrained by growing budget deficits and preoccupied with fighting terrorism, the state and local arena may be where reformers have their greatest chance of achieving success.

KEY TERMS AND CONCEPTS

clean election laws
cumulative voting (CV)
Federal Election Commission (FEC)
Help America Vote Act
Watergate scandal

DISCUSSION QUESTIONS

1. What are the major advantages and disadvantages of public versus private financing of campaigns? How would public financing of campaigns affect elections and representation in the United States?
2. Who controlled redistricting and how did the results of redistricting affect the 2002 elections in your state? What are the major advantages and disadvantages of partisan versus nonpartisan redistricting?
3. What are the most important differences between single-member, simple plurality elections and elections based on cumulative voting? What are the main advantages and disadvantages of SMSP elections versus cumulative voting?

SUGGESTED READINGS

Dudley, Robert L., and Alan R. Gitelson. *American Elections: The Rules Matter.* New York: Longman, 2001. Dudley and Gitelson provide a comprehensive overview of the influence of rules on the electoral process in the United States. Topics covered include voter eligibility, apportionment and redistricting, nomination rules, campaign finance, media access, ballot regulations, and the Electoral College.

LeDuc, Lawrence; Richard G. Niemi; and Pippa Norris; eds. *Comparing Democracies 2: New Challenges in the Study of Elections and Voting.* Thousand Oaks, CA: Sage Publications, 2002. This is a new collection of essays by leading scholars in the field of comparative electoral behavior. Individual chapters provide cross-national perspectives on topics such as electoral systems, candidate selection, campaign communications, and voter participation.

Magleby, David B., ed. *Financing the 2000 Election.* Washington, DC: Brookings Institution Press, 2002. These essays by the some of the leading students of campaign finance in the United States provide a comprehensive overview of the role of money in the 2000 elections. Individual chapters cover the 2000 presidential nomination and general election campaigns, the congressional elections, gubernatorial and state legislative elections, the role of interest groups, and reform proposals.

Wattenberg, Martin P. *Where Have All the Voters Gone?* Cambridge, MA: Harvard University Press, 2002. Wattenberg examines the reasons for low voter turnout in the United States and offers suggestions for reforms that might raise participation levels.

INFORMATION SOURCES ON THE INTERNET

Center for Voting and Democracy: www.fairvote.org. This site provides a comprehensive overview of redistricting practices in all 50 states along with summaries of the results of the 2001–2002 redistricting process. Extensive information about alternatives to single-member, simple plurality elections such as cumulative voting and proportional representation is also available here.

Common Cause: www.commoncause.org. Common Cause is a nonpartisan pro-reform advocacy group. The organization's website provides brief descriptions of existing state public financing systems as well as information about current efforts to reform campaign finance laws at the national and state levels.

Federal Election Commission: www.fec.gov. The FEC's official website provides a vast amount of information on campaign finance, election laws, and election results.

National Institute on Money in State Politics: www.followthemoney.org. This website provides a wide range of information on state campaign finance laws along with a database on campaign finance in all 50 states.

Index